DAVID WATSON
A Biography

Teddy Saunders and
Hugh Sansom

Hodder & Stoughton
LONDON SYDNEY AUCKLAND

British Library Cataloguing in Publication Data

Saunders, Teddy
David Watson: Biography
I. Title   II. Sansom, Hugh
283.092

ISBN 0-340-39990-2 Hbk
ISBN 0-340-57410-0 Pbk

Published by Hodder and Stoughton,
a division of Hodder and Stoughton Ltd,
Mill Road, Dunton Green, Sevenoaks, Kent TN13 2YA.
Editorial Office: 47 Bedford Square, London WC1B 3DP.

Photoset in Linotron Ehrhardt by Rowland Phototypesetting Ltd,
Bury St Edmunds, Suffolk.

Printed in Great Britain by
St Edmundsbury Press Ltd, Bury St Edmunds, Suffolk

Contents

Foreword

David Watson was one of those rare people whose warmth of character and strength of conviction drew people to him like a magnet. Years after his earthly mission was concluded, his influence is as real as it was when he stirred the conscience of all who heard his witness to the love of Christ.

Hugh Sansom and Teddy Saunders have provided us with a penetrating study of all the factors that combined to make David Watson one of the most effective Christian leaders in the twentieth century.

The lack of a father's love and influence is something that I experienced, and so I understand this gap in David Watson's life. In vivid language we are told of his enjoyable school life in Wellington, his father's school, and also of his Christian conversion under the influence of John Collins.

The growing stature of the Anglican priest proclaiming Christianity as a living relationship began to attract wider recognition through his ministry at St Cuthbert's, York. Soon it was clear that David Watson had a very special appeal so far as young people were concerned.

His missions in universities earned him recognition as a foremost teacher as well as a preacher. It was inevitable that the Church of England would recognise the mighty evangelist and bring him to the London area.

This biography, delving into his entire life, has been well researched and is lovingly written. It is a useful reminder that the quality of a man's life is more important than its length.

The last time I talked with David Watson was in the interregnum between his first serious cancer attack and his final illness. We met in the tea room of the House of Lords. I was recovering from cancer in my throat, and David knew how the Royal Marsden Hospital had helped me. He also indicated to me that, although he was enjoying a respite, he knew that he had a greater challenge to face.

The radiance of his faith shone in his face as we talked of our respective experiences. Such courage as he revealed owed its origin to his unshakeable trust in the resurrected Christ.

This biography does what David Watson would have sought: it tells his story simply, and it ends on a note of triumph. He left us in the knowledge that 'the best is yet to be'.

GEORGE THOMAS
VISCOUNT TONYPANDY

Introduction

We believe that David Watson's life and work are worthy of the closest attention by the leaders and members of Christian churches of all traditions. David exhausted himself in the proclamation of the gospel – the good news – and he had few party lines or loyalties beyond it. Those who discern in him a 'mellowing' towards social priorities are, we believe, naively mistaken into supposing that he had previously neglected them. For him, social action was an intrinsic part of, and indeed sprang from, the gospel, and he never deviated from his view that hope for the human race depended upon a response to God's offer of new life in Christ. The history of evangelicalism in the nineteenth century suggests that when the Church allows the gospel of Christ to control its life, the social actions which result from it are truly constructive. It should be recognised that the social reformers of that era were also the founders of the missionary enterprise of which the Church has subsequently been so proud. David Watson belonged in that tradition. Those who today sit lightly to gospel preaching need to realise that their social programmes are likely to fall without it.

David, in his ministry, fully accepted that varieties of doctrine and tradition are inevitable within a modern church. His remarkable acceptability as a missioner across all traditional boundaries of Christendom is evidence of this. Yet it was not the result of his adopting a 'lowest common denominator' for his message, but of his refusal to invade the cultural and traditional presuppositions of his audiences. Of course, the telling of God's good news again and again challenges human complacency and demands repentance, but it has little to contribute to the ecclesiological debates which have become the obsession of so much of the Church today. David's lifelong aim was the positive offer of the life-changing gospel. Nor was that gospel confined to the initial free gift of justification, which gave admittance to the family of God, but it included the availability of grace by the power of the Holy Spirit for every eventuality which the Christian would subsequently experience. 'With God all things are possible,' (Matthew 19:26), even those things firmly pronounced impossible by the pundits.

The late Canon John Poulton began the work on this biography, but he was a sick man when he was invited to undertake the task and, sadly, he died before he could make much progress with it. There is no doubt that, had he been able to complete it, the book would have benefited enormously from his wisdom and his wide knowledge of the Church. Unfortunately, this was not to be, but we are indebted to him for his brief beginnings. During the course of our work, a great army of helpers has emerged to throw light on some phase or aspect of David's life and ministry. We are deeply grateful to all who have written to us, been interviewed, provided letters or photographs, or commented on earlier drafts of our manuscript. David had touched so many people in many countries during his life that it has not proved possible to include everything that has been said to us. We doubt if the inclusion of more material would have contributed greatly to our interpretation of David's life and ministry, and it is an interpretation which we have tried to write to set alongside David's own autobiographical books.

We are therefore refraining from giving personal acknowledgment to our many helpers, except where their names are recorded in the text. However, one who has made a rather special contribution should be mentioned. Mark Saunders has put in hours of work, especially in support of his father. He has reduced the manuscript to manageable order on his word processor and then edited it to the satisfaction of both authors and, we hope, our patient publishers, to whom we are also indebted for their advice and encouragement.

We must also express our gratitude to Viscount Tonypandy for his warm and felicitous Foreword.

TEDDY SAUNDERS
HUGH SANSOM

I

Early Years

DAVID CHRISTOPHER KNIGHT WATSON was born on 7 March 1933 in an army officer's quarter in Catterick in Yorkshire, the son of Godfrey Watson and Peggy Simpson. Godfrey was a serving officer in the Royal Artillery whose recent postings, like so many others of those days, had included service in India and Burma.

The Watsons were a Cumberland family and had been so since the sixteenth century when they moved south from Scotland. Their patriarchal figure was Richard Watson, Bishop of Llandaff from 1782 to 1816. This interesting character became Professor of Chemistry at Cambridge University at the age of twenty-seven although, in his own words, 'at the time I knew nothing at all of chemistry and had never read a syllable on the subject', a commentary perhaps on the knowledge of this science among his contemporaries. Yet he soon managed to deliver a course of lectures and was duly elected a Fellow of the Royal Society.

When the highly prestigious Chair of Divinity at Cambridge became vacant, he set himself to capture the 'foremost post of learning in Europe' by applying himself to acquire knowledge in a totally different field. He was appointed in 1772 to be Regius Professor of Divinity, revealing a remarkable measure of ability to match his ambition and industry. Bishop Richard established a family seat at Calgarth Park near Windermere, which, with its 3000 acres, remained the home of the Watsons until requisitioned for use as a military hospital in the First World War. It is now sheltered housing for the elderly.

Godfrey, great-grandson of the Bishop, followed his father's footsteps into the army. After a distinguished career at Wellington College, where he became a senior Prefect and where he was remembered as a boy with 'an imposing personality . . . handsome appearance and commanding presence',[1] he went to the Royal Military Academy at Woolwich in 1915. Commissioned into the Royal Artillery, he served for three years in France and Italy during the First World War. In 1922 he was stationed in Burma where Peggy's uncle, Charles Cooper, was a distinguished Civil Servant, and it was at Rangoon in 1922 that Godfrey and Peggy met, when she arrived for an extended holiday with the Coopers. Peggy's family had army connections too, her father having served with the Royal Army Medical Corps as a doctor during the Boer War, but he had died when Peggy was quite young. At the time of her holiday in the Far East, she was only nineteen years old, and had been working as a dancing teacher in Cambridge, where she lived with her mother. The relationship flourished and after only a brief courtship (though not uncommonly brief by Indian Raj standards), the wedding took place at Maymyo, up-country from Rangoon, in July 1924.

So the Watson family settled into life in what were the last years of the British Raj in India, years in which the best and the worst of that regime can be distinguished. There was good government based on British justice and the legacy of Victorian Christian standards of integrity and honour. Peace was maintained, at a cost, among the immensely varied and multitudinous peoples of the vast sub-continent, and services of a civilised sort were built into what was then considered to be an uncivilised community. Railways were constructed which are still a major asset half a century later. Education and culture were encouraged, and health and welfare attempted on a limited but still colossal scale.

Soldiers, merchants, officials, engineers, doctors, teachers and missionaries left their homes and families to travel far away into an alien land where they endured heat and much frustration in pursuit of the ideal of the British Empire which they considered the enlightening element in a dark world. That they did so expecting and exacting much gain, both personally and nationally, cannot be disputed, but it is mistaken to pretend that the profit motive cannot be balanced by higher aims. Many of these expatriate British left their bones in India, or returned home broken in health and hope. Many left no lasting monument of their achievements, but rather earned the hatred and contempt of the Indians, but that in itself does not belittle the contribution made by the Raj to the permanent well-being of India.

Yet the other side of the coin presents an unhappy picture to the honest viewer. The British chose to live in splendid isolation from the Indians, making no friends among them and accepting no competition from them. 'The Club' was the centre of society and here a life of comparative luxury was enjoyed with such diversions and pastimes as were deemed appropriate. The Indians were 'natives' and 'never to be trusted', so no genuine attempt was made to train the middle management or to encourage professional skills.

In this elevated and privileged estate, values could easily deteriorate, and sometimes quite rapidly. The British middle-class ladies and gentlemen of the Raj soon discovered that whisky and soda was both cheap and effective, and that with its help it was not difficult to forget the code of ethics they had inherited from their parents. Women were not plentiful, and bachelor men had to wait long years for suitable wives, so that divorces and other scandals were common among the comparatively small circles that frequented the clubs.

For Godfrey and Peggy, home leaves and frequent postings to other garrisons made for much movement. A daughter, Diana, was born to them in 1925 and when she was about eighteen months old Peggy brought her back to England, staying with Godfrey's mother at Streatley near Luton. Eventually, Godfrey obtained a home posting to Putney, in south-west London, and they lived for a time at Barnes. Various other moves culminated in the posting to Catterick, where David was born.

Through his mother, Godfrey had been greatly influenced by the writings of Mrs Mary Baker Eddy and was a very convinced and practising Christian Scientist. The concept of the literal power of the mind over matter held a particular fascination for many in the period after the First World War. One of the consequences of this belief was that the true Christian Scientist did not accept the reality of sickness, holding that it was merely a product of the mind. Godfrey insisted therefore that David's birth should take place at home without the help of a doctor. Peggy was, however, allowed to have a Christian Scientist nurse, who lived in the house with them as the time came near. She had no training in midwifery, but the birth was fairly straightforward and Peggy remembered only the nurse's comment on noticing that the baby's shoulders were rather depressed: 'You are going to have trouble with his chest – just look at his shoulders.'

Two months later, Godfrey was posted to India again and Peggy took the children to her mother in Bedford while awaiting passage on a ship. They sailed from Southampton in September 1933, in a very crowded troop-ship, sharing a cabin with another mother and two small children. It was a noisy and uncomfortable journey through the Mediterranean and the stifling heat of the Red Sea. David proved to be a terrible sailor and was frequently sick. The ship docked at Karachi, and a long, hot and dusty train journey followed to Jhansi in northern India where Godfrey was stationed.

Life could be fun in India for the children of army officers, and a great welcome awaited them from the Indian servants who made a fuss of the baby, garlanding him with rose petals and calling him *Chota Sahib* ('little master') like all of his kind. Diana, now aged eight, had her own pony and sometimes could ride on elephants and join in the many children's parties at the club. When the hot weather came in April, all the mothers and children went up into the hills to stay at Bhowali until October, the journey each way being very exciting as the car negotiated many hairpin bends with steep drops on either side of the road.

When David was eighteen months old, another posting took Godfrey to Campbelpore near Rawalpindi, but it was decided that Peggy and the children should spend that summer in England, preparing for Diana to go to school. They made their base in Bedford again and when Diana had started at school, Peggy and David sailed back to India, where Godfrey was now at the School of Artillery in Kakul near Abbottabad. However, in 1936 news came that Diana was seriously ill with whooping cough and Peggy immediately set off again on the long and uncomfortable journey. The quickest way was by train to Karachi, by ship to Marseilles, and then overland to England. The whole trip took three weeks.

Meanwhile, David stayed behind with Godfrey under the care of a young Belgian girl, Antoinette, who was employed as his governess and always known by him as 'Toinon'. It was not an altogether successful experience in developing a father/son relationship. Godfrey's strong sense of discipline caused him to over-react one day when David went out to play without his topi, the pith-helmet which all the British wore to protect them from the sun. The beating made a deep impression on the three-year-old's memory and their relationship never recovered fully, particularly as several other eruptions followed in the next few months.

Diana's recovery was slow and, on medical advice, Peggy decided to bring her back to India for the winter. They duly arrived at Kakul, but Diana had her appendix out at Aden on the way, and took some months to recuperate. In the spring of 1937, Peggy and both children returned to England, to Bedford with her mother, and this was the last they saw of India.

Godfrey came home on leave that summer and they holidayed together as a family at Hythe. Then he was gone to India, where he stayed until the outbreak of war in 1939. David was not to see him again, except for a flying visit home after the opening of hostilities.

Throughout his life, one of David's most pronounced characteristics was the strong need he felt for a father to approve of and support him. Even when he was at the height of his powers, surrounded by friends and the recipient of public adulation, there remained a longing for warm fatherly love and companionship. From time to time he found a figure worthy of his trust and enjoyed a freedom which at other times was lacking, but there was never anyone capable of a commitment to him that was simply for his own sake, and was irrespective of other callings and loyalties. The big imposing personality for which Godfrey was held in such esteem among friends and colleagues had served only to distance him from his small son, who remembered him only faintly and then as one it was hard to please and easy to inflame. Out of necessity, he was absent for much of the time, but even when he was present he did not seem to realise that David hoped for so much from his heroic father and too often found only grim disapproval.

Soon after his fifth birthday, David started at kindergarten and quickly proved to be a bright and willing pupil. He was a pleasure to teach, showing zest and ability, and making great progress. In particular, his writing was exceptionally good. But his grandmother's death in 1939 caused another upheaval for the family and Peggy found a top floor flat in Bedford where they were to live for the next ten years. The wanderings were over, but complications set in when two other children – one a cousin, Christopher Cahusac – came to stay as evacuees, and later the house below became the wartime home of Rye Grammar School. Air raid shelters were built in the garden and had to be occupied whenever the sirens went.

In 1940, David started at the preparatory section of Bedford School where he quickly climbed to be top of his form, maintaining a position in the top six for all of his time there. The headmaster noted that 'there is just a danger that he may become a little priggish', but he showed good all-round ability with no obvious weaknesses. He developed an interest in sport, especially cricket, and enjoyed mechanical toys such as trains.

Like most families at that time, much interest was taken in the progress of the war. A large map was fixed on the wall and front lines were marked with flags of the opposing forces. The Germans always seemed to be advancing in those early days. Wartime Britain was not a particularly cheerful place in which to grow up, with darkened streets and restricted freedom reflecting the bad news. However, the war did provide a stream of heroes to be worshipped and villains to be hated. Above all, Churchill's indomitable appearance and remarkable voice lifted the hearts and delighted the minds even of small boys. So great a communicator could not but inspire all those who, like David, felt a desire to assume leadership in the future.

Then from India came bad news. Godfrey, by now a Lieutenant-Colonel commanding the Sixth Indian Field Regiment in Quetta, had fallen in love with a married woman who shared his Christian Science beliefs, which Peggy had never done. He wanted a divorce, which was granted in 1943. Extraordinary as it may seem, David was not to learn of all this for forty years because within a few weeks it had faded out of sight as news came of Godfrey's sudden death. He had been playing squash with a brother officer and became overheated. The resultant cold soon developed into bronchial pneumonia, but since as a Christian Scientist he refused all medical attention, it proved to be a fatal infection and he died on 11 February 1943. In David's own words, 'The disease which supposedly had no reality killed him, and the human mind was an insufficient saviour.'[2]

The Regimental Padre, who considered that Godfrey's death was totally unnecessary and virtually self-inflicted, refused to take the funeral service. Another padre was found but feelings ran high in the regiment and only one other officer attended the funeral, although Colonel Watson had been both liked and respected. Indeed, it is hard not to believe that this inglorious end to the life and career of a man of high quality and great ability was a wicked waste at a time when such men were of special value. Such is the danger of sub-Christian cult religion. David was to teach this lesson the more powerfully in later life because of its personal effect upon himself.

Godfrey Watson's failure to provide his son with appropriate fatherly support has already been recorded and the final indignity of his careless death did nothing to compensate for this when so many other families were being bereaved by acts of war. His example as a husband was another legacy which was to be of little help to David. Godfrey was so often absent on his duties and sat so lightly to domestic responsibilities that David came to suppose that this was the proper role for a husband. Throughout his boyhood it was his mother, and his mother only, who was the constantly available friend and resource. His father was on duty elsewhere. His mother was there to provide for him. That was the model he accepted and was to assume was right for his own home and family later.

Peggy, now left without a husband or a pension (for the divorce had taken effect before Godfrey's death), had to take a job in a local school to make ends meet. Diana left school in 1943 and immediately joined the Women's Auxiliary Air Force, relieving her mother of the need to maintain her. David continued at Bedford Preparatory School. Peggy's predicament needs to be seen in the context of the sufferings being endured by so many others at the time, but it is greatly to her credit that she adapted so well to her circumstances, which must have seemed a major humiliation. She had not been employed since she worked as a dancing teacher at the age of nineteen, before the eventful holiday visit to Burma in 1922, and she had lived subsequently, as she had previously, in middle-class society where servants were the norm and money was no great problem. The war changed much of this anyway, but Peggy's determination that her son should lack nothing that she could possibly provide for him deserves the admiration of many who have cause to be grateful for what David became.

Free from obligation to bring up her children in Christian Science, Peggy arranged for them to be baptised and confirmed into the Church of England and David was soon enrolled as a server in the local parish church. Neither the confirmation classes nor the weekly Sung Eucharist meant anything to David. Nevertheless, he assumed that it was something that had to be endured, and that it was probably good for his soul. Religion did not play a big part in prep school life either, but David was entering with zest into everything else the school offered. When in 1944 he was moved up into the Lower School, his marks in most subjects were good and the following year he was made Head of School. The headmaster commented that 'he exercised his authority with tact and firmness, and has shown considerable enterprise'.

Preparations were now well underway for the next stage of David's education. Godfrey had entered David's name for his own old school, Wellington College, but Peggy must have wondered how she could possibly afford the fees for a public school. However, it was pointed out to her that, as the son of a serving army officer who had died on active service, David was eligible for a Foundation Scholarship.

Wellington College, set among the woods and rhododendrons of Berkshire, was founded as a national memorial to the great Duke of Wellington who died in 1852, six years before the College was opened. It was the Duke's belief that the army needed officers who, before attending a military academy, had received a 'gentleman's education', in order to develop character which, in the Duke's eyes, was of greater importance than any professional skills. Since he had himself dominated the national scene during the first half of the nineteenth century by sheer force of character, rather than by an extraordinary brilliance of intellect, his opinion on such matters was carefully noted and accepted. His own career had been marked by remarkable application and a very sensible willingness to adapt his methods to whatever circumstances confronted him. He seldom seemed at a loss, even in moments threatening disaster. As a soldier, he is still thought to be the greatest among those who have served Britain. As a statesman, he suffered many reverses, but never lost his nerve nor forfeited the admiration of his countrymen.

Thus, Wellington College sought to provide a 'gentleman's education', which quite literally meant 'the education of a gentleman' as well as 'an education in how to be a gentleman', for those boys entrusted to its care and especially for the sons of serving officers. Its first Master, Edward

White Benson, who presided over the College until 1873, subsequently became Archbishop of Canterbury from 1883 to 1896. It was he who had inscribed over the imposing main entrance the words: 'The Path of Duty is the Way to Glory'. If, in the second half of the twentieth century, the word 'duty' has fallen into disuse, in 1946 when David Watson arrived it still had real meaning.

Generally speaking, the public schools had weathered the Second World War rather well. Pressing into service older teachers due for retirement, and recalling some who had retired, they maintained good standards of education and made sensible adaptations to their lifestyle and domestic structures. At the end of the war, they duly returned to the well-tried principles of the past, as staff returned from the Services eager to build a new future on traditional foundations. It was not until the Sixties that the liberalisation of society seriously challenged authority structures and caused the schools to rethink their methods. In 1946, fagging was still prevalent and unquestioned. Discipline was strong and in some respects rigid. Headmasters reigned supreme, almost unchecked by higher authority. Although among themselves and among their staffs they began to ask questions and think new thoughts, their priority was to recapture the excellence which had been known in the past, before the six-year interruption of war, rather than to launch out into bold policies and experiments patterned by the incoming tide of the future.

The public schools were really the vehicle for the promotion of Victorian greatness. They trained for leadership. They expanded the youthful understanding, not so much with technological facts, but with the dignity of classical thoughts. The duty to lead others was deeply inculcated by everything they did for their pupils; by the submission of the will to discipline, the exercise of the mind by learning, the broadening of the soul by the contemplation of the arts, the building of the physique through an emphasis upon exercise and team games, and the enlightenment of the spirit through the continual practice of compulsory Christian worship and instruction. All these, within the very closely knit community life of single-sex boarding schools, built up in every boy a sense of calling to leadership. Was it not by these values that the British Empire had come into being and needed to be maintained? Were not British justice and British freedom the products of this philosophy? If it is not actually possible to attribute to the great Duke his most famous alleged statement, that the Battle of Waterloo was won on the playing fields of Eton, there was sufficient truth in it to make the British public schools conscious of their traditions and of the responsibilities laid upon them.

David sat the Common Entrance Exam in the Easter term of 1946 and was placed sixth of the thirty-seven entrants for Wellington. He was given a place in Hill Dormitory (often known as 'the Hill' or 'the Dormitory'), his father's old house, and it was decided he would start there in May, two months after his thirteenth birthday.

2

Wellington and the Army

THE MASTER OF WELLINGTON during David's time was Major H. W. House, who had been appointed in 1941, but the staff member with whom David had closest contact was the tutor in charge of the Hill, his housemaster, B. C. L. (Bertie) Kemp. To both of these he became better and better known as he climbed the school and they increasingly gave him their confidence as he gained their respect.

First, however, he had to adjust his attitudes. He became again a junior among so many larger and more mature boys, of whom the seniors seemed to him like demi-gods, awesome and privileged. They were to be worshipped from afar, for the system had a way of suppressing any cockiness in juniors. Discipline was important and strict, perhaps the more so because of the strong army links and traditions of Wellington, and life was tough, with few luxuries and limited liberties. Nevertheless, it was a happy and coherent place, the discipline and sense of duty generating an atmosphere of everything being in its proper place and pupils knowing where they stood. It produced fine, upstanding, well-mannered young men, though not a great diversity of individual characters, initiative being channelled firmly through the chain of command.

David was always an enthusiast, dedicated to making the best of everything, and he quickly overcame any initial feelings of homesickness and entered fully into the excitements which were offered to those prepared to accept them. His grandfather, his father and one of his uncles had preceded him at Wellington and his father's name was printed up on the large board in the Hill, which bore the names of all previous Heads of Dormitory. Why should he not follow in their footsteps?

The Hill was situated in one of the original buildings at Wellington. It did not resemble what one normally thinks of as a dormitory, but consisted of long corridors of cubicles created by high wooden partitions. In these each boy had a bed, a desk, a chair, a window seat and a chest of drawers, giving a modicum of privacy. There were no variations for age or seniority.

There were forty-five boys in the Dormitory and it was with these, changing every year as some left and others came, that David's life was closely bound up during the next five years.

Inevitably, life was largely routine. Stringent rationing still applied, though no one went hungry. Breakfast was at 7.45 a.m., Chapel followed at 8.45 a.m. and lessons occupied the remainder of the morning. After lunch there was forty minutes' free time in the dormitories before organised games and other activities. Three afternoons a week brought further lessons from 4.30 p.m. to 6.00 p.m. Evenings were devoted to individual 'prep' in cubicles, and 'lights out' was at 9.30 p.m. for juniors and at 11.00 p.m. for seniors.

David worked hard and successfully, being a determined person who never wanted to be left behind. Nevertheless, he found time to join a number of college societies including the Film Society, the Music Society, the Madrigal Society, the Sing-Song Society and the Bohemian Union. He was, generally speaking, a friendly and acceptable companion, kindly and generous towards others. He made friends without much difficulty, particularly with Sam Osmond, an exact contemporary.

He was not a natural or brilliant athlete, but he applied himself enthusiastically to most sports and became an adequate and even good performer. He loved cricket and played for the Dormitory junior team. Later he played for the College Second XI and eventually became its captain, which office he enjoyed greatly. He was an effective fast bowler but, in spite of a good eye and a neat style, never really excelled as a batsman. He played for his dormitory at rugby (stand-off half) and at hockey, and later captained the College Second XI at hockey and the Third XV at rugby. Perhaps he lacked the ruthlessness and physical flair to be really good. He excelled, however, in table tennis, enjoyed shooting and squash, and in his spare time he took up golf. He also learned to ski when the opportunity presented itself. He played all games with that characteristic determination which he had begun to develop at Bedford and which he later carried over into his life's work. This, coupled with the gift of leadership which was so pronounced, made him more valuable as a captain of team games than his actual performance in each might have suggested.

By 1949, this leadership ability was given a chance to develop still further with his appointment as a dormitory prefect, though still only sixteen. The next year he became a college prefect and Head of the Hill, and then, following in his father's footsteps, David was made a member of the so-called Upper X, comprising the three most senior prefects. Yet power and authority did not take away his basic 'niceness', as Richard Harries, now Bishop of Oxford, recalls:

I was at Wellington with him in the same house. I was in fact his fag for two terms when he was not only Head of House, but Head of School. What impressed me then, and what remains indelibly in my mind now, is his respect for me as a person, his courtesy and his sensitivity. Wellington then was a very tough, not to say rough, school and fags were the lowest of the low. But David was an extremely gentle taskmaster.

James Wort, who taught mathematics at Wellington, remembers him not as a particularly outstanding pupil, but as 'one of the five nicest boys' of his whole time at Wellington. 'He was always doing helpful things for other people.'

At the same time, David was developing a flair for efficiency. This was not an obsession with order so much as the ability to get things done properly, without fuss or delay. He was an excellent organiser, both of people and programmes. Although he had no obvious natural charisma and no great personality with which to dominate a scene – as perhaps his father had – he communicated well with others at all levels and could persuade them to do things his way, which was usually, of course, the most efficient way.

He had a knack of establishing a rapport with people on a one-to-one basis by exploring mutual interests and experiences, and explaining, with candid charm, how his own problems were similar to theirs. This charm, or warmth, was to remain an enormous asset all his life and, when coupled with a fearless openness, was totally disarming. His sense of humour, expressed with a delightful chuckle, made his gift of communication irresistible. One of his contemporaries, James Ekins, recalls that he was a very balanced person, 'never prone to the wilder excesses in which the rest of us sometimes indulged'. In contrast to many boys at the school, David's appearance was always 'efficient' too – socks pulled up, trousers pressed and clean, hair brushed.

At Wellington, David showed no real interest in Christianity. Although he dutifully attended the compulsory Chapel services, he could not see that they had any relevance. In fact, they tended to generate an unconscious but fairly thorough knowledge of the Bible, even in those who most resented them. The most ungodly public schoolboys of the era could still quote the words of obscure Old Testament prophets. Nevertheless, David regarded them merely as a part of the culture of the public school and he found them powerless to help him in his search for some meaning and purpose in life. He remembered being stirred and impressed by a Franciscan friar who came to give a series of addresses in Lent, not only by what he said, but by his simple lifestyle, with the brown 'dressing-gown' and the open-toed sandals. But he 'wondered how on earth anyone with any intelligence could go around like that for the sake of Christ'.[1]

His interests were developing on lines rather different from most of his contemporaries. He became fascinated by philosophical questions and began to explore the teachings of theosophy and Buddhism. In particular, he was fascinated by the mysticism of eastern religions. An uncle of David's had been a devotee of Rudolf Steiner and introduced him to his writings. Man was the centre of Steiner's system and there was no need for God. In his last year at Wellington, David became excited by some of John Dunne's abstract ideas about time and the meaning of dreams. Still searching, but still really dissatisfied, he wondered whether there was any life after death and even took part in one or two séances to discover if he could get in touch with his father.

This unsuccessful spiritual search did not seem to have any ill effect upon David's academic progress. Although never academically brilliant, he did well in most subjects by virtue of hard and intelligent application and showed a particular aptitude for maths and science. He passed his Higher School Certificate, the equivalent of GCE 'A' levels, in Maths and Physics in July 1951. He won an Open Exhibition in Mathematics to St John's College, Cambridge. Although nuclear physics was too new and remote a subject to be included in the curriculum to any significant extent, David nevertheless pursued an interest in it. He decided to stay on at Wellington, where he had greatly enjoyed his time, for one extra term and was made Head of College.

He also became editor of *The Wellingtonian*, having served as assistant editor during the previous year. His editorial in the December 1951 issue was on the value and dangers of competitive games and the importance of team spirit and whole-hearted participation. There was already a maturity of style evident in his writing. He had taken English as a subsidiary subject in the sixth form and this gave him an appreciation of English literature which undoubtedly helped in his writing. He also won the Prize for Reading in his last term. The set passage in the senior competition was St Luke's account of the risen Christ on the road to Emmaus. In his comments as judge, Sir Gyles Isham pointed out how much more difficult it was to read the Bible publicly, in cold blood, than it was to read it in church. He felt that Watson (whose strong, rich voice was still untrained) was the only one of the competitors to have overcome the difficulties.

One side of David's life which remained underdeveloped at Wellington, and indeed until some time into his twenties, was the capacity to relate to girls of his own age. Much has been said of this limiting effect of single-sex boarding school education, and without doubt there is justification for the criticism. The schools are increasingly admitting girls to their sixth forms and some are deliberately turning to co-education as more liberal views prevail. For David the problem was the greater because of the limited social life he enjoyed at home. The family lacked a father, and also the financial resources with which to embark upon the enjoyment of local society to the extent that other families did. David's sister Diana was seven years older than he and although always kind and helpful to him, especially when he decided, with characteristic methodology and application, to learn to dance, she had her own life to live and her own work to do.

In 1949, Peggy, David's mother, married again. Through some friends in Beaconsfield she was introduced to a Colonel Hawkes, whose wife had recently died. There was a mutually felt need for support and companionship, but there were never any real bonds of love and affection and sadly the marriage was not a happy one. David was initially very pleased for his mother, not least because he knew it would relieve her financial burden. Although he used to play golf regularly with his stepfather in the holidays, he never built up a close relationship with him, and Colonel Hawkes certainly did not begin to fill the father-gap in David's life.

During the Christmas holidays of 1950–1 David and Sam Osmond, with two other friends, one of whom had a sister who brought along three of her school friends, went on their first skiing holiday at Oberlech in Austria. The four boys and four girls mixed rather awkwardly together and applied themselves, especially David, much more to the business of skiing than to the social opportunities presented to them. The holiday was the more remarkable for a massive avalanche which completely isolated the village of Lech for a few days and delayed their return to school until after the beginning of term. David was extremely worried by this default, partly because it was his first term as Head of the Dormitory, and three new and inexperienced prefects had to shoulder his burdens. In the event, it was a useful lesson to learn that other people could cope in his absence. Later in life he would frequently have to leave his church in the hands of others when he was away for several weeks on missions.

When Sam came to stay with David in Eastbourne, where Peggy was now living after her marriage, they managed to persuade some girls from a domestic science college to accompany them to a dance at the Grand Hotel, which they all enjoyed. In his last summer at school, David organised a short holiday for three boys and three girls on Hayling Island but, though this feat greatly impressed his contemporaries, David's relationships with members of the opposite sex were never very relaxed.

When David left Wellington, the Master, Major House, wrote in his final report:

He has had a distinguished career here, with real breadth of interest and under-standing. I am sure that he will make his mark at Cambridge and later, especially if he does not allow his academic programme to suffer from competing claims on his time – which can easily happen in a University to a versatile and receptive undergraduate. As Head of School, he has given me much help and a sense of assurance. He has been most thoughtful and foreseeing and shown balanced judgement and perception. I am very sorry that his time is up and wish him all good fortune.

Bertie Kemp, Tutor of the Hill, wrote: 'His advice on any point was always worth listening to. He was one of my best Heads of Dormitory and, amongst the staff, he was considered to be one of the best Heads of College.'

It was no great surprise when it was announced in June 1952 that the Queen's Medal, awarded to the most outstanding boy of the year, had been awarded to D. C. K. Watson. Queen Victoria had established this prize 'to hold up to the admiration of the students and to their emulation, so far as they are capable of emulating such virtues, the great qualities of the Hero and Statesman in whose name and to whose memory the College has been instituted'. The names of all the medal winners are displayed on a prominent board in the College, and David would have been delighted to have known that in 1984, the year of his own death, the Queen's Medal was awarded to the son of his old friend, Sam Osmond.

In view of Wellington's strong links with the army, the cadet corps played an important part in school life. It was also something which David enjoyed and in which he did well. He ended up as Company Sergeant Major, with Sam holding the senior post of Regimental Sergeant Major. National Service was still compulsory in 1952 and both chose to do the two years' service before taking up their places at Cambridge University.

In February 1952, therefore, David and Sam were called up to the Royal Artillery (Gunners) Training Depot in Oswestry, Shropshire. They met at Euston Station to catch the train north. King George VI had died the previous day, and the papers were full of obituaries. This, together with the February cold and the chilling prospect of starting again as a very junior recruit, made for a dismal journey. As they had expected – and as always happened – the recruits were chased around and shouted at over the first few weeks. Special care was taken to make it clear that young men from posh fee-paying schools were not the elite – quite the reverse. Barrack room inspections and competitions became so important that there were nights when the recruits did not dare sleep in their beds for fear of not getting everything perfectly squared up again in time for the morning inspection. Life was certainly not comfortable.

Conscription for National Service had not previously been enforced in peacetime but there were circumstances which made it inevitable in the aftermath of the Second World War. Some considered it sound that every male citizen should become involved in the defence of his country for a period of his life, and that a spell in the forces would be good for the characters and attitudes of British youth. Others believed that with only volunteers available, the armed forces would be so depleted that their present worldwide tasks could not be undertaken. There were differing opinions in high circles about the validity of these views, but eventually National Service ceased to interrupt the lives of British young men, partly because the worldwide tasks began to disappear as the British Empire shrank into history. But in 1952 there was still the fearful, if sometimes entertaining, experience of learning to serve their new Queen as best they could.

Eventually David and Sam were summoned to attend an Officer Selection Board down in Hampshire. Both were selected, so after twelve gruelling weeks at Oswestry, they reported to the Mons Officer Cadet School at Aldershot. There was more drill, of course, under the supervision of the famous RSM Brittan, whose voice could be heard for miles. Six weeks' basic training with drill and lectures was followed by six weeks' more specialised training in gunnery, which involved some mathematics and, not surprisingly, David did well at this. Towards the end of the course, he was appointed Senior Under Officer and was awarded the Stick of Honour, which was presented to him at the passing out parade by Field Marshal Lord Harding. He was commissioned to H Battery, 3rd Royal Horse Artillery – one of the army's most elite regiments – and posted to Germany. Sam was posted to a different regiment in Ghana, and so their paths separated for a time.

At Mons, David had begun to enjoy life again after the rigours of Oswestry, but he was thoroughly to enjoy his time with the 3rd RHA in Germany, and by his own account led a very full and exciting life. His Commanding Officer, Lieutenant-Colonel G. W. Goschen, wrote to the Director of the Royal Artillery (who was an old friend of David's mother) to say that he was, 'a charming person, everybody likes him, he always seems to enjoy everything he does and there is not much that goes on in the regiment that he has not got a hand in. In fact, you could not wish for a better chap.' Army life seemed to suit David and at one time he was seriously thinking of applying for a permanent commission. He tells two stories of his exploits which illustrates the style of life the young British officers enjoyed. The first describes a wild chase through the streets of Hamburg after a group of officers had visited a night club. 'The German police cars had a tough time stopping our pepped-up Mercedes, though we eventually capitulated to about twelve of them. It was the nearest to a James Bond car chase I have ever been in.'[2]

The second story is of the time he managed to sink his four guns in a thick black bog while manoeuvring them in an exercise. 'I had never before or since seen tanks become submarines within a matter of seconds; it was immensely impressive, and I doubt if any other junior officer has accomplished the same feat with such dramatic effect.'[3] Despite this misadventure, his Commanding Officer later wrote:

I have served with no other junior officer of whom I have a better opinion than 2nd Lieut. David Watson. He knows his job, enjoys doing it, and is the possessor of the sort of personality that makes anyone he meets feel the better for it. I would be delighted to have him in my Regiment as a regular subaltern and was extremely sorry to see him go.

The level of success achieved by David both at school and in the army is remarkable and largely stemmed from two different capabilities which, when combined, proved irresistible. On the one hand, he had the capacity to work hard and with real zest at whatever was committed to him and to apply a sharp intelligence to every task. This meant that he was always on top of the job, although not necessarily always right.

At the same time, he had a humble personality which was able to win the confidence and approval of those with whom he was dealing. He was better able to communicate his views and ideas than many men more gifted than himself because of the warmth and attractiveness with which he presented his case. There was no pomp about him, and no arrogance to alienate those who disagreed. The simplicity of his style and the humour he introduced into every situation made him acceptable, and his leadership effective.

As yet, however, he was not excited by considerations of truth and error but simply by the activity of motivating people to creative deeds. He had not yet found the philosophical base from which to make full use of these twin qualities, application and humility. He remained 'C. of E.' in the army and dutifully attended the Regimental Church Parades, but he drifted further from God during these two years. The padre, who, unknown to David at the time, was suffering from a severe nervous breakdown, did nothing to convince David of the reality or relevance of the Christian faith. There remained an emptiness in his life.

David's atheism had been born out of the rather flaccid religion prevailing in twentieth-century British society, rather than because he was totally convinced that no God existed. He knew that he could not prove that there is no God, any more than he could prove there is one. It is revealing that it should have been the need for proof which concerned him. The scientific emphasis which so widely influenced the thinking of the western world demanded that everything should be subjected to a process of cerebral criticism to see if it held together. If no convincing reasons for the truth of a proposition were forthcoming, doubts could and should be entertained. One did not necessarily have to be in possession of all the facts to hold a particular view, only to be unable to discover any adequate evidence to the contrary. The onus was firmly on the proposer to prove his point and his data had always to be scrutinised most carefully.

This approach is, of course, entirely valid for science, but it was not really designed for the consideration of religion. Science quite rightly demands proof; religion properly demands faith. If an aeronautical engineer told you that he had no proof that his aeroplane would fly but that he simply believed it would, you would justifiably conclude that he had missed his calling and travel by some other means. In just the same way, a religion that does not involve faith but which makes logical sense is dubious. So religion, obliged by the scientific mindset to prove that there is a God, which it could not do, became the object, not of faith, which is its essential method, but of criticism, which it could not survive.

Public school religion in particular was often reduced to a rather tepid ethical code sustained by some not unpleasant traditional ceremonial. It did not lack scholarship or integrity but it seemed to an honest observer, and David was certainly one of these, to lack life. What it had to·say was almost irrelevant to daily problems. However much one might wish to believe in God, it became more and more difficult to do so in the absence of the necessary proof. It was this vacuum which dictated atheism.

On one occasion, when suffering from a hangover after an especially wild party, David found himself saying out loud, 'O God, there must be a better life somewhere.' But that almost involuntary prayer remained unanswered for a few months more, and David came out of the army at the end of 1953 describing himself as a humanist and an atheist. In spite of his successes in it, life did not yet seem to have any purpose.

3

Cambridge

IN 1954, NINE OUT OF TEN Cambridge undergraduates were men. The modern development of the old traditional colleges into mixed societies simply had not begun. Even the newer colleges were intended for students of either one sex or the other. Moreover, the traditions of the university were preserved in fairly strict rules of conduct which, although severely dented in the immediate post-war era, were still applied to each new generation. Gowns appropriate to each college had to be worn by every undergraduate venturing out after dark and they had to be back in their rooms by midnight. They also had to obtain written permission to go away for a weekend during Full Term.

For young men straight from school, these rules seemed insignificant and university life a breath of the fresh air of freedom, but for those who had already tasted adult life and held positions of responsibility during their National Service, it was not so easy to submit to the disciplines and restrictions of the life which they were now to embrace. Nevertheless, the university rules were, on the whole, well observed.

In fact, although National Service was to continue until 1960, a growing number of school leavers elected to defer their call-up until after graduation, partly perhaps in the hope of avoiding it altogether, and partly to continue their studies without the enforced interruption. The contrast in ages, though not so marked as in the immediate post-war period, therefore still existed within the community. The 'older men' were often distinguished by an air of confidence and sophistication, by their cavalry twill trousers and sports jackets, and by their spontaneous gatherings in each other's rooms for drinks – usually cheap sherry disguised in a decanter. Girlfriends came up from London on Sundays on the so-called 'popsie express', which arrived at Cambridge station at 11.20 a.m.

Three years previously, David Watson had stayed on at Wellington for an extra term to try to upgrade his Exhibition in Mathematics into a full Scholarship, but in this he had been unsuccessful. The surprising, though not altogether unwelcome, result of this was that St John's College informed him that although his Exhibition still stood, they would no longer allow him to read Mathematics. The question arose, therefore, as to what subject he should read instead. During his last year at school, he had begun to develop a strong interest in philosophy and to enjoy the discussion of philosophic questions with one of his sixth form tutors, Robert Moss. It was with some enthusiasm now that he opted to read for the Tripos in Moral Sciences. This was basically a humanist course, which eminently suited him and involved the study of, among other things, philosophy, psychology, logic, ethics and metaphysics.

The university as a whole, and St John's College in particular, arranged its accommodation, both for undergraduates and for dons, in a series of courts with the public rooms (Chapel, Hall, Library, Common Rooms, kitchens, etc.) built into these. In each court, a series of staircases led to the students' rooms in pairs, one at the back and one at the front, originally used as a bedroom and sitting-room for each man. Post-war Cambridge, however, had been forced to turn each room into a bed sitting-room in order to provide for the considerable expansion in numbers occasioned by the arrival of hordes of ex-servicemen and the subsequent growth in further education. This proved perfectly satisfactory and has persisted ever since. It did, however, involve two men living comparatively closely together and perforce having to share their lives and facilities more than with others. David had been delighted to discover that a friend and brother officer called Tom Abraham was coming to St John's at the same time as he was and they arranged to share rooms together. Tom had been at Marlborough and was a talented skier and squash player. David also found Sam Osmond at Cambridge, though in a different college.

In the film *Chariots of Fire*, Cambridge freshmen were shown being welcomed with a sort of fair in which the various clubs and societies – sporting, intellectual, artistic, social, political, dramatic, religious, and anything else that could be conceived and organised – sought to attract and enrol the 'freshers'. Since each term lasted only eight weeks, there were only three terms in each year and most undergraduates only stayed 'up' for three years to complete their degree course, any social or cultural interests needed to be pursued early and with some vigour, if at all. The first week of a new academic year saw the newcomers invited to a large number of meetings sponsored by the various societies.

David and Sam agreed to attend as many as they could with a view to enjoying the proffered refreshments, but resolved in advance to join none of them. Thus, at four o'clock one afternoon David found himself at 'a nondescript tea-party organised (I thought in my sophistication) by undergraduates with bright eyes, perpetual smiles and silly badges in their lapel buttonholes'.[1] He had been in Cambridge for only a few days – a confirmed atheist studying for a degree in humanist subjects. That tea-party was to change everything.

The post-war years had seen in Cambridge a remarkable growth in the size and influence of the religious societies. A good sermon at the University Church of Great St Mary's would often excite more interest than a political debate at the Union Society. There were active denominational societies representing every tradition within the Christian Church, and there were chapels and chaplains in almost all the colleges. In addition, there were two well-established interdenominational bodies. The Student Christian Movement (SCM) had a broad-based platform and much official support and approval. It emphasised the liberal intellectual standing of the churches and the need for Christians to be involved in society at all points. The Cambridge Inter-Collegiate Christian Union (CICCU), which had no official approval, held to a more conservative theology and an evangelistic approach, emphasising the need for a personal relationship with God. The story of the CICCU (pronounced 'kick-you') has been told by J. C. Pollock in *The Cambridge Movement*[2] and by Oliver R. Barclay in *Whatever Happened to the Jesus Lane Lot?*[3]

The difference between the SCM and the CICCU mirrored the differences within theology in the university faculty and in the Church; between the liberals and the evangelicals. Put epigrammatically, as is the evangelical wont, it was the difference between 'views' and 'news'. Liberal theology, which had controlled the faculty for many years, was based upon the scholarship which submitted Christian truth to the human mind. As with other academic disciplines, 'views' were thus produced, in the light of previous scholarship, which carried the authority of truth until other opinions came forth to supersede them. It was intellectually honest, of course, and true to the faith as understood by the academic mind, though it varied enormously in its allegiance to what the evangelicals saw as biblical revelation. What united it, apart from the supremacy of the intellect, was the scorn of the liberals for the conservative and evangelical theologians – usually kindly scorn, but sometimes less so. The CICCU was considered naive and obscurantist in the light of modern scholarship.

Conservative evangelical theology held rigidly to the authority of Holy Scripture 'in all matters of faith and doctrine', as the Church of England puts it. The mind, therefore, was subject to the Bible and not the other way round. If this principle was followed, they believed, a revelation was uncovered which could best be described as 'news'. It was God who revealed it, rather than the human mind which discovered it. It was 'good news' or 'gospel', which the keen mind could and should study in the light of the findings of modern scholarship, but needed to do so with the presupposition of faith in a divine revelation.

It was to a CICCU tea-party that David Watson went, all unwittingly, in October 1954. He has told the story at some length in *You Are My God* and it is therefore more appropriate here to point to its significance rather than to spell out its details. After tea, the freshmen were invited to listen to a brief talk by a young Anglican clergyman, John Collins, Curate of All Souls Church, Langham Place, in London. Although David subsequently remembered little of what had been said, he was strongly drawn to the speaker himself, by his simplicity and sincerity. It was all so pleasantly done and seemed real and attractive rather than religious. As he left, he politely shook the speaker's hand and entered into a brief conversation with him. He had not expected a gentle but very direct question as to his own beliefs. This opened the door to an invitation to breakfast with the speaker at his hotel in the morning. He was shaken but impressed, and could not refuse.

At breakfast John Collins, again with studied simplicity and a winsome smile, explained to David what he felt he had never heard before: that God loved him, that he offered him total and free forgiveness for everything that had caused a broken relationship between them, that this forgiveness had been purchased by Christ upon the cross and that if he would accept this offer, he could have Christ as his Lord and friend. This step needed to be taken very deliberately by opening both his heart and his life to God. To support each point, the Bible was quoted, and simple but practical illustrations were given.

'It all seemed far too simple,' wrote David, years later, 'and there were still a host of philosophical questions as yet totally unanswered.' But the humanist left the hotel clutching a little explanatory booklet and with his mind racing. That evening, alone in his room, he read the booklet, *Becoming a Christian* by John Stott. 'It was compellingly clear in its logical reasoning. Steadily I realised that, if these things were true, I wanted them to become real in my own life.'[4] He knelt by his bed and prayed the pattern prayer at the end of the booklet.

Lord Jesus Christ, I humbly acknowledge that I have sinned in my thinking and speaking and acting, that I am guilty of deliberate wrongdoing, and that my sins have separated me from Thy holy presence, and that I am helpless to commend myself to Thee;

I firmly believe that Thou didst die on the cross for my sins, bearing them in Thine own body and suffering in my place the condemnation they deserved;

I have thoughtfully counted the cost of following Thee. I sincerely repent, turning from my past sins. I am willing to surrender to Thee as my Lord and Master. Help me not to be ashamed of Thee;

So now I come to Thee. I believe that for a long time Thou hast been patiently standing outside the door, knocking. I now open the door. Come in, Lord Jesus, and be my Saviour and my Lord for ever. Amen.[5]

It is important in the subsequent history of David Watson to have a clear understanding of this experience of conversion. He became not only a minister, but also a teacher and evangelist. Through him, many the world over came to faith in God through Christ, and still do as they read his books and listen to his recorded addresses. For him this conversion, far from being the last word in his own experience of God, was not only the beginning of a life of faith, but also set the pattern and style for his theological insights and the message which flowed from them. He learnt that the Christian religion is not a series of propositions but a living relationship. The philosopher had discovered that the 'host of philosophical questions' which were left unanswered by his breakfast conversation were pushed aside unanswered, some rendered irrelevant and of no further interest, and some to be fully answered at a later stage by a great burgeoning friendship with the living God himself.

The key to the effectiveness of John Collins' message to David had been its simplicity. There was no attempt at all to enter into discussion with a professed atheist with a view to convincing him of the validity of Christianity. No brilliant arguments were put forward. No complicated religious system was considered. A straight offer of friendship between God and man was made over breakfast. Its very terms were deliberately simple. The great mystery of the cross was unveiled with the aid of a piece of dry toast, laid upon the upturned palm and transferred to the other palm to the accompaniment of the words from Isaiah 53:6, 'the Lord has laid on him the iniquity of us all', in order to illustrate how guilt had been transferred from sinner to Saviour.

This is a concept of unfathomable depth about which endless thought and discussion has taken place, but there at breakfast it was as if a piece of a jigsaw had suddenly fallen into place. Simplicity and profundity are not adversaries, but brothers in truth. It was this that really caught David, in spite of his intellectual difficulties and religious prejudices. God, the creator of all, actually wanted him for a friend, had paid all his moral debts upon the cross, and would come to share his life with him if he wanted him to. Throughout his life and ministry, David sought to preserve this simplicity of the gospel in every presentation of it. His endless studies were with a view to delving deeper into its meaning, and bringing himself further under its authority, so that he could be more effective in achieving true simplicity in expression and in emphasis.

People often said to David how much they would have liked 'a Damascus road experience' – a bright light and voice from heaven. But David himself saw no bright light nor heard any heavenly voice. He never felt that he or anyone else needed to have done so. When he got around to studying St Paul's conversion in Acts 9:1–30 and Acts 22:1–21, he realised that the bright light and the voice from heaven were only concerned with the *beginning* of a new relationship with God, rather than with its fulfilment.

Some used to argue with him that conversion experiences are emotional decisions, which tend not to last and can be dangerous. David believed that some emotional pressure is involved in every big decision, but he was certainly not swept into faith on any wave of emotion. No doubt his heart beat a little faster as his mind raced around the implications of what he was discovering, but this was a decision of the will: to accept the free offer of forgiveness like St Paul before him. Others believe that such a decision needs to include acceptance of the discipline of the Christian Church. With this David had some sympathy, for he was increasingly to discover the need for every human to be disciplined in whatever he or she attempts, but he knew that such discipline in matters of religion is a secondary thing. Unless the relationship is first established, the very purpose for the discipline does not exist and the power to achieve it cannot be discovered.

A more generally held objection to the conversion experience is that it is not actually needed, and that it merely provides an excuse for the converted to behave badly. A conversion experience at some point in one's life, it is said, merely distracts from the daily need to live a life pleasing to God. Proponents of this view are in danger of working on the assumption that God is concerned with man's moral performance in life and not so much with his spirituality.

In this scenario God is a judgmental authority, before whom what is necessary is to live as decently as possible in order to be worthy of him. Nevertheless, since God is not unfair enough to expect the impossible, most people, within their abilities and after due effort, will be acceptable to him anyway. Jesus is an example set before us to inspire us on, but his standards, being beyond reach anyway, are not to be taken too literally. Be respectable, be sincere, be, humanly speaking, as successful as you can, but God is reasonable and benevolent and it is our genuine endeavour that counts.

What David discovered during those few October hours, and it was quite a shock to him, was that moral performance does not come into it at all. What he was being offered, without any conditions, was a free gift of forgiveness and thus friendship with God. He discovered also that it had already been purchased for him by Christ on the cross. All he needed to do in order to receive the gift was to acknowledge himself to be a sinner. Moreover, to be a sinner was not necessarily to do great wrong, but simply to live outside the friendship of God. However, you actually needed to know yourself to be a sinner in order to know yourself forgiven.

His conversion, therefore, was a change of kind and not of condition. He had become a Christian, whereas he had not been one before, but he was not yet a good Christian, or a holy Christian, or a joyful Christian, or even an understanding Christian. He felt just as he felt before. However, his condition was to change gradually as his faith and understanding grew. His moral performance in life hitherto was entirely irrelevant to his new status. He had not earned it, nor could he have done so, but he had received it by acknowledging an incurable unworthiness. He was taking God at his word, taking him on trust, believing that he would not be let down. This was to be his unchanging gospel.

When, having prayed 'the prayer' he felt no different, he was disappointed, and when next morning he still seemed unchanged, he felt he had been let down. It was very perplexing. Yet he trusted he had been right to take the step. For several days he persisted in this state of suspended hopefulness, not knowing what else to do, but not experiencing any of the great feelings of change which he had expected.

He kept his promise to John Collins to let him know if he had taken the prescribed step and was delighted to get an encouraging letter from him with the information that he had asked a friend to call. On the same day, a note lay on his desk when he returned from lectures revealing that the friend was David Sheppard, the renowned cricketer of Cambridge, Sussex and England, and a striking personality with a considerable presence, who had long commanded the respect of schoolboy cricketers and especially those based in Sussex. As the note promised, he returned after lunch and David gratefully, if not a little awestruck, accepted his offer of help and friendship.

David Sheppard was then in his final year at Ridley Hall, Cambridge, training for ordination into the ministry of the Church of England. His comment upon David was: 'I don't think I have ever before met anyone who was so confused!' As David says in *You Are My God*: 'my religious ideas were . . . an incredible tangle of various beliefs, interwoven with a few strands of Christianity here and there.'[6] Yet the change from humanistic atheism to faith had taken place and a hunger for more understanding quickly developed. He agreed to go weekly during term to Sheppard's rooms in Ridley to read the Bible with him and to learn to pray. As he came under instruction and encouragement in this way, his faith began to develop.

One of the first signs that something real had happened to him was that he had, quite naturally and without effort, stopped swearing in the perpetual way common to the British soldier. He also found that 'a new love for people slowly began to dawn in my heart'.[7] Each week for the rest of the academic year the two Davids would read a different chapter of the Bible, discuss the subject matter and pray about the lessons learnt. David found the teaching invaluable, but also used the sessions to explore all sorts of questions which his new-found faith created for him, and to talk over what he should or should not do to deepen it. He came to see that he owed much to David Sheppard's care for him and wrote in his autobiography: 'It is impossible to stress how vital these sessions were for me. Without them, humanly speaking, I should never have survived as a Christian.'[8]

Another practical thing which David Sheppard did for David in those early days was to encourage him to join the CICCU. At first he found that he had little or nothing in common with the other Christians in St John's who were members of the CICCU. They seemed to him to be rather too intensely religious and they did not share his interests, particularly sport, of which he played either hockey or squash nearly every day. The very idea of going to a prayer meeting seemed quite extraordinary at first and it did seem a little excessive to have one every lunch-hour.

His first experience of one was quite an eye-opener, with scores of young men praying audibly, one after the other, without using set prayers. He quickly became acclimatised to it, however, and learnt to accept with joy the style of extempore prayer as natural to the Christian who enjoyed a friendship with God through Christ. This the CICCU taught him by example. In addition to formal prayers that were highly polished both in the beauty of the language and delivery and in terms of theological accuracy, there was the natural desire of the children of God to address him as 'Abba, Father', and in words that simply spring from a living family relationship. David was to learn to use informal prayer regularly and with great profit for himself and his companions.

The CICCU also provided for its members a series of evangelical speakers of considerable ability. Each weekend one would come to give instruction in the Bible and, even more important, to preach an evangelistic sermon in Holy Trinity Church. During the three years that David was at St John's, and the further two he was to spend at Ridley Hall Theological College, he only missed these sermons when genuinely prevented from attending. Not all of them were of the highest class or of equal effectiveness. They were preached by men of varying expertise from many denominations: some laymen, some clergy and some bishops, some from overseas and some with little or no academic background. They presented between them a multi-cultural treatment of the gospel, and yet in their common Evangelical inheritance they knew no other gospel. By the time David left Cambridge, whatever may have been the merits of other training he received for his life's work, he was deeply taught in the truth of the gospel and well experienced in different ways of expounding and proclaiming it. This he owed to the CICCU Bible readings and Sunday evening sermons.

A second vital lesson he learnt from the CICCU was an ecumenical attitude towards other Christians. Here was a body of Christians from a wide spectrum of ecclesiastical and cultural backgrounds, amongst whom the prim and self-conscious Old Wellingtonian was to find a warmth of fellowship and breadth of understanding beyond what the wider Church could offer him. Divided by much, they clung together in Christ. The Bible was their authority and the gospel their 'stock-in-trade' and they refused to be diverted from either by the very considerable liberal pressures with which they were constantly assailed by religious leaders in the university. Thus, the members of CICCU, by refusing to abandon their conservative allegiance to a Bible-revealed Christ, were in fact providing a truly ecumenical experience in all they did. It was here, bit by bit as his faith and understanding grew, that David found the Body of Christ.

Very few senior members of the university agreed with or supported the CICCU. It was essentially an undergraduate movement. Yet one rather quaint figure, the Senior Under-Librarian of the University Library, Dr Basil Atkinson, was a stalwart friend to all its members and a great resource of wisdom both to them and to the movement as a whole. He was one of the university's two experts on ancient languages but, more important in this context, he was a deeply prayerful Christian.

Eccentric to a degree few other dons achieved, he used to ride through Cambridge on an old upright bicycle, dressed in a blue pinstriped suit and a green pork-pie hat, and his voice, strong and with extraordinary emphasis placed upon almost every word, was often mimicked by his many friends. He used to read the lessons at St Paul's Church on Sunday mornings, and when it was known that on a particular Sunday he was to read Daniel chapter 3, the attendance was greatly increased. Stories about him abound to this day among his old friends.

Basil Atkinson was an unrepentant Protestant who held all things Catholic in strong disapproval, but his opinions were always seasoned with love. Ironically, it was from him, perhaps more than any other, that David eventually learnt to include the Roman Catholics in his respect. 'David,' he would say melodiously, 'they believe what we believe, but they have systematised it all into unscriptural methods. The cross gets hidden in the Mass, forgiveness in the confessional, and penitence in penance. Even Christ himself is obscured in Mariolatry [Reverence of the Virgin Mary].' Basil became a real and lasting friend to David, the older eccentric academic and the young respectable activist united by a common love for Jesus and the Bible. They used to say that you could tell the state of the CICCU by its appreciation of Basil: when the CICCU was strong and healthy and full of zeal for evangelism, its leaders had a great respect for Basil and valued his advice; but when it was struggling with dissension and lacking evangelistic zeal, Basil was probably being ignored or treated only as an elderly outsider.

Thus, the Cambridge experience developed. David struggled with his studies and found them a real challenge to his burgeoning faith. As the latter grew almost daily into a deep experience of 'the unsearchable riches of Christ',[9] he was all too conscious of the tension between it and what he was being taught in the lecture halls. He was very fortunate in having as his supervisor in St John's a former President of the CICCU, Malcolm Jeeves, a deeply committed Christian who helped him greatly to integrate his faith and his intellect. Philosophy was training his mind to think logic-ally and for this he would always be grateful, but it could not necessarily explore areas such as religious experience, which did not belong within its discipline.

David completed Part One of the Moral Sciences Tripos in June 1956, doing 'reasonably well in the exams in spite of my increasing preoccupation with Christian work (and still a lot of sport)',[10] and then switched to reading theology. By now his mind was fixed upon ordination into the ministry of the Church of England. David Sheppard's example to him in this respect had been extremely powerful, but so had been the most exciting and formative influence upon him during those early years as a Christian, the schoolboy camps at Iwerne Minster.

4

Camp

DURING HIS FIRST TERM AT CAMBRIDGE, and within a few weeks of his conversion, David Watson was invited by David Sheppard to help at a public schoolboys' camp shortly after Christmas, at which the Christian faith would be taught and practised. Camping in January may sound a rather uncongenial pursuit even for public schoolboys, but actually the word disguised a somewhat different activity, having been taken into the post-war era from the vocabulary of the 1930s. The event was held in winter and summer in a pleasant country house at Iwerne Minster in Dorset. During term-time the house was a minor public school, Clayesmore, and so provided all the facilities nearest to the heart of a boy – playing fields, gymnasium and common rooms. However, it was always known as 'Camp' because that particular series of holiday parties had begun years before under canvas. It is still known by that name although, partly to distinguish it from other 'Camps', it has also become widely known as 'Iwerne' (pronounced 'Youwern').

By this time David had already arranged to go with his room-mate, Tom Abraham, on a skiing party which was also to include some 'stunning girls'. So, to strengthen his invitation, Sheppard enlisted the support of David MacInnes, the son of the Archbishop in Jerusalem, who, one year ahead of David Watson at Cambridge, was to become a great friend to him. Both Sheppard and MacInnes had been recruited to Camp during their first year at university and both considered it to be the best possible training ground for a young Christian, so it is not altogether surprising that their combined efforts prevailed.

David was already seeing his Christian faith as the most consuming interest of his life. He was devoting some forty-five minutes each day to prayer and Bible reading and allowing his enthusiastic temperament to make him as wholehearted a disciple of Jesus Christ as he had been a head boy of Wellington College and a promising young officer in the RHA. So, after Christmas at home, during which he had been able, to his great delight, to explain his new-found faith to his mother, he packed his bags and set out for the first of what was to become a long series of thirty-five Camps. For many years he simply could not stay away.

Camp had been founded and was still being run by the Rev. Eric John Hewitson Nash, whose personal leadership controlled and inspired it throughout. Contrary to what might be expected for such an assignment, Bash (as he was universally and affectionately known by all) was a mild, quiet man with a thin voice and none of the obvious accomplishments supposedly needed for boys' work. He was not a big personality, not athletic or mechanically minded, not social or entertaining, not in any way 'with it' and without any great intellectual powers, although he had taken his degree at Trinity College, Cambridge. He had a limited stock of small talk and was somewhat shy and awkward in mature company and especially with women. Nevertheless, he had a fine sense of humour, was a good questioner and could draw people out to talk about what interested them. He was not himself the product of a great public school, though in speech and manners he might well have been. It is appropriate to salute those who in 1932 appointed him to the staff of the Scripture Union to develop work among public schoolboys, and who supported him and trusted him thereafter through many criticisms. He was to remain with Scripture Union for thirty-three years and became a towering figure in the Church.

His great friend and colleague, John Eddison, himself a product of Bash's work as well as his First Lieutenant in it, recalls the words which were written in the Press about him and his ministry at the time of his death:

Bash . . . was a quiet, unassuming clergyman who never sought the lime-light, hit the headlines, or wanted preferment; and yet whose influence within the Church of England during the last fifty years was probably greater than any of his contemporaries, for there must be hundreds of men today, many in positions of responsibility, who thank God for him, because it was through him that they were led to a Christian commitment.

Those who knew him well, and those who worked with him, never expect to see his like again; for rarely can anyone have meant so much to so many as this quietly-spoken, modest and deeply spiritual man.[1]

Bash was a remarkable and unusual man, whose eccentricities are still a constant source of amusement to his former campers, but above all, he was a deep man of prayer. He lived for Camp and for his boys, to each of whom he became a friend of rare value and complete trustworthiness. Even his theology was selective in order that it should be effective, for the simplicity of his gospel presented Jesus only, as Saviour, Lord and Friend. Vital, victorious, loving and available, Jesus was the person with whom life was to be lived in this world and the next. It was attractive and acceptable stuff.

Intensity was firmly rejected for there was much hilarity and enormous enjoyment at Camp. Bash's great sense of humour and the happy atmosphere he loved to generate contributed to the natural image of the Son of Man which he aimed to present. Hilarity is not to be confused with frivolity, and nowhere was this to be seen more clearly than in Bash's insistence that the boys should have a wonderful time at Camp in order that they might associate the Christian religion with happiness and joy as much as with serious considerations. David's later style of ministry owed much to this principle. His grasp of the importance of all the realities of human existence, including humour, tended to banish such fraudulent attitudes as religiosity and pomposity.

In these days the comment has to be made that although Bash was unmarried there is no reason to suppose that he was homosexual. None who knew him were ever given the remotest reason to suspect that his motives were anything but the highest. While he was infinitely kind and sympathetic towards all he sought to counsel, his approach was quite unemotional, in fact clinical and at times almost detached. He had made decisions years before about marriage, and he was so dedicated to his work and to winning boys for Christ that nothing was allowed to distract him or spoil his ministry to them. Everything was geared to that end. Consequently, Camp had a record of wholesomeness of which any boarding school would be profoundly jealous, and many other organisations also.

The evidence for the effectiveness of Bash's work is to be seen in the innumerable company of men fed into the leadership of the Church. In industry and politics, in medicine and the other professions, in education certainly and in the ministry of the churches above all, they are to be found. Some have become bishops; more perhaps than a superficial count would disclose. But, perhaps more particularly, it is necessary to recognise a surprising number of men of great quality, of whom David Watson is an obvious example, by whose leadership the greater Church has been enriched beyond telling.

It was, therefore, into this man's orbit that David came, all unsuspecting but definitely hopeful, in January 1955. Bash was to become the nearest that David ever found to an earthly father. He was to exercise upon him an extraordinary influence as he trained and inspired him for ministry. For David, fatherless and insecure, Iwerne was to become a safe place where he found a new family and a new identity. Compatible with everything he knew already, he could there entrust himself to a caring welcome and find himself accepted into a truly Christian brotherhood.

But first he had to submit himself to menial tasks: potato peeling and saucepan scrubbing. He expected, from his background and experience, to be appointed to some role in which he could be a help to the boys, but of course Camp was in the hands of those who knew that spiritual maturity was more important than natural gifts. He did not yet qualify in that respect, or indeed in the Easter Camp that followed. During the war, when domestic help was hard to find, Bash had instituted a third tier between the leaders, or 'officers', and the boys. Undergraduates from Oxford and Cambridge who were not yet suitable for the spiritual work among the boys, but who might well become so if given an opportunity to prove themselves, were recruited in a semi-domestic role. They were full members of Camp for all purposes, but they also assisted the kitchen staff (who were professionally employed) with much of the labour involved in feeding up to 200 people. David, though warned in advance, had not quite expected what he found but he enjoyed it nonetheless and entered enthusiastically into every aspect of Camp.

Camp was organised around 'prayers', morning and evening. The word was used loosely, for apart from one short prayer in the middle, the forty minutes was occupied with some choruses, very well led and sung, and largely biblical in substance, and a short talk from one of the officers. The series of talks was drawn up by Bash himself, who also selected the speakers. They were designed to bring the listener from perplexity concerning the Christian faith, through a recognition of his need, to an understanding of Christ as Saviour and a commitment to him as Lord. He was then instructed in Christian living, shown the importance of Bible reading and prayer, challenged to victory over sin and to service in Christ's kingdom, and given a striking portrait of God's great love for him which would never fail. David soon perceived that John Collins' discussion with him over breakfast, John Stott's booklet *Becoming a Christian*, and David Sheppard's subsequent systematic teaching and encouragement all had their genesis in Bash's careful training.

It was the quality of the talks which impressed him so much. It was not the erudition which was outstanding, but the communication. Bash trained his officers to speak from well prepared notes, which had been prayerfully put together. No talk was acceptable to him unless it seemed to carry divine power in its delivery, and this would depend upon the prayerfulness of the speaker more than upon his natural ability or technical skill. He would never put down a bad speaker, though occasionally, if the talk was too long as well as too dull, he would try to interrupt and halt it, much to the amusement of other officers. He once gave one of his most established speakers (a public school chaplain) a little note just as he stood up to speak. In it he read: 'Be winsome, genial, gracious, engaging, clear-cut, logical, doctrinal, not too fast.' Given no time to prepare for such a performance, the advice was largely wasted, but it became one among hundreds of stories circulated in the 'officers' room'.

His own talks, which occurred usually not more than three or four times in the course of a ten-day Camp, were shining examples of the art of public speaking. It was, as Prebendary Dick Lucas has written, 'the attractiveness of the speaker's personality, reinforcing the phrasing and the arguments, which gave the words their unusual impact'.[2] John Stott recalls how Bash 'went out of his way to encourage others, especially young men at the threshold of their ministry. However much one floundered, he was nearly always generous in his words of appreciation, although bold in constructive criticism when the situation demanded it.'[3] Bash's instructions included the length of talks – fifteen minutes – and that they should have no more than three points feeding the overall subject, each of which was to be illustrated from everyday life, and especially from the everyday life of a boy. Anyone reading John Eddison's books will quickly realise how well the author had learned to illustrate his talks and become a pattern for others. With such examples to follow, it is not surprising that David Watson developed over the years into a brilliant speaker.

It is a further mark of Bash's genius that he knew he should work through and from within the Body of Christ. The nature of his calling to the boarding schools made it impossible to belong to a particular parish or to identify his flock geographically, as St Paul and other missionaries had done. Consequently, he formed his 'officers' room' (using the term to refer to the community of officers) into a caring community bound together by a love for Christ, a loyalty to himself, and a common vision for the work of Camp among the boys. Some of his senior officers came, as he did himself, virtually every holidays for ten, twenty, even thirty years. It was the thrust of their lives. Others, like David, found themselves giving it priority over everything else for as long as they could, and never letting go of the sense of belonging to a brotherhood when excluded from attending. Bash somehow held them in bond, sharing his work and his vision in partnership with them under the sovereign love of Christ. In York in the Seventies David set out to recapture and develop this concept, the pattern discovered lying somewhat dormant and dusty within his early training at Iwerne, expanding it to be the characteristic of the whole church.

For his third Camp, in the summer of 1955, David was introduced into the officers' room. Officers ran the entire Camp, in detail as well as in general. If an officer was, say, in charge of tennis, he would undertake all the work and take all the initiative to make tennis a success. He might have an assistant if the load was considered a heavy one, and if, for some reason, he needed casual help on a particular day, he had only to ask in the morning officers' meeting and two or three hands would go up. Everything was run that way, and David played his full part.

In addition, officers were all allotted to the leadership of particular boys' dormitories and would take special pastoral care of each of the boys in them. They were to be their hosts, getting to know them and making sure that they were enjoying Camp, but they were also their pastors, helping them to understand the talks and to respond to them. This care of each individual boy was not, of course, unique in work amongst boys, but it was of the greatest importance at Iwerne. None of the boys was neglected, and officers might spend time and energy in activities in which they had no real interest, simply to win the friendship of a particular boy.

David learnt through this discipline to count others more important than himself, and to make sure that he did everything he could to make the boys realise the full value of Camp. He seemed to have a natural aptitude for this, particularly for the pastoring side of it, due, no doubt, to increasing prayerfulness. Bash, recognising his potential, eventually appointed him to be one of the two officers who worked directly under him in the Commandant's dormitory.

Bash's time was inevitably given to the leadership of the work as a whole, so that his dormitory needed really good officers who knew his mind. Here were always to be found the boys who, in their particular school, exercised a measure of spiritual leadership among their fellows and especially those from Camp. Depending upon the school, and varying from year to year, this might include leadership of some form of Christian group. They were being trained in Bash's dormitory for this responsibility and hopefully for greater things thereafter.

David Fletcher, who eventually succeeded Bash when he retired, had filled this role for a few years and David Watson became his partner in the dormitory. They enjoyed praying and working together, but even more the privilege of such close fellowship with Bash. The emphasis upon personal care for each individual and the practical lessons for exercising it without pressure were both creative and liberating.

David himself testifies to the values of Camp in his life and ministry in *You Are My God*, regarding them as:

Undoubtedly the most formative influence on my faith during the five years at Cambridge . . . They were tremendous opportunities for learning the very basics of Christian ministry. Through patient and detailed discipling (although that word was never used) I learned, until it became second nature, how to lead a person to Christ, how to answer common questions, how to follow up a young convert, how to lead a group Bible study, how to give a Bible study to others, how to prepare and give a talk, how to pray, how to know God's guidance, how to overcome temptation, and also, most important, how to laugh and have fun as a Christian – how not to become too intense, if you like. I also gained excellent grounding in basic Christian doctrines, with strong emphasis being placed on clarity and simplicity. I may never fully realise how much I owe to the amazing, detailed, personal help that I received over those five years . . . if God has given me a useful ministry in any area today, the roots of it were almost certainly planted during those remarkable five years in the camps. It was the best possible training I could have received.[4]

The 'clarity and simplicity' which David mentions above were another distinctive emphasis of Bash himself. It was not only in the preaching of the gospel but also in the understanding and teaching of it that simplicity was needed. For Bash, it was a 'simple gospel', which needed to be made available to the believer so that you could feed upon it, as it were, 'in thy heart by faith with thanksgiving'.[5] Since it was intended for everyone, it must not be obscured by long words or abstruse discussion so that uneducated people could not grasp it. Profound as the implications of the gospel are, it is not so much a thesis to be understood as an offer to be accepted.

Bash was passionately dedicated to the evangelical movement in the Church of England, whose 'stock-in-trade' was the gospel, as John Stott once put it. As such, Iwerne stood firmly within the evangelical tradition of the churches, searching the Scriptures for the revelation of God which would offer salvation to a stricken world. Evangelicalism crossed most denominational boundaries and united those who shared a common understanding that within the Scriptures were 'all things necessary to salvation: so that whatsoever is not read therein, nor may be proved thereby, is not to be required of any man'.[6] Evangelicals differed from each other on many matters not crucial to this gospel of salvation – such as church government and baptismal practices – but they were united in their loyalty to scriptural revelation and to the Christ it revealed.

Their fortunes down the years ebbed and flowed with the theological fashions prevailing in the churches and they were often at their best when the Church needed them most. In the mid-twentieth century, when the influence of the 'Wesleyan' or Evangelical Revival from more than a hundred years earlier had spent itself, there was certainly a need for the rediscovery of the biblical gospel. At the end of the century the fruits of the work of Christian Unions and many other such initiatives, often dependent upon lay leadership, are clearly to be seen.

Nevertheless, Bash discerned very early that evangelicalism was in danger of over-emphasising the more intellectual aspects of the Christian faith. Not surprisingly, the movement had formulated for itself a body of Christian doctrine, drawn from a study of the Bible, which provided the boundaries within which it existed. Such doctrinal precision, necessary to counter the determined assaults from opposing theologies, had the effect of restricting the interests of its members to those issues spelt out so clearly in the literature it produced. This lent strength and effectiveness, but also threatened to foster rigidity and negativity.

The Bible itself is exclusive in the sense that it addresses and emphasises certain areas of human existence. It also makes abundantly clear that there are very different prospects and expectations for believers and non-believers. However, it also demands a genuine love within the fellowship which is to transcend all disagreement. Bash believed this transcending love to be a gift of God to each – a spiritual emphasis which would become seriously weakened if a theological emphasis replaced it. Revival would never follow the winning of any argument, but rather depend upon deeper and deeper commitment to Christ. In this distrust of intellectualism he had much in common with St Francis of Assisi in fearing the crippling effect of a slide into gnostic tendencies.

Nevertheless, though not an intellectual himself, Bash recognised the value of intellectual achievement. He rejoiced when his men showed skill in this field, especially when they were able to destroy some demon of error and unbelief with which he believed the Church was plagued. From the Thirties on, his officers' room included a high proportion of men with First Class degrees at Oxford and Cambridge and men highly qualified for intellectual leadership among their peers. He knew that such scholarship was indispensable to the progress of the movement as a whole, uncovering and expressing the real truth, and setting the Church free to build the real kingdom. But he feared greatly that if evangelicals made the study of truth their chief aim, they would come to defeat the very purpose for which they did it.

This became David's conviction also. An untiring student, he never allowed knowledge to be more than a maidservant to faith. He firmly believed that his personal commitment to Jesus, the relationship which sprang from it and his teaching of the gospel were more important to himself, to the Church and to the world than anything else. It was in pursuit of this goal that he sought spiritual renewal at a later stage, and it was the word of God to him to 'seek my face'[7] which brought him such great blessing at the end of his life.

5

Ridley Hall

As 1955 MOVED ON, David gradually moved towards ordination. When he began to consider his future career, he thought first of teaching. He had enjoyed a term teaching at Wellington just before starting at Cambridge, and had also spent part of one vacation teaching English to foreign students at a language school in Eastbourne. Now he was enmeshed in Camp, and because of Bash's emphasis upon the key role of the public schools, he felt that he could perhaps best serve Camp by becoming a teacher at one of them, as many other Camp officers had done.

The possibility of offering himself for ordination had first been raised by David Sheppard at one of their weekly sessions, but at that stage David still had a horror of having to speak in public. His first-ever speaking engagement after his conversion had been on 30 November 1954 in the village of Swaffham Bulbeck, near Cambridge, where a student at Ridley Hall was leading a small CICCU team which included David and Richard Bewes. They each gave a simple testimony of how they had come to faith in Christ, but David recalled how his mouth was dry, his knees knocking and his hands shaking.[1] Nevertheless, a young man in the Royal Air Force committed his life to Christ.

It is interesting that the cause of his hesitation in considering ordination had been this fear of public speaking, and extraordinary that a man later to be perhaps one of the most distinguished speakers of his generation, and already quite used to leadership and command, should have suffered from such a doubt at this stage in his life. To the end of his life David lacked confidence about his speaking, needing to bestow hard work and great determination upon it. He was grateful for every word of affirmation, even when he was at the height of his powers.

On Trinity Sunday 1955 David happened to attend a service in the magnificent Chapel of King's College. He had never been to a service there before and did not recognise the preacher. In the Church of England, Trinity Sunday is often reserved as a day of prayer for the ordained ministry, and on this occasion the preacher was Cyril Bowles, Principal of Ridley Hall and later Bishop of Derby. The sermon was an 'unemotional but powerful'[2] one on the need for more men in the ordained ministry. God spoke so clearly to David through this sermon that he was convinced that, despite his fears, he should offer himself as a candidate for the ministry. After much prayer, and after talking to friends, including the Vicar of his home parish, Holy Trinity, Eastbourne, he applied to the Central Advisory Committee for Training for the Ministry as the first step in testing this call from God. In June 1956, he was invited to attend a residential selection board and was subsequently recommended for training.

He applied to Ridley Hall, the college at which David Sheppard had been trained and many other Camp officers, including John Collins and even Bash himself, many years earlier. It had the great advantage of being in Cambridge, where he was now Bash's representative among Iwerne campers. He was awarded a grant of £344 a year from central Church funds for ordination training to support him during his two years at theological college. He entered Ridley in September 1957, and continued for his first year to read Theology in the university, which he had begun the previous year.

A tension developed for him in this subject for he faced biblical criticism for the first time, and many of the set books were written by those who did not share his evangelical outlook. He wrote: 'Much of the dry, dusty stuff that we were studying seemed thoroughly destructive. What on earth did it have to do with the knowledge of God?'[3] He admired some of the professors for their saintliness and their scholarship, and he enjoyed how Henry Chadwick (incidentally an old Iwernite, and later Regius Professor at both Oxford and Cambridge) 'made the theological controversies of the early Church live in an astonishing way, impersonating the fathers and heretics as though he had known each one of them'.[4]

David did not find it valueless being made to re-examine most of the basic issues of the Christian faith, some of which he had begun to take for granted, and he learned to weigh up the arguments on both sides. Undoubtedly it sharpened his mind. In addition to reading the prescribed set books, he would always try to read parallel books written by more conservative authors. This study made him more convinced than ever of the intellectual integrity of the 'simple gospel'. This helped his faith to grow. He eventually got only a Second Class, Grade Two, in the Theological Tripos, which gave him his degree. Some of his friends were surprised that he had not obtained a higher mark, as he undoubtedly had a good brain, and a contemporary at Ridley, Keith Sutton, now Bishop of Lichfield, feels that this disappointing result was a clear indication of the struggle going on in his mind at the time.

During his second year at Ridley he had no academic work in the university to do and so was more fully involved in the life of the Hall. David describes his time at Ridley as 'largely through my own fault . . . a difficult and negative time',[5] although this comment has surprised some of his contemporaries.

> I disliked the formality of Ridley chapel services every day; I rejected any teaching that I considered remotely 'liberal'; I found the staff giving theoretical answers to questions I was not yet asking . . . The staff were patient with my spiritual arrogance and critical attitudes, and I am sure now that I would have grown in my knowledge of God far more had I been a little more humble and positive in my approach.[6]

It is certainly true that the staff at Ridley were more liberal in their theology than the evangelical students and this tended to maintain a tension between the two parties which was not conducive to spiritual health and progress. Unfortunately, there was an unattractive arrogance among some of the conservatives which did not help their cause. Young people often give this impression. Regarding themselves as the trustees of God's great revealed truth, they found that their teachers did not appear to share this privilege and impatiently reacted against them. Certainty in Christianity can be a dangerous thing for any believer if enjoyed in the flesh rather than the Spirit but, equally, uncertainty is crippling to Christian ministry. The biblical revelation is based upon certainty, but balances it with enough uncertainty to restrain the believer from sin. He has not gained his position by merit, but has received it by faith. David was not the first to allow himself in his frustration greatly to exaggerate the gap between the trainers and the trainees, and then to regret his unspiritual attitudes in later life, but he never came to believe the liberal theology which provoked these or at any stage to regret the lack of it.

David began his theological studies with the assumption that the Bible is the word of God. He acknowledged the authority which the Bible must have over him, not only in his actions but also in his thinking. Having accepted that limitation, he could not allow his mind to operate in academic study as though he was free to think exactly what he liked. His frustration at Ridley Hall was that the syllabus dealt chiefly with academic theological questions, and did not appear to begin where he began, with actual submission to the Bible. Indeed, academic study was not what he wanted from Ridley. He never wanted to be a theologian; he wanted to be an evangelist and a teacher.

For David, the task facing the Church was to build faith, for which he needed to receive the biblical revelation. The study of theology as a branch of philosophy was no doubt interesting and even valid, but it was not what a prospective builder of God's kingdom most needed. It is the difference between being taught French and being taught how to teach French. He did not despise the learning of his teachers so much as become impatient with the academic liberalism which denied him the opportunity for studying what he believed to be so important for his future ministry.

The truth is that he had been and was still being trained by Bash. Anyone enjoying the privilege of that experience, with the endless work and practical training in evangelism and pastoral care providing the context for theological thought and debate, would struggle to avoid the danger of frustration from purely theoretical training which challenges the premises upon which the work is done. Of course, there were things which a parish priest needed to be equipped for (marriage, baptism, bereavement, etc.) that a Iwerne officer, whose 'parish' consisted solely of public schoolboys, did not. Nevertheless, the model for Christian ministry that Iwerne presented was sound. David was lapping up the principles and the practices of Camp with the eagerness of a participant who finds the joy of success attending his efforts. They must be right because they worked. In contrast, the liberal training for the ministry which he was required to undergo actually seemed to have nothing positive to say. It seemed an expensive and long-drawn-out process for very limited gain.

Years ago, the theological colleges offered training for much shorter periods, and with a more limited aim. Men from universities would come to such a college for three or four terms as a preparation for ordination; a sort of extended retreat rather than a period of theological education. The emphasis was upon devotion and piety. It is true that 'sound learning' and piety were thought to be indivisible, but for ordination it was the godliness which was considered essential, however valuable academic achievement might be. Many ordinands did not read theology at university but some other discipline, and at their theological college what they learned was only an aperitif of theological input to whet their appetites for the years they were to spend in their studies after ordination. Even then, it was mainly the Bible and the Prayer Book that they studied.

David believed that lessons should be learned about the best method of training men and women for the ministry, and his comments on page forty of *You Are My God* are relevant:

More emphasis is being placed (and in my opinion still needs to be placed) on first-hand experience of church work as part of the training. This was the method of Jesus, who lived and worked with his disciples. They watched him on the job, listened to him, were sent out by him, reported back to him, learnt from their mistakes, and so on. It was not 'first theory, then practice'. The learning and doing were closely interwoven.[7]

He certainly thought that more in-depth training in the situations where the original call was received, and where possible in the parishes where they are to work, would be far more beneficial to candidates.

It does not seem that he wrote further on this subject but in later life, and especially when he had encountered the less rigid system employed by Fuller Theological Seminary, Pasadena, he would from time to time debate with his friends the inadequate training provided for its ordinands by the Church of England. Young people offering themselves full of zeal for the work of the gospel are incarcerated for two, three or more years in a college which is required to teach them and test them in a theological syllabus, most of which they may never think about again. The staff of the colleges are excellent and able men and women, some of whom make very good bishops later, but most are best qualified to teach theology rather than to train a person in a practical syllabus similar to that which David enjoyed at Iwerne. Even when they attempt it, their enterprise is seriously handicapped by the artificial circumstances of college life. David's ambition to found a 'Fuller in London' was only frustrated by his death.

Nevertheless, David's sojourn in the wilderness at Ridley was not all gloom. Cyril Bowles, the Principal at that time, writes:

I formed a high opinion of him, partly because of his obviously strong personal religion, but also because of his apparent maturity and stability of character. He had a fine and clear mind. I did not doubt that he would make a good and effective clergyman. I thought he showed a marked ability to teach and I made my own private assessment that he might well in the future be appointed to the staff of a theological college. That he became a leader never surprised me.

Most of David's fellow-students remember him for his disciplined life – Keith Sutton, whose rooms looked across at David's, says that the light was always already on in David's room when he switched on his own each morning. Richard Bewes remembers that David was 'assiduous in Bible study, thinking out his theology. He was alert, cheerful, very active and contributing vigorously to the college life.' Another contemporary describes him as having a single-minded concern for Christ, with a strong spiritual discipline. 'He was a gracious person with a good sense of humour, but at times he could seem a little aloof.'

During the second or final year at a theological college, arrangements are made for each ordinand to find the particular church in which he or she should serve their 'title' – their first curacy. Originally, a 'curate' was a clergyman who had the charge, or 'cure', of a parish – that is, in England, a rector or a vicar. Now, however, the word is used to denote an assistant clergyman. In the Church of England a young male ordinand is ordained 'deacon' and then serves a probationary year before subsequent ordination to the priesthood. The probationary nature of the first year is virtually a formality, for very few do not get 'priested' at the end of it. The bishop of the diocese usually requires the curate to serve a further two years in the same parish. The choice of a first curacy is therefore considered to be of great importance in the ongoing training, and in practice is the most valuable experience in the system.

Some ordinands are recommended to a vicar by their bishop, and are happy to leave this decision to him, having neither the desire nor the needed perspicacity to exercise the choice themselves. Often this works well. David Watson, however, had not enjoyed membership of any particular local church and therefore could not easily identify a bishop as his own. Officially he had been sponsored for ordination by the Bishop of Chichester, since his mother's home at Eastbourne was in that diocese. However, he had made many contacts through Cambridge and Camp and was perfectly at liberty, under the guidance of his college principal, to pursue some of these. He looked prayerfully at three in particular.

The first was in north London, and seemed to offer him opportunities among young people and in local schools which attracted him, but in the event he did not consider it at length in the light of the other two. The second was an invitation from John Stott to join him in the distinguished and influential ministry of All Souls, Langham Place, in the West End of London. All his life, and without any reservation, David maintained a deep respect and admiration for John Stott, considering him to be the greatest and most influential Christian leader in Britain during the twentieth century. In the mid-Sixties their paths diverged due to a disagreement on emphasis, but David continued to read all Stott's books and to recognise his unparalleled leadership. Indeed, he was more delighted during his final years to be privileged to renew fellowship, and be invited to share in some of Stott's work, than he was by many other compliments and invitations. To be asked in 1959 to serve his curacy under him was extremely attractive.

But the third and most attractive contact was with John Collins, the man who had led David to faith in Christ. After a curacy with John Stott, John Collins had, since 1957, been Vicar of St Mark's Church, Gillingham, in Kent. Superficially the parish did not look very exciting. With a population of about 14,000, it lay in the centre of the town on a densely populated slope rolling down towards the muddy Medway and the dockyard. The church was a lofty Victorian building of blackened red brick, capable of holding 1,000 at the Christmas Carol Service, but on other Sundays difficult to heat and discouragingly large for a small congregation. It stood prominently at one end of the High Street, with the railway station at the other. From its roof, the view presented a wilderness of chimney pots in every direction, only broken in the south by the gas works and the distant towers of the oil refinery on the Isle of Grain.

There was no building of distinction in the centre of the town, for the beautiful medieval church was hidden away at least a mile from the main shopping area. So there was some truth in the local saying that 'If Kent is the garden of England, Gillingham is the compost heap.' Rows of little houses, dating from the 1850s to the 1870s, stood with their front door opening on to the pavement, or with a tiny front garden and gate. They had been built for dock workers, and indeed many of the men still worked in the dockyard. Thanks to the presence of the Royal Navy, thirty-seven pubs refreshed them each evening and at the weekends. At one time, the BBC used part of the parish on dark wet nights to film *Coronation Street*.

St Mark's was no different from the many working-class parishes in Britain where the Church exercised little influence and was neither understood nor appreciated. It was tolerated of course, and generally speaking valued as just one of the many organisations which in certain circumstances might perhaps be a help to some; but its real worth had disappeared with the last century and had now been replaced by the Welfare State. Even educated people had ceased to patronise the Church or to believe its teachings, so why should dockers and their families think differently? Behind the church there was the usual unattractive hall, previously a school and now partly in ruins. The vicarage was a square brick building, dated 1876 on its fine drainpipes, surrounded by a sizeable garden inconsistent with the style or scale of the housing in the parish.

But then there were the people, and if Gillingham seemed drab, the people certainly were not. They were warm-hearted, colourful, genuine, many of them with their roots in East London, brought to the Medway in past years by jobs in Chatham dockyard, and exhibiting all the famous Cockney quick-wittedness, humour and repartee. Sociologically, the sort of vicar needed was a 'man of the people' who would present no unacceptable contrast to and speak the same language as the parishioners. But in 1957 the trustees appointed, and the Bishop of Rochester instituted, the Rev. John Theodore Cameron Bucke Collins.

The son of a Church of England vicar, John Collins had been educated at an English public school and at Cambridge. He speaks with a quiet middle-class accent. He is not a scholar, but a man who reads well and thinks long. He served a spell in the Royal Air Force after the war, training to be a pilot, before going up to Cambridge. He was President of the CICCU, at that time the largest society in the university, and in the opinion of Basil Atkinson he was the best President the CICCU ever had. After six years' curacy at All Souls, Langham Place, during which he became John Stott's right-hand man, he took on the struggling dockers' parish in Gillingham and utterly transformed it. He then accepted a village church with a congregation of about a dozen or so at Canford Magna, which was fast becoming absorbed into the Bournemouth–Poole urban sprawl. From 1971 to 1980 he filled the little church, built daughter churches in the parish, and persuaded Canford public school, with its 500 boys and girls, to share a lively evening service with the parish.

Called in 1980 to take on the leadership of Holy Trinity, Brompton, in London's Knightsbridge, he built, with his colleague and successor Sandy Millar, a major evangelical witness within London standing across, as it were, from All Souls, Langham Place, in style and emphasis, but sharing its eminence in size and influence. It may well be asked whether any other vicar of his generation has a comparable track record; though it seems likely that in heaven such comparisons will not be considered appropriate. At Brompton, he entered into other men's labours and enriched them. At Gillingham and Canford, the work was, under God and along with his staff, his own. To them, he would wish to attribute much credit for the developments and increase, but if he was able to enjoy the support of some of the best men in England as his curates, they chose to come to him because of the training he gave them and the fellowship he offered them.

David Watson, having been converted through John five years previously, now chose to become one of his curates. The ordination was in Rochester Cathedral on 27 September 1959 and was conducted by the Bishop of Rochester, Dr Christopher Chevasse. Some fifteen years previously he had been chairman of the working party which had produced the report *Towards the Conversion of England*, a far-reaching document, sadly neglected by the Church, which called on the Church of England to recognise that evangelism must be at the heart of its ministry.[8] 'Possessed of a new hope in God's power and purpose, the parochial clergy will be enabled to look upon their ministry with new eyes, seeing the parish as a sphere for evangelism, and themselves as called to be fishers of men.' David Watson, who read the Gospel in the service, was one who saw his ministry in those terms, but the bishop could hardly have foreseen that the new young clergyman was to become one of the outstanding British evangelists of the twentieth century. However, he clearly knew that the clergy of St Mark's, Gillingham saw 'the parish as a sphere of evangelism and themselves as called to be fishers of men'.

6

St Mark's, Gillingham

DAVID WATSON HAD THE UTMOST CONFIDENCE in John Collins and in his methods. If he found his new parish daunting, that was because it was so different from anything which he had so far experienced. He did not think of it as impossible to influence, and John had already been there for two years testing the water, as it were, with the assistance of his senior curate – none other than David MacInnes. Because the parish had to provide free accommodation for curates and none was immediately forthcoming, John and his wife, Diana, released part of the ground floor of their capacious vicarage and made their home on the first floor. MacInnes was installed in the large former drawing-room of the house and Watson was to occupy the former dining-room. A young doctor, Graham Scott-Brown, preparing to become a missionary in Nepal, was another resident.

For David, this community of friends under one roof, sharing a common task and enjoying the same insights and methods, was particularly attractive. It was an extension of the Iwerne officers' room, secure and close and effective. It was also his first taste of normal home life – though the busy, overcrowded vicarage was not exactly an ideal site. Above all, it was great fun. The sheer level of enjoyment was a tonic to set beside the long hours worked, the importance of their calling, with its influence upon life and death, and the constant effort to relate adequately to their parishioners.

John Collins and David MacInnes were aware that David came with a high reputation for organisation and self-discipline. They therefore decided, for their own sakes, to pull his leg gently at the first staff meeting. For the first week, they drew up an arduous programme covering every minute of each day from 6.30 a.m. to 10.30 p.m. Alas, the joke backfired. David accepted the working schedule without question and by Friday was sailing along triumphantly whilst Collins and MacInnes, almost dead with exhaustion, decided they would have to call a halt, and, to Watson's glee, owned up.

This incident illustrates a characteristic of David Watson at this time of his life. Whatever the pressures of work, he had the capacity to be in control, to be confident and relaxed, with laughter not far away. He was punctual; his letters were answered promptly; 'papers' were efficiently produced in his neat handwriting on key subjects; his filing system worked; and the notes for his talks were always impeccably and fully written out in time. His daily timetable was clearly undergirded at every point with prayer and he rarely seemed to put a foot wrong. When he did, moreover, it was often as a result of his idealism.

One of his first tasks was to help dismantle the harvest decorations and take the flowers and fruit to the elderly parishioners. He had been recommended, unless it seemed inappropriate, to say a brief prayer in each home. Within a few days, John began to get some comments: 'Your new curate is a very nice young man, but I didn't like the way he prayed.' It transpired that David had based his prayer upon 2 Peter 1:10–11 (King James Version) concluding with a petition that the old folk might 'enjoy an abundant entrance into the everlasting kingdom'. They were not so anxious to go just yet!

He did make one complaint, however, about his schedule. Assigned to share the ministry in the monthly Family Service, David came solemnly to John with a carefully compiled list of reasons why he should be left out of this. He didn't see himself as gifted to work among children, and felt no calling to do so. 'I feel called to work among adults and students, not children.' John knew it would do no good to argue each point, so with a smile he reminded David that he would decide what training David needed. It was just as well. David became a brilliant speaker at the Family Services and much of his future ministry was built upon this strength.

Not many people can speak effectively to children and to their parents together, and he achieved this because even his earliest talks sprang from his painstaking study of the Bible. Who would think of making Leviticus chapter 14 the basis of a twenty-minute sermon to a group of ordinary people, including children? But David did so – most memorably. His opening verse was Leviticus 14:35 (taken from the King James Version): 'It seemeth to me there is as it were a plague in the house.' His visual aid was, of course, a house, cunningly constructed (probably by a fair, devoted member of the flock) so that by turning a leaf the various brightly coloured rooms could be seen. These captured the attention since decorating one's home was a popular pastime in Gillingham. The congregation was then treated to a conducted tour of the house by the Old Testament priest who, of course, found sin in the form of 'hollow strakes, greenish or reddish' (Leviticus 14:37, King James Version) in many a dark corner.

There was great stillness and attention. Nobody who heard that talk could have escaped the conclusion that sin needed to be taken seriously, and could only be 'cleansed' through the costly death of Christ.

From John came training at an exceptionally high level, based upon what he had himself learnt from Bash and from John Stott, and put together carefully with ever more discriminating detail as experience of parish work forced him to examine and adapt himself to people's needs. The big question was not only, 'Is it true and accurate?' but also, 'Can they understand it and will they want to obey it?' Every word became suspect until it meant to the hearers precisely what they were intended to hear, and every method was suspect until it was shown to be achieving its purpose. Thus, even preaching, however interesting and well applied, was found to be inadequate as a method of instruction for some of the worshippers who had left school at fourteen. An overhead projector was installed in St Mark's and sermons from such masters as John Collins, David MacInnes and David Watson, while still being expositional, were illustrated with coloured pictures and diagrams and, later, drama, such as would not be commonplace in adult education. Nothing was taken for granted in their efforts to proclaim the gospel of the kingdom.

David Watson came to the ministry with a reputation as a speaker made in that most exacting of testing grounds, the Library at Iwerne, and fostered at Cambridge. It had been achieved by long hours of prayer and study and continual self-criticism, and few men would have felt at that stage in his experience that a higher standard was needed. Yet at Gillingham he was having to compare his performance not only with his vicar's winsome and persuasive addresses, which were rather more effective than his own quick-fire and dogmatic style, but also with David MacInnes' flowing deliveries, so beautifully put together that they seemed quite irresistible. MacInnes scarcely seemed to have any worries about preaching, or to need to work very hard at it. His natural fluency was truly remarkable and the humour which punctuated his sermons was so spontaneous and so relaxed that it never offended and always attracted. David Watson, the perfectionist, was challenged by the excellence of his colleagues and came again and again to John for help.

John was nothing loath. There is a streak of the autocrat within him – a gentle and benevolent one, but an autocrat nonetheless. He would submit each of David's sermons to careful criticism, mentioning the strengths first, and going on to two or three areas where there was room for improvement. He would never bring up too many weak points, as he didn't want to discourage, but he looked for, and in this way obtained, a high standard of preaching from his curates. David received such criticism joyfully and profited greatly. Years later David MacInnes was to write: 'To listen to David's early teaching at St Cuthbert's, York, was to hear the clear intonation, style, and even sometimes the illustrations of John Collins.'[1] Such is perhaps the natural outcome of good vicar/curate relationships.

But another problem required a solution. However well thought out and put together David's material might be, when he raised his voice in a large building (and there were no microphones in those days) his delivery tended to relapse into the monotonous pattern of the falling cadence. Also there was a suggestion of the clipped words of an army officer. Another member of the vicarage community took him in hand. Diana Collins had studied speech and drama at the Royal Academy of Dramatic Art, and brought to bear upon David what she had learned about voice production and speech training. Characteristically eager for anything which would help, and well aware that his voice was a precious instrument given him by God for the proclamation of the gospel, David was assiduous in doing the exercises which she set him. Every morning at a particular time the vicarage would hear strange sounds emanating from his room as he practised his breathing and resonance. As a result of his diligence, there was eventually nothing in his voice which detracted from his message, but a power and flexibility which greatly enhanced it and enabled him to speak for long periods without tiring.

Years later, British Rail decided to introduce recorded announcements on board their new InterCity 125 trains between London and Scotland and invited David Watson to record them. British Rail had originally approached Richard Baker of the BBC, and indeed there is a remarkable similarity between the voices of the two men. Christians used to listening to David's tapes were surprised to hear him welcoming them aboard the train and informing them of its stopping places. As far as is known, Diana received no commission.

One of the most significant lessons learnt at Gillingham was about people. The army had taught him something about men, but here he was visiting ordinary homes and becoming deeply involved with men and women and their families. He was learning to live among them, to share their experiences, and to communicate intimately with them. They were friendly and full of humour, yet tragedies and tensions were as common there as anywhere, and a Christian minister needed eyes to see below the surface, and a heart to care. Life was tough and the people were poor, for Gillingham had only recently emerged from a period of unemployment and great poverty following the war. In the Thirties, young men would wait at the station for hours in the hope of earning sixpence by carrying someone's bag. Many of the little terraced houses were neat and clean and warm, but some were dark and shabby, and visiting involved treading one's way through lines of nappies and other washing hanging inside or out in the yard. David Watson made the effort and overcame his initial unease with such surroundings. He loved the people and they loved him. They laughed at him and teased him, and he paid them back in their own coin. But they listened and learned from him because he was clearly genuine.

David was given responsibility for the church's Pathfinder group of young teenagers, with a biblical syllabus to work through. They graduated on their fifteenth birthday into the Youth Group, with which he was also asked to help, but which was firstly the responsibility of David MacInnes. It had been run before MacInnes' arrival by David Smith, a lay Reader at St Mark's, and his wife, Jean. They were still fully involved, and their home was always open on Saturday evenings for those who were beginning to show spiritual interest. There were games for them to enjoy, refreshments and conversations, and a short Bible study. Many of the young people, unable for various reasons to talk to their own parents, used to share their problems with the Smiths. Numbers coming to their house on a Saturday grew steadily until there were as many as forty-five crowded into the small sitting-room, most of them sitting on the floor. The last to arrive often had to climb through the window because they couldn't get through the door.

There were as many as 140 or so, of both sexes, at the Friday evening Youth Club meetings. Some had come for a fight or at least to make mischief, but were usually diverted by the relaxed good humour which prevailed. This reflected the way in which David Smith and David Mac-Innes were able to gain the respect of the club members. They had received no special training for youth work, but relied upon their native intelligence and the deep pastoral concern which their own Christian faith had implanted in them.

David Watson was fairly apprehensive at first, wondering whether he had any gift for youth work of this nature – all his experience so far was with public schoolboys and undergraduates. He had no idea how to relate to the girls and not much in respect of the boys. But he had the example of David MacInnes to follow, and he was determined somehow to succeed, however hesitant he might feel. He soon perceived that his only enemy would be any tendency to be pompous and his greatest ally his sense of humour. He and David MacInnes were mercilessly teased, mocked and tried, but the good temper with which this was received enabled relationships to be built.

Every club evening included an epilogue at which the three Davids took it in turns to speak. On one occasion, immediately before it was due to begin, there was a commotion outside and a lad at the back picked up a brick and dashed out. Sensing that something was up, David MacInnes followed in rapid pursuit. That was precisely what he had been expected to do, and those remaining in the rambling old hall immediately locked all the doors. However, one was overlooked and left unlocked and unguarded. By sheer providence David MacInnes went straight to that particular door, got back inside, and calmly distributed the hymn books for the epilogue. He then told those guarding the doors to call the others back in. When they came (followed by David Watson, who had been in another room and quite uninvolved), they were amazed to see David MacInnes sitting there as though nothing had happened. They thought there must be something special about him if he could pass through locked doors. Not all such episodes ended with victory for the leaders, but with patience, good humour and much hard work, the club prospered.

David MacInnes excelled at leading these short epilogues, and David Watson, always keen and quick to learn, soon became almost equally good. Not all who attended the Youth Club showed great interest in spiritual things, but many did. One lad who entered the Merchant Navy attributed his stability and integrity entirely to what he had learned at the epilogues. Another, who used to come at the age of nineteen carrying a flick knife and talking always of fights, soon revealed a deep need hidden beneath a brash exterior. An illiterate eighteen-year-old accepted Christ as his Saviour following a simple illustrated epilogue which David had given. This young man had been thrown out of his home at fifteen and had lived rough with a gang of boys until someone invited him to St Mark's Youth Club. He found an unexpected friend in David, who started to visit him every morning to teach him a verse of Scripture.

Learning from this that there was a serious lack of suitable materials for helping such people, David put together some simple dramatic sketches and jingles set to popular tunes in an effort to teach them the biblical message. He also seized every opportunity for more thorough conversations with individuals away from the group, sometimes at the Smiths' house or on an occasional walk or outing. The annual Pathfinder houseparty particularly provided a good opportunity for this. He wrote:

However good and effective our Epilogue may be in the club, nothing is a substitute for detailed, prayerful, personal work. Giving a talk, it is said, is like throwing water from a bucket over a row of bottles; a few drops may enter into some. Speaking to individuals, on the other hand, is like pouring water from the jug into the narrow neck of each bottle. Indeed it is important to keep in the forefront of one's mind a right sense of priorities. 'Compared with evangelism, everything else happening in the church is like rearranging the furniture when the house is on fire.'[2]

Having come to Gillingham with no proper training or advice in church-based youth work, David realised the need for a resource book to help others in similar circumstances. Using his own experience at St Mark's, and with the help of responses to questionnaires sent to other youth workers, he wrote his first major book, *Towards Tomorrow's Church: A Practical Guide for the Church-based Youth Club*. It was published in 1965 by the Falcon Press (Church Pastoral Aid Society) and included a fore-word by David Sheppard, who was then Warden of the Mayflower Family Centre in Canning Town. The book dealt with the aims and methods of organising a youth club, and had a chapter on the teenage temperament.

Nevertheless, it would be a mistake to imagine that his ministry was only amongst the young. He regularly visited a number of elderly couples and, with the other clergy, spent time most weeks at the euphemistically named 'Over Fifties' Club'. At one of his talks a widower named Fred, aged about seventy-five, became a Christian. He had worked all his life in the dockyard, was poor in health, suffering from depression, and was generally rather pathetic. He asked whether he could 'help the church', so David suggested that he should come up to the vicarage twice a week and sort out piles of old newspapers which, in decent condition, could be sold for recycling. One of the consequences of Fred's depression was that he frequently slipped back, losing the assurance that Christ was with him and had forgiven and accepted him.

For many months it was a common sight to see David sitting with Fred on a pile of newspapers in the vicarage garage. For about fifteen minutes he would teach him, showing him verses from the Bible on which he could rest his faith. When, despite jokes and illustrative stories, concentration failed, David wrote out the verses in large letters on pieces of card which Fred could read again when assailed with doubt. He gave him John 6:37 – 'Him who comes to me I will not cast out';[3] Isaiah 41:10 – 'Fear not, for I am with you, be not dismayed, for I am your God; I will strengthen you, I will help you, I will uphold you with my victorious right hand';[4] and Hebrews 13:5 – 'I will never fail you nor forsake you'.[5] During the day Fred kept these cards in his pocket ready for use, and at night he propped them up against the clock. In this way, little by little, with many lapses, he eventually came to 'joy and peace in believing'[6] before he died.

Meanwhile, the congregation of St Mark's was growing fast, both in numbers and in depth of faith. David played his full part in this, not only in the services and through his preaching, but in visiting and ministering to the people in their homes. His stepfather had given him, rather unexpectedly, a gift of £150 to buy a car. It was quite a lot of money in those days, for a curate's stipend was under £400 a year. David consulted John as to the appropriateness of owning a car in Gillingham and then spent £80 on a 1938 model Morris 8, leaving himself £70 for running expenses. David MacInnes had an even older Morris and these two cars became quite a feature in Gillingham, providing transport for visiting distant parishioners, and making days off away from Gillingham much more viable.

Once, the two curates were invited together for lunch by a forthright old lady who, many years before, had cooked for one of the Archbishops of York, and who therefore held strong views on clerical behaviour. She lived at the other end of the parish, so they travelled together in David Watson's Morris. When they arrived she asked them abruptly, 'How did you come? By bus? Or did you walk?'

'Well, actually, we came in my car.'

'Oh, I see, so you are the kind of curate who has a car, are you?' she mumbled disapprovingly, making them both feel like bloated capitalists. Looking out of the window to see what sort of classy sports car this upper-crust curate owned, she could see only a very ancient, battered little Morris. 'Is that it?' she asked. 'Is that it? I thought you said you came by car?' Her peals of laughter made David realise he was accepted, after all.

The car, often an object of scorn and derision, was just about the only thing about David which was dilapidated. He was always neatly and properly dressed. When asked to speak, he spoke for the right time and was clear and to the point. His addresses were accurately applied to his hearers. In his room, too, everything was in place, with no sign of confusion or indecision. At this time of his life he presented the image of a confident and meticulously efficient man. He had great energy and health, was a regular squash player and an enthusiastic participant in any other available sport. He never cracked up or became ill – in sharp contrast to his health a few years later. He worked very hard and was always learning. He carried his notebook with him everywhere, writing down anything which appealed to him and might prove useful, including the jokes he was told.

Life in the vicarage was comparatively frugal. They all used to have breakfast together in the mornings, were given lunch by kind parishioners, but cooked supper for themselves in the evenings. The only dish the Davids could normally manage was an omelette, but occasionally they tried to vary the menu. Diana once had to protest when they experimented with cauliflower cheese in a pressure cooker, and every room in the house was pervaded with a smell which made her think that the Russian army had arrived and was taking its boots off. They tried to keep accurate household accounts, which was not easy, and one day found themselves discussing together how much a pinch of salt would cost. There was no central heating in the high vicarage rooms, so they had to try to keep themselves warm with paraffin heaters and overcoats when working at their desks in winter. Because all three clergy were on low stipends, they also had difficulty building up their libraries, which were, of course, the tools of their trade. Second-hand theological book catalogues were avidly read when they came through the post. All too often John Collins and David MacInnes would rush to the phone to order a book, only to be told, 'Sorry, but a Mr Watson from Gillingham has just reserved that.' David, always the early riser, had been first to gather and read the post.

During these three years David began to learn how to relate to women of his own age, and to value them as people. Needless to say, he was attractive to them, and sometimes this was reciprocated. John remembers David asking his advice and having discussions with him on marriage. Characteristically, he was determined not to be swept off his feet by a pretty face, even a pretty Christian face. He wondered whether he ought to marry at all. He realised that he was a man who had the capacity to work from morning to night with a packed programme. He saw readily enough the force of St Paul's argument in 1 Corinthians 7, so unpopular in this century, that the single life has considerable advantages, both for men and women, leaving them free to serve Christ.

He thought at that time, too, that he might possibly be one of those men whom Jesus mentioned in Matthew 19:12, who were 'able to receive' such teaching, because he could face the self-discipline and the measure of loneliness inevitably involved. He had also noticed the phrase in 1 Corinthians 7:37 'being under no necessity' and saw it as a holy and valuable condition. He had already begun to feel that God was calling him to work not on the mission field or in an industrial area, but amongst students, and perhaps in a parish in the setting of a university. He nevertheless felt that marriage, should it come, ought to enrich the ministry that God had given him. He began to pray, and felt it right to pray regularly, that God would lead across his path a girl who was not only as much concerned about Christian work as he was himself, but who would be able to face up to the demands that such a ministry would place upon them both.

In *You Are My God* David tells the story of a hazardous incident when a tall drunken Irishman – a man of great physical strength – made a sortie on the vicarage. Opposite the front gate was a pub and one Saturday, about twenty minutes before midnight, having imbibed for some hours, he persuaded himself that John Collins had run off with his wife, and he

David aged 8, 1941.

Wellington College prefects, 1951. Sitting on the left of the headmaster are Sam Osmond and David.

ABOVE
Mons Officer Cadet
School, "D" Battery,
1952. David fourth from
left in the front row;
Sam Osmond far right
in the centre row.

David with his mother
and step-father, 1956.

ABOVE
After David's ordination
at Rochester Cathedral,
27th September 1959.
Left to right:
Richard Bewes, Herbert
Cragg, David, Cecil
Bewes.

RIGHT
Corrie Ten Boom's visit
to Gillingham. Pictured
here with David, John
Collins and David
MacInnes.

David leaves Gillingham
for Cambridge.
St Mark's parishioners
make their farewells.

ABOVE
The Round Church,
Cambridge.

LEFT
David and Anne
on their wedding day.
Pictured here with
David's mother.

decided to get her back. The outer door of the vicarage was shut and bolted on Saturday nights. This door was massive and Victorian, studded with iron and, apart from lacking a portcullis, was well equipped for a siege. So the Irishman picked up a piece of rock from the edge of the drive and threw it repeatedly against the door, eventually snapping the bolts. He then proceeded to break down the inner door, smashing the glass panels.

David, armed with a broom, was preparing to do battle in the hall, while John stood behind the door on the bottom step of the stairs, ready to tap the Irishman on the head with a heavy piece of ebony wood which he had brought back from Tanganyika earlier that year. Happily, the police responded promptly to a 999 call, and within minutes a car arrived to take the Irishman away. Diana was the heroine of the occasion. The bathroom was over the front porch. With great presence of mind she poured cold water on him steadily from above, and when the next day he appeared in court, he said to the magistrate: 'Your honour, I don't remember much, but I do know that it was raining heavily at the time.'[7]

Through it all, David loved being at Gillingham. If the church was set in an unresponsive type of parish, where growth was generally thought to be difficult, if not impossible, that only made it more rewarding and more exciting. The centre of St Mark's, great Gothic barn that it was, began to be comfortably filled on Sunday evenings. Present, of course, were some professional people, particularly from the Royal Naval barracks at Chatham and the headquarters of the Royal Engineers, both of which were within the parish; but this only emphasised that the true composition of the congregation was the ordinary people of Gillingham. Everyone was valued, both as people and as Christians. John Hughes, now Vicar of St John's, Harborne, who with his twin brother David, now Vicar of St James', Didsbury, was a member of the youth club, remembers the excitement of life at St Mark's. They were the sons of a Royal Navy captain, and they loved St Mark's and its people.

Yet something may have been missing. Sue Lynn Allen, who came to St Mark's as Parish Worker at about the same time as David, certainly felt that this was so. She had been converted at the great Billy Graham Harringay Crusade in 1953 and subsequently had been helped by the teachings of Joe Church, William Nagenda, Roy Hessian and others associated with the East African Revival. This was essentially a holiness movement. The churches in Rwanda and south-west Uganda had been paralysed by immorality and drunkenness and with tensions which understandably arose between the whites – missionaries with traditions of paternalism – and the blacks; pride on the one side and resentment on the other. After much prayer, the Holy Spirit brought conviction of sin and the assurance that forgiveness and blessing would follow when Christians 'walk in the light', according to 1 John 1:7.

'Walking in the light', according to Revival teaching, implied spiritual honesty, repentance and confession, themes which are clearly emphasised in 1 John 1. Whereas 'walking in the light' often involved pointing out the sins and failures of one's fellow-Christians, 'confession' (1 John 1:9) was interpreted as the public and open confession of one's own sins, and even sinful thoughts, to others. This undoubted movement of the Holy Spirit brought great blessings to the churches of Rwanda, Burundi and Uganda and spread to the neighbouring countries of Kenya, Tanzania and even parts of Zaire. Hypocrisy was exposed, many people were converted, countless lives and communities were transformed, miracles were experienced, and amongst the Africans a most attractive holiness, integrity, openness and quickness to speak about Christ developed. The full story of the revival has recently been told in *Fire in the Hills* by H. H. Osborn.[8]

Sue longed to see these lovely qualities brought to Gillingham, and much discussion as to how this might come about took place at staff meetings. While rejoicing in this marvellous movement in Africa, John and the two Davids doubted whether the phrases in 1 John 1 would bear quite the weight that the East African Church put on them. Moreover, they knew that open confession required delicate pastoral handling and, for one reason and another, these discussions made no progress.

David matured significantly during his time at Gillingham. His increasing understanding and mastery of various aspects of the ministry made for job satisfaction of the highest order. The fruit of his evangelism, teaching, writing and prayer was evident in the church, and especially among the young people. He found that he could relate to all ages, and to all sorts of people, winning their respect and often their affection. He had proved the validity of his call to ordination, and the power of the gospel. But it would, nevertheless, be true to say that all spiritual advance was within the framework of what he had already learned at Iwerne and Cambridge. If anybody had said to him that there was a whole dimension of the Spirit with which he was scarcely acquainted, or even recognised, he would have been mightily surprised. The Collinses and St Mark's were to receive a singular visitation of God's Holy Spirit after David had moved on, as indeed was David himself, but while he was there neither he nor they had any suspicion of the extent of a further territory yet to be explored. However, there was one memorable event in 1960 which whetted their spiritual appetite and began to open their eyes.

The previous autumn Graham Scott-Brown said to John, 'If a Dutch woman whom I met in India ever visits England, I should like her to come here.' About four months later, he announced that she had indeed arrived, and was on her way to Gillingham. At that time, Corrie ten Boom was unknown, and John and Diana were rather hesitant about having her. After all, she was nearly seventy. How well would an elderly spinster fit in with the life of the vicarage, which by now included two small children as well as everybody else? Would she be able to sustain a whole week of meetings? However, with some reluctance, they agreed. Corrie turned out to be a delightful visitor: gracious and full of joy.

Night by night, in the corrugated iron hall adjoining the vicarage, she taught from the New Testament, illustrating her chosen themes with adventures of her life in Holland during the German occupation, and in Ravensbrück concentration camp. The story of how God 'shed abroad' his love in her heart, enabling her to forget her own misery and to care for her companions, and even to forgive the guard who had tortured her sister Betsy to death, has since been told in *The Hiding Place*.[9] The clergy at St Mark's had often spoken about the primacy of love in the Christian life. But this was different. This was a love which had been tested in a fiery furnace of suffering and had worked. Night by night the hall was packed, and the whole parish opened like a flower in the sunshine. David records:

As it transpired, Corrie was the most wonderful, gracious and normal guest you could possibly have imagined. It was hard to think of her suffering all the brutalities of the Nazi concentration camp. She seemed so gentle, so good, and with a delightful sense of humour. Her talks, illustrated by simple and unforgettable visual aids, made a lasting impression on us all.[10]

A number of people were converted that week, but far more significant was the effect of her life, particularly on those with whom she was staying at the vicarage. She gave them a glimpse of this other dimension. She spoke of the fullness of the Spirit much as others did, but she also seemed to receive detailed, specific messages from God. 'There will be thirteen coming to the Lord tonight', and there were – twelve in the meeting and one afterwards. She clearly had a remarkable prayer life. She had, in fact, been given another language, a language of the Spirit, with which to pray and to praise God, but she never mentioned it at the time, realising quite rightly that it might well have been counter-productive. Nevertheless there was a gleam of glory, and David saw it. He continues:

Most of all, she was someone who walked daily with her Heavenly Father; and sometimes in conversation, while we were expressing some anxiety about something, she would turn so naturally to prayer that it took us a few moments to realise she was no longer talking to us, but to God.[11]

Corrie was strongly of the opinion that there was need to battle in prayer and action against the powers of darkness, both in normal temptation and in the more sinister spheres of spiritualism and the occult, with which she had been fighting in Germany since the end of the war. She had come to believe that, filled with the Spirit, any gift of the Spirit she needed would be made available to her. She knew from long experience in ministry how necessary and valuable all the gifts could be – gifts of that Spirit who glorifies Jesus. And at the heart of her own devotional life was the restful certainty that Christ lived in her, and that as she trusted him, his beauty and power would be seen.

When John and the two Davids, suitably dog-collared, were seeing her off at the station in Gillingham, as the train started moving she leaned out of the window, her broad-brimmed hat narrowly missing the signal at the end of the platform, and called out to them in a clear, strong voice: 'Now remember, don't wrestle, just nestle!'

7

The Round Church

THREE YEARS WAS THE NORMAL SPAN of a first curacy, although this could be extended, and then a second curacy was expected, or some specialist work may have been undertaken for a year or two. During his third year at Gillingham David Watson considered very carefully an invitation from David Sheppard to join him as Chaplain at the Mayflower Family Centre in Canning Town. The role was really whatever he could make of it because the Centre was still in its infancy and the gifts and personalities of its leaders, especially Sheppard's, were still forming it into what it would become. Clearly, however, the work of the Chaplain would be among the local people and in the building up of a congregation. David felt himself still called to share the vision he had been given at Camp, to reach and win educated young people in order that, from among them, Christian leaders could go into all sectors of life in the nation. He decided to turn down David Sheppard's offer and to look for a curacy, if possible, in a church which attracted students.

It was not long in coming. When it came it seemed too good to be true. And yet it was to be one of the most difficult periods of his life, as well as one of the most rewarding. When he had been up at Cambridge, he had been a frequent worshipper at 'the Round' – the Church of the Holy Sepulchre, just across the road from St John's College. It is one of the three remaining round Norman churches in the country, architecturally fascinating, but rather small, with a seating capacity of about 150.

The Vicar was Cuthbert Mark Ruston, a genial, caring man with a bubbling gift of humour which made him anyone's idea of a perfect uncle. Not a great preacher, he was nevertheless a clear and penetrating speaker who was able to hold the attention and interest of the many students who attended the Round Church every Sunday in term. Nor did he neglect the parishioners who looked to him for pastoral care. Indeed it was as a pastor that his great work was done, for he always seemed to have time and he had a wonderful resource of deep, practical wisdom in the context of Christian living, which he would produce gently but with an honest directness which usually penetrated to the target. He was unmarried and had a little house in Jesus Lane where he entertained constantly. He was Vicar of the Round for thirty-two years until 1987, and served also as Rural Dean of Cambridge, Canon of Ely and Honorary Chaplain to the Queen. He died early in 1990 of cancer.

Mark was very interested in getting David to the Round for his second curacy. Being himself an ex-officer from Iwerne and still in touch with Bash, he had kept an eye on David as someone whose gifts would perfectly fit the task he had in mind. He wanted someone able to preach at university level, able to pastor and teach the growing number of undergraduates with whom he was in contact, and able to run a Children's Church. So, after proper consultation and hours of prayer, it was arranged between them and the Bishop of Ely, who duly licensed David on his arrival in September 1962. He was housed at Tyndale House, a residential Biblical Research Centre maintained in Selwyn Gardens by the Inter-Varsity Fellowship. This was within reasonable distance of the Round by that habitual means of transport in Cambridge – the bicycle.

David was now twenty-nine years old and had developed into an untiring worker and a very promising speaker. His preaching had advanced by leaps and bounds at Gillingham and was generally considered to be very good. He had a willingness, indeed an eagerness, to spend time with small groups in the colleges or with individuals in their rooms or his, teaching and explaining Christian doctrine or leading an unbeliever to Christ. Evangelism was his priority, and the work of Christ in redeeming the sinner the main theme of any message which he delivered to any audience.

Now that David was back in the academic world of Cambridge, the same old debate between the liberals and the conservative evangelicals confronted him once more. While he would use the more liberal commentaries and the latest theological works, he would often turn from them in frustration because they did not contribute to the task upon which he was engaged – winning men and women into a loving relationship with the living God. He believed that the Bible was all about God's unending efforts, by one means and another, to bring mankind back into the free and full fellowship which he had enjoyed with them before the fall. In Christ, God had achieved it for those who would receive it. That was the gospel, the 'good news'. But where was the 'good news' which the academics were showing him? He did not reject the theologians themselves, and would defend their right to hold their own opinions, but meanwhile he had work to do.

This was the time of *Honest to God*, the book by John Robinson, Bishop of Woolwich, which, mild though it undoubtedly was to those engaged in theological debate, and positive though it was in some respects, suddenly exposed liberal thinking to public scrutiny because it was written by a bishop.[1] Robinson harnessed the theology of the German scholars Tillich and Bultmann to challenge some of the credal presuppositions of the Church. Whereas it is traditionally believed that the transcendence and the immanence of God are held in tension in the Christian faith, each balancing the other, Robinson wrote that God was no longer to be thought of as 'out there'. He believed that in human experience God was to be found in 'the ground of our being', though not by virtue of the incarnation so much as by creation. He had little use for the institutional life of the Church and he sat rather lightly to revelation. It was not his best or most convincing book, and possibly it was giving expression more to a time of uncertainty in the Bishop's own thinking than to his mature and considered judgment on Christian theology. But it caused ripples in Christian circles and beyond.

Countless streams of earnest and honest young men sought out David for counsel and encouragement when faced with this bombshell. For long hours he would explain and reassure. Some could not take it and allowed their faith to evaporate. Others recaptured their equilibrium and soldiered on. David felt that little or nothing had been gained by the whole episode. Much of his time was wasted, much anxiety expended, and all that seemed to have happened was that many Christians lost confidence in the Church of England. *Honest to God* was published at the beginning of a decade in which the Church suffered an unprecedented decrease in support as far as its congregations were concerned. It is not possible to describe this as cause and effect, but perhaps it was more than mere coincidence.

Meanwhile, David was asking spiritual questions of his own. Mark Ruston remembered David telling him that, although he knew God had given him a gift of evangelism to reach those who had not yet accepted the gospel, he did not feel that he had got any specific message for Christians. This may seem a surprising sentiment for one with such a promising and obvious Christian ministry stretching before him. Nevertheless, he remembered the new spiritual dimension which he had witnessed during Corrie ten Boom's visit to Gillingham, and longed for that in his own life, and to see it in others too.

When he read the New Testament, it seemed to him to tell of Christians who were much more than simply converted. They seemed to have power to do extraordinary things, and to grow into world figures far beyond what might be expected of Galilean fishermen or Judaic Pharisees. Much of what St Paul wrote, though always consistent with the concept of the new creation, seemed to present areas of holiness and spiritual blessings beyond what David was experiencing himself. Hence he did not really know what to say on these subjects to help others.

Many years before, John Newton, the slave trader turned Christian minister and hymn writer, had described Christian living very clearly:

> To run and work the law commands,
> Yet gives me neither feet nor hands,
> But better news the Gospel brings,
> It bids me fly – and gives me wings.

David found this inspiring, but honesty made him wonder what were the wings he had been given. Far from flying, he seemed still to be running and working. He was doing it for and with his dear Lord and Saviour and it brought him great joy to see the kingdom being built. But flying? And with what wings?

He began to read the stories of some of the great revivals in history, fascinated at the way in which God had poured out his Spirit on so many people at one time. He began to pray that God would do the same in his day. He discovered that there were others with the same concern for revival, and from time to time he would meet with Basil Atkinson and Herbert Carson, Vicar of St Paul's, Cambridge, to pray. Often they were joined by Bill Butler, Rector of Little Shelford, a village just outside Cambridge, who would tell them more of the revival in East Africa in which, as a missionary, he had been deeply involved. David heard that at St Mark's, Gillingham, nights of prayer for worldwide revival were being held, as they were also at All Souls, Langham Place.

For David the move from Gillingham to Cambridge had been a severe jolt. At Gillingham he had shared the work and the home in the vicarage with such congenial friends that it was really an extension of the Iwerne officers' room. He often spent his days off with David MacInnes, as well as his working time, and John and Diana were so warm and gracious that it seemed like a big happy family. They worked hard and very long hours, but that suited David's temperament exactly, and they were always learning, especially from John, but also from each other.

In Cambridge the whole ethos was different. Mark was a dear man, wise and kind almost to a fault, but nearly a generation older and single as David was, so that the family atmosphere was missing. The issues in the church were different too, where debate and discussion predominated and cerebral activity always threatened to take over from spiritual blessings. David was not a little lonely and depressed in these circumstances. Nevertheless, he used to shoot off to Gillingham on his days off sometimes, and Mark was keen for him to keep his hand in at Iwerne when he could.

As well as the Family Service, Children's Church for children and their parents, which was an alternative to Sunday School at the Round, David was also given responsibility for a group of fifth and sixth form children from local schools. Many of these were the sons and daughters of dons in the university and they were generally very alert. He enjoyed teaching this group and was so successful at answering their questions that at one time there were fifty to seventy of them meeting regularly with him, and many became committed Christians. He also played a full part in the preaching in the Round, though in term-time visiting preachers usually occupied the pulpit in turn.

As his gift for evangelism developed and the facility for speaking with confidence grew within him, he found himself ever more eager to extend his ministry to the deepening of the Christian life within a believer. It was not a matter of ignorance or of complete emptiness on the subject, for the experience of God which had begun at his conversion had certainly not dried up and was still the mainspring of his life. But it did seem to be stuck at a particular level. No amount of good advice from outside, or of spiritual exercises within, seemed to shift it.

David began a close personal study of the Beatitudes in St Matthew 5:1–12. He read *Studies in the Sermon on the Mount* by Martyn Lloyd-Jones, minister of Westminster Chapel,[2] who insisted that, in the Beatitudes, 'you have a description of what every Christian is meant to be'. Lloyd-Jones emphasised the vast difference between the Christian as described by Jesus and the non-Christian, whose ideals and ambitions seemed so opposed to what Jesus offered as the way to true happiness and spiritual blessing. David spent several months studying and meditating on the first four Beatitudes, and gradually began to see that Christ was speaking deeply to the innermost spiritual condition of the heart.

He deals with the developing thought patterns in *You Are My God* on pages 51 to 53. To be 'poor in spirit' meant to recognise that in spite of any human success, even in religious areas, he was actually bankrupt in spiritual terms. 'To begin with,' he says, 'this was a far cry from my own opinions about myself . . . So God began to rebuke me for my spiritual pride, my arrogance, my self-righteousness and my critical spirit.'[3] From this he had to 'mourn' or lament as the logical step required in the Beatitudes. This was an active response to what God was saying to him. He found himself literally weeping 'for my spiritual poverty': 'Grief is a love-word. I knew that God still loved me more than I could possibly imagine, but there was much in my life that hurt him; and the knowledge of that broke me. More deeply than I can ever remember, I began to repent of everything that I knew was wrong in my life.'[4]

Those to whom this experience is relatively unknown may find them-selves in doubt as to whether it is really healthy. Introspection can be as crippling as a physical affliction, and those subject to its repeated applica-tion may indeed become unhealthy and unbalanced people if the exercise is a selfish indulgence unaccompanied by any real positive purpose. Simply to consider one's own weaknesses and errors outside the context of a vital and motivating relationship, such as a marriage or even a business partnership, is to invite a cumulative breaking down of confidence. This is gradually to become indecisive or autocratic, to a lesser or greater extent, according to temperament. But where the authority of God is admitted and the purpose of life is to please him rather than oneself, life is trans-formed by a positive, healthy and benevolent mindset. It should not, there-fore, be a surprise to find in the biographies of Christian saints a record of deep spiritual conflict, without which their contribution to human his-tory would have been considerably impoverished.

For David, the tears were occasioned precisely because the relationship with his Maker already existed and was very real to him, rather than because it was illusory. He did not grieve because God did not love him, or had rejected him, but because the love was so strong that he hoped to respond to it more deeply. It was a positive giving of himself at which he aimed, rather than selfish indulgence. This is common to Christians of every age and of every tradition. Mark Ruston is on record as saying that he considered David Watson to be the most spiritual man he had ever met. Perhaps this is not surprising.

From 'mourning', the Beatitudes lead to 'meekness'. To repent is insuf-ficient without the will to cement into place a decision to obey God in every detail of life. David writes:

The meek person is someone who is so mourning his spiritual poverty that he is willing for God to do what he likes in his life. That man will not protest or complain; he will not dictate his terms of reference; like the Virgin Mary he will say, 'Let it be to me according to your word' . . . God brought me to the point where I was genuinely willing to say, as far as I understood it, 'Not my will but thine be done.'[5]

A decision of the will is stronger than any opinion of the mind, although it has to be applied and re-applied in all the circumstances of life. Not for nothing does the Church of England require of each of those being mar-ried that they declare publicly 'I will', whereas less enlightened authorities are satisfied with 'I do'.

Yet still a dynamic of positive action on the basis of the three steps into poverty, mourning and meekness seemed to be needed, and David found this in the fourth Beatitude – 'hunger and thirst for righteousness'. 'I spent much time in prayer, asking God to do something new in my life ... But as much as I was willing for anything to happen, nothing did. I was disappointed, perhaps a little disillusioned; but the hunger never abated.'[6] He points out that at this time, the winter of 1962–3, there were others, independently of himself though some well-known to him, who were making the same pilgrimage. Without working through the same Scriptures, nor coming to the same conclusions in detailed terms, they were similarly hungering as he hungered, for the deepening of spiritual life. Learning of this, his own expectations grew.

Hard and earnestly as he prayed to be filled with God's Spirit in a fresh and more comprehensive way, not knowing exactly what he meant by that but believing that his prayers would be answered, the silence from above remained unbroken. Perplexed and frustrated, he one day shared this with a friend. While he was doing so, he himself realised what was 'the missing link'. He remembered the Virgin Mary. The promise of God had come to her clearly and she believed it, although none of the signs of a pregnancy were yet evident. Finding herself in precisely the same circumstances as those she had been in before the coming of the archangel, and knowing nothing beyond the words he had spoken, which presented her with great problems and threatened her with considerable danger, she launched into a wonderful song of praise and thanksgiving to Almighty God. That was faith – to take God at his word before anything happened to fulfil it. Perhaps the conception itself took place not when Gabriel announced it, but when the first notes of the Magnificat sounded in the halls of heaven. Gabriel had spoken in the future tense; Mary's response is in the perfect tense of completed action.

Once again, I confessed every sin I could think of, and asked for God's forgiveness, even the sphere of my unbelief. I told him I was willing to obey him, whatever the cost. I then asked him to fill me with his Spirit, *and began to praise him that he had now done it*. As I went on praising for perhaps ten or fifteen minutes, I had a quiet but overwhelming sense of being embraced by the love of God. There were no startling manifestations.[7]

The presence of God with him and the joy this brought to his soul was quite unmistakable, and he not only basked in it, but also began irresistibly to want to tell others of it. Some welcomed his good news with characteristic and spontaneous gladness, notably Basil Atkinson. He found that David MacInnes had had a similar experience on precisely the same evening, and that the Collinses and many of their friends at St Mark's, Gillingham had corporately entered into a new experience of the love of

God, becoming 'gently aware of being filled with the Spirit'. Over the succeeding weeks, many received his news with joy.

But many evangelicals were embarrassed by it, perhaps partly because, having arrived at a balanced and convenient spirituality, they were not hungering after anything else. Others were rightly anxious to be sure that David had not stepped over a boundary into something unbalanced and eccentric which, if persisted in, would not only limit and distort his ministry, but could even lead him into such error that he would lose his ministry altogether. The Church from the earliest days has confronted the problem of various heresies, and in more modern times the evangelicals have been bedevilled by 'holiness' movements, which have diverted some of them from the outward vision explicit in the gospel to an obsession with their own spiritual condition. Among them have been those who have taught some theory of a 'second blessing' needed by believers before they could truly be recognised as 'full gospel' Christians. The theological questions raised by these problems are considered in Chapters 8 and 9, but for the moment it is relevant to say that included in the company of those cautious in their response to the news of David's experience were Mark Ruston and, in one sense more significantly, Bash.

Mark was a mature and cautious man. Upon his shoulders lay much of the responsibility for the leadership of the evangelical cause in Cambridge, and especially within the university as far as the witness of the CICCU was concerned. He had been nurtured in days when evangelicals had their backs to the wall, and found it necessary to have a careful and responsible approach to their relationships with others. It was not craven reluctance but sound wisdom which dictated his attitudes. For his promising right-hand man to move into a greater freedom of expression, to say the least, about the Holy Spirit, demanded caution on his part. Let David settle down a bit and become quite sure of the balance of his new emphasis before he launched into it all too publicly. Mark welcomed his greater joy but imposed a limited embargo upon his speaking about it.

For Bash, whose friend Mark had been over a great many years, it was equally difficult. A real enthusiast for anything that indicated genuine spiritual progress in anyone, and especially in one as close to him as David had become, he knew the crippling dangers possible in a 'second blessing' experience and always wanted it analysed and, if necessary, eliminated. He had a definite distaste for anything 'Pentecostal' in character, not only because he felt it was doctrinally unsound but, much more important, because of what he considered its unrestrained excesses of style. He could not allow Camp, under any circumstances, to become stained with anything which might alarm parents or headmasters, a prospect which to him seemed likely to bring it into such disrepute as to threaten its very existence. Anyway, tongues and such like seemed perfectly ridiculous. He did not exclude David from the officers' room, hoping that its influence would soon reveal to David the unwisdom of anything excessive, but he restricted his liberty to discuss these matters at Camp. In fact these reservations were shared and continued to be so by many in the evangelical mainstream, so that from this point on David found himself viewed with suspicion by some whose support he might otherwise have enjoyed, and excluded from the fellowship in which he felt he naturally belonged.

Yet David did not see his step of faith into the fullness of the Holy Spirit as diverging from the traditional evangelicalism he had learnt at Camp and from Bash himself. For someone to become a Christian by inviting Christ into his heart and to share his life was little different in fact from the traditional Anglican teaching contained in the Prayer Book services. It was only a rather practical way of understanding this. Evangelicals laid great emphasis upon the importance of taking this step, went on to encourage every Christian to believe and to know that God accepted all those who took it, and then taught them that by the Holy Spirit's power they received new life in every sense. They were spiritually born again. This was symbolised by the sacrament of baptism and confirmed with the laying on of hands. There remained the necessity of being filled and refilled by the Holy Spirit for each day's work and witness. As far as David knew, he was merely realising his assets. He perceived that the New Testament Christians enjoyed a condition that was different from his own when he came to Cambridge in 1962, though only in degree and not in kind. Consequently, he sought to enter more fully into what they enjoyed and what he knew he already enjoyed in part.

So his joy was in the fulfilment of what, as an able and increasingly experienced teacher of Bible-based Christianity, he longed to experience in his life because it was promised in the Scriptures. It was only new to him because he had not experienced it before to such a degree, but it never seemed to him to be different in kind from his previous life as a Christian. It was a major step forward for him, certainly, but not a step upward into a different category. It could only be classed as a 'second blessing' in that it came between the first and the third in a long series.

Soon this was all to be called in question.

8

Charismatic Renewal

VERY SOON THEY STARTED THE INQUEST. It was inevitable that such a deep and joyful experience of God should lead those who had received it into asking themselves and others just exactly what had happened. They needed a clear understanding of the blessing if they were going to teach it to others and spread the good news to the wider Church.

One possibility was the traditional view of spiritual experience, whereby the blessing was an intensification of what they already knew of life with the indwelling Christ. This might be called the 'Keswick' view, in promotion of which the Keswick Convention is held every year in the Lake District 'for the deepening of spiritual life'. Thousands of Christians gather to seek a more dedicated life, which indeed they often find. This results in many vocations to the ministry and to the mission field, as well as to a generally deeper commitment to Christ among those participating. It is biblical, balanced and consistent with classical evangelicalism.

David was now in frequent consultation with John Collins and David MacInnes, and with Michael Harper in particular. Michael was one of the staff of All Souls, Langham Place, who had experienced the 'fullness of the Spirit' a little earlier than the others, as a result of the prayers of the group of members there who had founded the Anglican Prayer Fellowship for Revival. These included a saintly couple called George and Mary Ingram and two laymen, Bill Grant and Eric Houfe. Michael had discovered what was unknown to John and the two Davids at this stage, namely that the wind of the Spirit had been blowing more strongly in America and many similar experiences to their own had been recorded there. It seemed to spring out of the growth of the Pentecostal Churches, a somewhat disparate group of congregations, all of which based their identity upon a 'second blessing' experience, with which was associated the phrase 'baptism in the Spirit', and the possession of the spiritual gifts listed by St Paul in 1 Corinthians 12.

They mushroomed after the turn of the century into a large number of denominations worldwide, distinct from each other but owing a common loyalty to Pentecostalism. The movement grew so strongly in both North and South America that they far outnumbered the traditional Protestant churches in some places. Bishop Lesslie Newbigin delivered a series of lectures in 1952 (subsequently published by SCM as *The Household of God*) arguing that there were now three main streams of Christianity: the Roman Catholics (adherents of the 'body' or institution); the Protestants (adherents of the Word); and Pentecostals (adherents of the Spirit). The rest of the Christian world was beginning, albeit very slowly and hesitantly, to realise that Pentecostalism could not simply be brushed aside as an insignificant and blemished form of Christianity, practised mainly by theologically uneducated people.

In Britain there had been manifestations of Pentecostalism for some years, but these seemed to lack endurance and the teaching was considered suspect. Principal George Jefferies held huge rallies in the Albert Hall and collected many supporters, but his influence tailed off. Some of his friends used to teach that there are two Holy Spirits in Scripture, one the third Person of the Trinity, and the other the second Person, the Spirit of Christ. A more lasting work was done by Smith Wigglesworth, a plumber from Bradford who became a member of the Salvation Army. But the strong opposition of the evangelical Bible teachers such as F. B. Meyer, A. T. Pierson, Oswald Chambers and Graham Scroggie made it very difficult for Pentecostal churches and established the Keswick view as orthodox. Perhaps even more significantly, these Pentecostals established no bridgehead in the Church of England, which in size and standing dominated the British scene.

In 1959 in Van Nuys, California, the Episcopal (Anglican) Rector of St Mark's Church, the Rev. Dennis Bennett, preaching on Passion Sunday, told his startled congregation that he had been filled with the Holy Spirit and had spoken with other tongues, just like the Apostles on the Day of Pentecost. One of his curates registered his protest by taking off his vestments in the middle of the service and publicly resigning; another curate, preaching at another service later in the day, told the congregation that this sort of thing could not be tolerated in a respectable church; and the church treasurer suggested to Bennett that he ought to resign, which he later agreed to do. This may not have been the first occasion when a 'Pentecostal experience' happened in a traditional denomination, but the publication by the Bishop of Los Angeles of a Pastoral Letter banning all speaking in tongues under church auspices gave the incident considerable publicity.

It soon became apparent that Dennis Bennett's was no isolated experience; many other ministers and lay people in different parts of America had had similar manifestations of being filled with the Holy Spirit. News of these happenings slowly crossed the Atlantic, and there were three references to tongues in the *Church of England Newspaper* in 1961, including one article which was a testimony by Bennett himself. His full story was later published in his book *Nine o'Clock in the Morning*, which was widely read in Britain during the 1970s.[1] So too was *The Cross and the Switchblade* by David Wilkerson,[2] which had a great influence on the beginning of the Catholic Pentecostal Revival in the United States.

A new magazine, *Trinity*, was launched by a group of Pentecostal Episcopalians in 1961 and copies of it were brought to Britain the following year. This magazine, the first to promote Pentecostal views amongst the historic churches, was eagerly read by those who were longing for a spiritual revival, but inevitably it reached only a limited membership. The Editor of *Trinity*, Mrs Jean Stone, invited a leading evangelical scholar, the Rev. Dr Philip Hughes, to visit California in 1962 to see what was happening in the Episcopal churches. Hughes, an Englishman and a respected senior theologian from the stricter wing of evangelicalism, wrote an article for *Christianity Today* on his return, describing the profound impression his visit had made on him. 'Dare we deny,' he asked, 'that this is a movement of God's sovereign Spirit?' But it was his subsequent editorial in the British theological journal *The Churchman* in September 1962 which made many evangelical Christians take notice of what was happening in America. Writing in the third person, Hughes said: 'What he witnessed points in only one direction, namely that the Breath of the Living God is stirring among the dry bones of the major, respectable, old-established denominations, and particularly with the Episcopal Church.' Permission was given for this editorial to be reprinted and circulated, and the demand was so great that eventually 39,000 copies were printed.

At about this time Michael Harper, through a study of St Paul's letter to the Ephesians in preparation for a parish weekend conference which he was leading, discovered something of what it meant to be 'filled with all the fulness of God'.[3] When shown a copy of *Trinity* he realised that, although he had not yet received the gift of tongues, his experience was the same as that described in the American magazine. He began to take a considerable interest in the American scene, and by the time John Collins, David Watson and David MacInnes came into his orbit, he was already very familiar with the Pentecostal terminology and theology. He was an enormous help to them as they sought to explain what they had discovered of the Holy Spirit's transforming power.

At first they naturally inclined towards the Keswick view, that is, that their experience was an intensification of the spirituality they already knew. But the more they heard of the Pentecostal interpretation, the more they felt drawn to it. There seemed to be three points at which it related so clearly to their recent experience. First, they could see the close connection in time and in type between the Americans who enjoyed the Spirit's fullness and their own claims. God's Spirit was at work. Secondly, they found themselves receiving a blessing which, though they had sought it and prayed for it, had been worked in them objectively 'from above', rather than been generated subjectively from within. Thirdly, some of those who had shared this blessing with them, particularly at Gillingham, had also received the gift of tongues. Michael suggested they should seek the advice of the great Dr Martyn Lloyd-Jones, a towering figure within evangelicalism, who was minister of Westminster Chapel.

Lloyd-Jones was an eminent surgeon who had in middle life entered the Congregational ministry, bringing to this work his very considerable intellect and a keen theological insight. He was a preacher who succeeded to the Free Church tradition of biblical scholarship with a somewhat calvinistic approach, and he drew very large crowds to his Bible expositions in Westminster. He was now beginning to be elderly, but he retained all his faculties and exercised a wide influence. In more recent years he had surprised many by espousing the Pentecostal position in some respects, without otherwise losing any of his trenchant Evangelical views.

An appointment was made to see him and the four Anglicans duly arrived together. Lloyd-Jones asked each of them to tell their story in turn and, when they had done so, he gave them his testimony of a similar experience he had had after the revival in the Hebrides in 1949. He then looked at them straightly and pronounced: 'Gentlemen, I believe you have been baptised in the Holy Spirit.'

It may be that this was the moment when the Charismatic Movement in Britain was born. There had been recently a spontaneous growth of Pentecostal groups which were developing into the major movement usually known as the House Churches, and many of the struggling Pentecostal churches were over the next twenty years to experience considerable prosperity. However, the 'Charismatic Movement' is the name by which those members of the traditional historic denominations who embraced some of the distinctive Pentecostal theology, if not necessarily its style, were to identify themselves. The word comes from the Greek 'charismata' (best translated 'love-gifts'), which is used by St Paul in 1 Corinthians 12 to describe the gifts of the Spirit, which have come to play so significant a part in the life of the movement. The title was already widely in use in America.

In Britain this movement for renewal found its roots in the Anglican Church, but soon spread to all the other major churches. Whereas in America the Episcopal Church is not a stronghold of evangelicalism, it was within the evangelical wing of the Church of England that charismatic renewal developed and spread most rapidly. Two of Michael Harper's colleagues at All Souls also entered into a new experience of the Spirit at about this time, and it was not long before one or two Anglican parishes were touched by renewal, among the first being St Mark's, Cheltenham, and St Paul's, Beckenham, in addition to St Mark's, Gillingham. With rapidly growing interest in this new work of the Holy Spirit, and the need for increased fellowship, teaching and support for those involved, Michael Harper resigned from his post at All Souls in 1964 in order to devote himself more fully to a ministry of writing and teaching to encourage those already involved, and to try to persuade others that this was an integral part of true Christianity, and completely consistent with the beliefs of the historic churches. The Fountain Trust was set up and a bi-monthly (later monthly) magazine, *Renewal*, was launched.

Lloyd-Jones' epic pronouncement, made with his customary force and authority, had the effect of registering the movement as truly Pentecostal in thrust. David Watson, at least, was unhappy from the start with this definition. He could not believe that 'baptism in the Spirit' was biblical when used in this way. He rejected also the view that the 'gifts' were marks or consequences of being 'baptised in the Spirit'. In *You Are My God* he devotes a chapter very largely to this problem, balancing Lloyd-Jones' teaching on the subject with John Stott's. The longer he lived and the more experienced he became in the ministry, the more he regretted the loose use of the phrase 'baptised in the Spirit'. He found that it divided the Church down the middle, whereas he was convinced that one of the offices of the Spirit of Unity was to reconcile the various factions within the Body of Christ.

David writes in *You Are My God*:

The expression 'to baptize in the Holy Spirit' comes only seven times in the New Testament, six of them linked with the baptism that John the Baptist said the Coming One would bring [Matt 3:11; Mark 1:8; Luke 3:16; John 1:33; Acts 1:5; 11:16; 1 Cor 12:13]. John had come to baptize with water as a sign of repentance, but Jesus would baptize with the Holy Spirit to introduce people to the blessings of the New Covenant. At Pentecost this promise was fulfilled, and this was repeated only in the house of Cornelius, at the Gentile equivalent of Pentecost ... (Acts 11:16).... From those six references it seems clear that the baptism in the Holy Spirit refers to Christian initiation. It is the spiritual event by which all people are brought into Christ, whether Jew or Gentile. This is even more clear in the seventh reference: 'For by one Spirit we were all baptized into one body – Jews or Greeks, slaves or free – and all were made to drink of one Spirit' (1 Cor 12:13). Nowhere is it suggested that Christians were, or could be, baptized in the Spirit after their conversion to Christ.[4]

David thus comes down categorically in favour of John Stott's arguments in his booklet *The Baptism and Fullness of the Holy Spirit*.[5]

The question arises, of course, because there are many references in Scripture to a certain dualism in Christian initiation which is borne out in experience today. Jesus' own baptism seems to be a moment when the Holy Spirit came to empower him for his future ministry; the Apostles were chosen and called to discipleship long before Pentecost; Saul of Tarsus was converted on the Damascus road and received the Holy Spirit under the hands of Ananias three days later; and so on. In more modern times, there are a great many Christians whose biographies tell of moments of empowering years after their conversions or equivalent. It may be valid to point out that John Wesley had become a convinced Christian, an ordained clergyman, a missionary and a church planter in America long before he experienced what is usually called his conversion, when he felt his heart 'strangely warmed'. Lloyd-Jones, in his book *Joy Unspeakable*,[6] devotes much space to this dualism in Christian experience, and makes a convincing case. Indeed, dualism of this sort merely mirrors the natural world and the gap between birth and maturity. What needs to be asked about it, and what Lloyd-Jones appears to neglect to ask, is what sort of change is being discussed.

John Stott may not be the first person to point out that there are two sorts of change. There is a change of status, or of kind, and there is a change of condition, or of degree. Christian conversion is a change of status. Everything intrinsic in being a Christian is then conveyed to the believer who becomes 'a new creature'.[7] This is the work of God, through Christ, ministered by the Holy Spirit and requiring only the response of faith. David's point about the seven references in the New Testament which refer to being 'baptised in the Holy Spirit' is that they all refer to this kind of change, to Christian initiation. Christian baptism is the sacrament of the Holy Spirit. But this is not to deny that other changes occur subsequently in every Christian's experience. The problem is 'the unscriptural use of language'[8] which divides the Church into two classes of Christians when the New Testament knows but one; and which distinguishes between the 'haves' and the 'have-nots', rather than encourages the 'haves' to have more.

Thus, the phrase 'baptised in the Holy Spirit' may not be a proper description of an experience of the Holy Spirit that is subsequent to and separate from conversion. Nevertheless, it is a valid description of the condition in which Christians should find themselves when converted. The usual and less divisive phrase is 'filled with the Spirit', as of a receptacle which may be full or not so full; a matter of degree. The word 'baptism' without question was used in the New Testament to signify 'initiation' or 'immersion'. Thus the Christian whose life is initiated by the sacrament of baptism in the Holy Spirit is to live submerged in the Spirit, but to use the word 'baptism' to refer to a crisis experience comparable but subsequent to initiation is unwarranted. One is a change of status and the other is a change of condition. If used as metaphors describing a condition, rather than theological words defining a crisis, baptism and fullness describe the same thing – one an external application to the person and the other an internal state. Both represent the degree to which a Christian should be in submission to the will and power of the Holy Spirit.

David, precise and accurate, was seeking to clothe his recent experience with words which could define it and saw the dangers ahead, already in evidence in Pentecostalism, if the wrong language was used. He strove to avoid the effects of it as, more and more, the Charismatics divided the churches to which they belonged. Yet he saw the fullness of the Spirit into which he had entered as a wonderful gift of God's love to him. Not only was he prohibited by love from any desire for controversy with his brother Charismatics, but he was bound by love to them in their common cause to proclaim their discovery to the rest of the Church. The evangelist certainly had something to say to other Christians now.

Whatever language others might use, David spent more and more of his time encouraging and enabling others to receive this fullness. He writes in *You Are My God*:

Most Christians would agree that we all need to be continually filled with the Spirit, since that is the plain injunction in Scripture (Eph. 5:18). But not all Christians expect anything much to happen. Many believe and teach that it is purely a matter of 'imperceptible growth into Christ'. That is not, however, the constant testimony of countless Christians all over the world who have experienced some form of spiritual renewal, whatever it should be called.[9]

In fact, what it was called became less of an issue than he suspected at first. Many Christians, who had not enjoyed a conversion experience so dear to the hearts of evangelicals, came gladly to receive the fullness of the Spirit and were not so particular in choosing their language in describing and teaching it.

For David every Christian grace, blessing or benefit came and was received in the same way. It came from God as a gift, and was simply received by faith. This was what had happened at his conversion – 'If these things were true, I wanted them to become real in my own life' (see page 22). Friendship with God was offered to him; he had simply hauled it aboard by faith. Similarly, when the fullness of the Spirit (whatever that was) had become his earnest desire, he had received it with the same simplicity of faith which the Virgin had demonstrated at the Annunciation. Whatever was on offer, he would receive.

He began to understand the whole Christian life in those terms. Spiritual power was not to be generated by an intensification of dedication, as Keswick seemed to teach. No measure of discipline would pluck blessing out of a reluctant God. No striving, no mourning, no fasting, not even praying, would move God to action out of pity for a deserving case. Even repentance was not some form of ransom to be paid, some sort of qualification to be gained, before God's stony heart could be melted. God is already immeasurably more gracious and merciful than man can understand. He is only too eager to bless in all sorts of areas of human life, some totally unexpected, and the list of his promises is almost too long for counting. This is the crucial truth. He gives and gives, and Christians must just keep on receiving. Every good gift is from above, and is to be received below. It is a living friendship which pours out gifts upon the beloved.

Put in these terms, it is not difficult to see why David and his friends kept trying to say that what had happened to them was from outside themselves rather than generated within. To describe it as 'the fullness' was only shorthand for an experience of the Spirit's ministry to them which was truly comprehensive and 'full'. Potentially, nothing was omitted from it. Actually, since it was a change by degree, it was incomplete and they still needed to receive ever more grace. But the disciplines of prayer and penitence were to be operated *within* a friendship with a loving and giving God, and never with a view to establishing or re-establishing it. It was a glorious friendship, a joyful and ever more fulfilling one.

So David found himself increasingly caught up into the charismatic movement, speaking at its conferences and pouring out his loving counsel to individuals and audiences alike. In the very early days, he wrote to John Collins, 'several in Tyndale have received the fullness of the Spirit, another in the Round Church did with me last night, and I am seeing 4 more of our congregation this evening who are "hungry and thirsty".' He wrote in another letter, 'I'm praying, "Lord give me Cambridge", and I simply rejoice in His perfect timing for sending me up here.'

9

Charismatic Controversy

BUT THINGS BECAME A LITTLE HOTTER in Cambridge. John Collins had been booked to speak at a clergy breakfast there and took the opportunity of telling some of the story of Gillingham's corporate blessing. The opposition exploded into vocal life and an even closer bond grew between those who had received the deeper experience of the Holy Spirit, as they began to feel rejected by those who felt that this was a dangerous and false doctrine which could only divide the Church. David wrote again to John:

Your letter was such an encouragement as I had had an hour with Mark Ruston yesterday. Yes, he accepted the fullness of the Spirit, but simply could not accept that our old nature had been crucified with Christ – and the same with Dick Lucas. Mark is now reading Romans 6, with my copy of Nygren[1] and I am praying much for spiritual illumination. He is sweetly and humbly hungry, and has asked me to pray for him.

Martyn Lloyd-Jones had given them two special warnings which exercised them greatly. First, they were to guard themselves against any false teaching on sinless perfection, and secondly they were to remember that the sanctifying work of the Holy Spirit must go on continually, as St Paul urges: 'go on being filled with the Holy Spirit'.[2] With the second, they were all agreed. However much they rejoiced in the moment when they found themselves filled with the Spirit, they were equally determined to maintain the condition of being filled into the future. Some might teach that it was a once-and-for-all experience by which they would be permanently and indelibly changed, but they knew that the Christian life was a relationship demanding continual recharging. To suppose otherwise was to court disaster. But Lloyd-Jones' first warning, though not totally unrelated to the second, presented them with greater difficulty.

Balance is needed in any true understanding of holiness. Bible teachers use many words, and convention speakers issue clarion calls, which the humble victims need to sift and reduce to practical meaning. A sense of humour comes in handy. What is obvious is that there is a tension between what Christians have to do themselves and what God has done for them. 'Be holy, because I am holy'[3] may be used as a summary of man's responsibility. But St Paul's repeated emphasis upon all that God provides in Christ for the Christian to appropriate by faith includes: 'our old self was crucified with him [Christ], so that the body of sin might be rendered powerless, that we should no longer be slaves to sin'.[4] David's letters to John Collins and Michael Harper have several references to this subject, and undoubtedly a debate took place between them and spilled over to those such as Mark Ruston to whom they were trying to communicate the meaning of their new experience.

It was true that many evangelicals made shipwreck of Romans 6. Some almost rejected it, holding that it had little or no relevance because it was unclear what St Paul really meant. Others moved with it into some degree of 'sinless perfection'. Many found themselves so filled with love for God through the infilling of the Holy Spirit that they desired only to please him and never to disobey him. They began, somewhat naturally, to believe that their old self had indeed been crucified with Christ so that they were set free from serving sin. However, most commentators agree that St Paul is consistent in Romans 6 with what he wrote in Romans 5, namely that sanctification is part of justification. What God has done for us in Christ in providing full and free forgiveness *extends* to a full and free victory over sin in daily living.

Romans 6 therefore does not teach instant holiness as a state of life fully supplied by Christ and enjoyed by Christians as a matter of course, but instant victory made available by Christ and to be appropriated by Christians. They are to 'count [them]selves dead to sin, but alive to God in Christ Jesus',[5] and to go into each day and every circumstance ready to enjoy this victory by a simple act of faith often repeated. Yet it is not the act of faith upon which St Paul focuses so much as upon the status of the person 'in Christ'. To such a person sin is alien, but not impossible. 'Do not let sin reign in your mortal body so that you obey its evil desires ... rather offer yourselves to God as those who have been brought from death to life ... as instruments of righteousness.'[6] You are in Christ, St Paul is saying: be what you are.

It seems that this did not remain an issue for long in spite of the early concern about it. The Charismatic Renewal has not been much occupied with theological debate about holiness, and there is little evidence that David found the matter very fascinating. Renewal was, for him, rather a threefold blessing of Christ's love, Christ's power and Christ's Body. He became aware of being overwhelmed by God's love as the Holy Spirit made God more real to him, involving his emotions as well as his intellect. He had a feeling of being loved, rather than merely a knowledge of it, and he knew that nothing could ever separate him from that love.

Through the Holy Spirit he experienced a new power in his ministry, particularly in evangelism. He channelled everything vertically now, referring every task and every problem up to God first, listening to him and obeying what he was told. He really enjoyed God, and his ministry became part of the 'family business' with all its resources behind him. No longer did he have to summon up his own power for ministry, but he was able to relax into the Spirit's power and see things happen. Not that this relieved him of responsibility for effort, especially not in sermon preparation, but it became a smoother process and the fruit of it was more assured.

David found he had also a new sensitivity to the whole Body of Christ. He had drifted rather naturally into a partisan attitude as an evangelical, holding views about other Christians which automatically fenced them off from him. Now, though his views did not change particularly, his attitudes certainly did. Anyone sailing under Christ's banner was his brother to be loved and helped, rather than to be attacked. Was he not also in Christ? He came more and more to dislike controversy and to eschew it. What he had to say was always positive and true to what he believed he learned from God in prayer and Bible study. It was never trimmed to suit the wind, but neither was it provocative if he could possibly help it. He was determined to avoid getting into heated arguments, finding them especially painful because they made loving more difficult.

David was, as always, working at high pressure, with many regular engagements for Bible Readings at College CICCU meetings in addition to his duties at the Round Church, and now he had prayer meetings every night with those at Tyndale House and others who had been filled with the Spirit or wished to be so. He became appreciably more tense than he had been at Gillingham. Moreover, knowing the intellectual level of his congregation, he felt the need for more time and effort to be put into every sermon and address. In some weeks, he would have as many as ten speaking engagements. He became aware too of the attacks of Satan upon himself as he began to experience bouts of depression occasionally. It was increasingly difficult to relax and unwind and there was added strain in that he did not have the same supportive fellowship around him as he had at Gillingham. He could not share everything with Mark, although their relationship remained good and warm.

Then there came more fuel for the fire of the opposition. After some months of prayer, David began to experience the gift of tongues. Of all the spiritual gifts, this was the most inexplicable and unacceptable to other Christians. David writes in *You Are My God*:

In our Western Christianity we have become so cautious about subjective experiences because of their obvious dangers that we tend to rule them out altogether. However, no one can read the New Testament without seeing that it is shot through with specific and often dramatic experiences of the Spirit. It is because of the comparative absence of these that the Church today stands in such desperate need of renewal.[7]

If the spiritual gifts seemed to threaten the orderly practice of biblical Christianity, so particularly did the suppression of the mind in moments of prayer when the voice spoke to God in a language which the speaker could not understand. To the non-charismatic Christian, it was so supernatural that it was weird. It could even be satanic. It was doubly suspect because the Pentecostals taught that tongues was the mark of baptism in the Spirit. Thus, it seemed, an unscriptural, divisive and elitist teaching was compounded by an unnatural and irrational activity which masqueraded as prayer. It was totally unnecessary too, for why could one not speak to the Father in a language one understood?

In *You Are My God*, David gives a simple and almost simplistic account of how he discovered tongues for himself:

I asked God to give me a language in the Spirit through which I could worship and praise him. I began to praise him in English, and then let my mind relax while my spirit went on praising with the first syllables that came to my tongue. They could be any syllables; there was nothing special or mystical about them. After some thirty seconds I stopped: 'David, you are just making this up!' I said to myself.[8]

After a short argument with himself he began again and 'went on making these noises for about thirty minutes or more'. He had done again what he had done when he was converted, when he was filled with the Spirit, and on countless other unrecorded occasions during his life. He had taken God at his word, risking himself on the assumption that it was a trustworthy word, and acted. For David, that was what faith really meant; it was the fundamental principle of Christianity.

In this instance, he had responsibly come to believe in the availability of the gifts, in the indwelling power of the Holy Spirit since he became a Christian, and in the benevolence of God's gift to him of tongues. As it happened, it became 'a natural and helpful part of my daily devotional prayer life – a marvellous way of abiding and resting in the Lord'. At first the sounds he made did not seem very 'edifying', since he couldn't understand them, but the worship which they enabled him to give the

Lord 'unusually refreshed' him. What could be more simple? Yet the storms of controversy raged over tongues for years and have still not died down. Certainly in Cambridge they made great issue out of tongues, perhaps particularly because they were an assault on the use of the mind, to which many intellectuals took very grave exception. To relax the mind and speak 'trans-rational or supra-rational' sounds was horrifying. Whatever Scripture said and good Christians experienced, such could not be tolerated.

David studied the question of spiritual gifts. He wrote:

The more I studied the New Testament the more I became convinced: the teaching that these gifts were only for the apostolic age was no more than a rationalisation of their absence for so long. The arguments against them were thin and questionable; I could see that all the gifts could be just as edifying for the Church today as in the first century, and many of them just as effective for the evangelistic thrust of the Church today as in the Acts of the Apostles.[9]

David believed he was on very strong ground here. Since the biblical revelation contains positive identification of these 'charismata' and encouragement for their use, how could anyone claiming to base their authority for faith and doctrine upon the Bible deny the use of them? Is not the New Testament shot through with supernatural signs and wonders? If they were to cease when the Canon of Scripture was established in the Church, would not the same Scriptures which record them also forecast their disuse?

The spiritual gifts are listed in the writings of St Paul for the use of the Church. In 1 Corinthians 12 he mentions nine of them in verses 7–10: the word of wisdom, the word of knowledge, faith, healing, miracle working, prophecy, distinguishing of spirits, various tongues, interpreting tongues; and in verses 28–30 some of these again with apostleship, teaching, helps and administrations. In chapter 13 he may perhaps be saying that love is a greater and 'more excellent' gift. In Romans 12:6–8 he gives another list including prophecy, service, teaching, exhortation, giving, leadership and showing mercy. In Ephesians 4:8–12, yet another list is given in which apostleship, prophecy and teaching are linked to evangelism and pastoring. St Peter also mentions spiritual gifts in 1 Peter 4:10–11, in which he lists speaking and serving, and goes on to refer at some length to suffering.

Several things should be said. First, some on the lists are ministries which develop from the use of a gift itself. David Watson clearly understood evangelism in very much the same terms as he came to think of prophecy. It was given, needed to be used, and would only bear fruit if God gave the increase. Secondly, some on the lists appear to be natural gifts which are enriched by the Spirit; while others are firmly supernatural. Thirdly, only tongues are for the benefit of the individual believer; all the others are for ministry. It follows from this that tongues are the gift which most interests the individual, but they are of least significance in the Church. The rediscovery of these gifts by the Pentecostals and their subsequent use by the charismatics have opened up great possibilities for the Church. They have also presented it with many problems, for the truth is that it is very difficult to produce and to agree a rational system for the use of supernatural power.

David believed in their use because they were scriptural. He used tongues regularly because he found out how to do so and because they refreshed him. He made very little use of other gifts – the more supernatural gifts – until rather later in life, partly because he had difficulty discovering their practical usefulness in order that he could weave them into the fabric of the ministry he was already undertaking. Gradually he did discover this, but always his ministry of evangelism absorbed his energies. In *Discipleship* he writes: 'Since these gifts come entirely from God, we must depend upon his Spirit for the right exercise of them before they become true spiritual gifts for the benefit of the church.'[10] He and many others have sought over the years to understand how to exercise the gifts rightly. Understandably, failure has accompanied success on this journey and mistakes have been made.

Of course, the dangers of the spiritual gifts are obvious to anyone giving them any consideration. The misuse of them is both unedifying and deceptive, causing disorder and mistrust in the Church. St Paul's first letter to the Corinthian Christians was written into a situation of such licence that he was forced to rebuke them sternly. The twelfth chapter was particularly corrective of an unhappy mixture of spiritual enthusiasm and sinful exuberance which was ruining public worship. Everyone wanted to speak with tongues and give prophecies. Disorder took over from decent, reverent order. St Paul pointed out that the Spirit was not a spirit of disorder, but of harmony within the Body. He would give one gift to one worshipper and one to another, and although each of them was available to them all, not all of them were to exercise them. The juxtaposition in the Acts of the Apostles of the 'falling' of the Holy Spirit upon believers and their almost immediate use of the gift of tongues has given rise to the view that the one is dependent upon and the mark of the other. But nowhere is this stated. It has merely become an assumption.

Nevertheless, the fact that there are incipient dangers in the supernatural gifts does not actually invalidate them. Indeed, misinterpretation of the gospel itself is so common, and false teaching on almost every subject so prevalent after nearly 2000 years of Christianity, that dangers abound on every side. However, the need is to identify and avoid any dangers, rather than advocate the neglect of God's gifts because of the possible consequences of misuse. Increasingly David found that anything supernatural, being by definition messy and even shocking, tended to frighten and provoke opposition. The gift of tongues, to him the simplest and most insignificant of the gifts, but one which brought invaluable blessing in his own spirit, became the focus of great wrath and bitterness. He was even turned out of Tyndale House because the authorities there heard he had used tongues privately in his prayers, in spite of his decision to keep 'very quiet about it'. Craven counsel said it would be dangerous. Mark Ruston, gracious as ever, immediately took David into his bachelor establishment.

It was not at all easy for David to live in this cauldron and he went conscientiously back to his Bible to see if he could be wrong. He could not be quite sure that, however firm was his experience, his explanation of it was sound and biblical. He longed to be allowed to share openly his new-found, God-given love for the Lord, and his sense of peace and joy at the Lord's love for him. As far as he could tell, the two-way relationship of love between himself and his Maker was totally biblical, but since that meant that those who opposed his view must be wrong, he could not be quite certain he was not wrong himself. Perhaps it was more likely, and certainly more desirable, that the process of deciding these matters by the unending use of words was wrong.

There was a price to pay for renewal in those early days. It is always costly to be a pioneer. It may well be asked whether what David received adequately compensated for what he suffered. For him there was never any doubt; although the pain caused by the criticisms and by the controversies which followed were a definite trial to him, he never wanted to withdraw from the riches of the inner experience which he received. Bishop Ralph Taylor was right to identify an evangelical as one who believed in 'the inwardness of true religion', and David had always shared in the hunger for a greater reality of inward experience. There was a natural tension between what he read in the Bible and understood clearly in his mind, and what he actually experienced in his life. The promise of Jesus, 'My peace I give you,'[11] he believed with all his heart but experienced only partially. Indeed, much of the 'fruit of the Spirit'[12] was clearly evident in his life; but not in its entirety. As he laid greater and greater emphasis upon the authority and trustworthiness of the Word of God, the contrast between what he believed and taught and what he enjoyed inwardly caused him real disquiet. Yet it was the inwardness of his faith for which he stood.

He learned through charismatic renewal that everything, indeed more than he had supposed, was ministered to the believer by the Holy Spirit. Everything that was ministered to him by the Spirit was to be received by faith. So all that was promised in the Word was to be enjoyed inwardly by faith. The Spirit made the fruit appear on the branches of his life because he gave the Spirit space to do so. This was not news to him, but it became new in him. He believed it actually and daily. The tense contrast between Word and experience faded into the reality of a Spirit-filled life. It was the most precious thing in the world to him; the pearl of great price. He was to find the gifts of the Spirit a practical foretaste of heavenly life as he began to walk where the early Christians had walked.

What he could not understand was why his evangelical friends did not seem to want to do so too.

He was particularly hurt that Bash took sides against him. Bash seemed to him to be wholly sympathetic to the biblical injunction to be filled with the Spirit. The story has often been told of Bash as a student at Ridley Hall frequently defaulting from early morning chapel. One day, an irate Vice-Principal came straight from chapel to his room and found him still in bed. Bash is said to have opened one eye and murmured sweetly, 'It's not chapel, man, it's abiding.' However fanciful this story may be, it exactly describes Bash's way of life – he lived abiding in Jesus. His constant theme and unfailing practice was to demonstrate that abiding in Jesus was the norm for Christian living, from which every deviation was to accept a lesser standard.

David felt that 'abiding' was a biblical word for Corrie ten Boom's 'nestling'. He thought that by seeking and receiving a closer relationship with Jesus he would be fulfilling Bash's greatest wish for him. But such proved not to be the case. Bash felt that this new movement exaggerated the simplicity of abiding in Christ by adding a dimension which did not belong in the usual, balanced and normal experience of biblical Christianity. He distrusted Pentecostalism, believing it to be unscriptural and unsound, and he found tongues quite ludicrous and repulsive. He had never spoken to his earthly father in unintelligible gobbledegook, and he had no intention of insulting his Heavenly Father by doing so.

Bash was no longer young, of course, and his extraordinary life's work had been built up in the face of the constant danger of losing the liberty he had been granted by the headmasters of the schools to recruit and to influence their boys. Even long after that danger had diminished considerably, it still existed in principle, and Bash saw no purpose in provoking any explosion of it. What if Camp became known for practising unusual religious activities uncharacteristic of the Church of England even in its broadest embrace? He could not jeopardise the whole work for the sake of some eccentric individuals, however well meaning and deserving.

So when David came back to Iwerne in the summer of 1964 for what was to be his last Camp, there was a certain coolness. He had been expecting to enjoy again the warm fellowship of the officers' room, which was his spiritual home, and to be strengthened by contact with his spiritual father, who meant more to him than anyone else. No one was rude, of course, and naturally there were none of the Cambridge confrontations, but it was a little different. Then one evening in the officers' prayer meeting, another officer, whose home was in Gillingham, prayed a prayer which was rather more charismatic in style than that used at Camp normally. Bash, very gently, and much as he sometimes did in prayer meetings, said, 'Will officers please not pray such emotional prayers?' To most of those present, and probably even to Bash himself, it was not a coded message, but a simple instruction from the leader. But to David it was different.

David writes of this incident that,

... although slight in itself, [it] seemed to oppose all the new-found joy and freedom in worship that had become so important to me. I felt a deep grief within my own spirit, and sensed that this was only a pale reflection of the much more serious grief of the Spirit of God. Whether or not I was right about this, I suddenly felt in a spiritual strait-jacket. At that moment I experienced something like a steel band tightening round my chest, and I began coughing. That night I continued coughing, and it steadily grew worse so that sleep became more and more difficult.[13]

It was the beginning of the scourge of asthma which plagued David, sometimes more and sometimes less, for the rest of his life. He had never had asthma before, though his chest was not naturally strong. Now it developed quite frighteningly, and the local doctor was puzzled enough to put him on the danger list. David knew that it had been brought on by the spiritual and psychological shock he sustained in the prayer meeting, and the implications for his relationship with Bash.

It is a mark of David's inner need that, when he realised that his way ahead was to be separate and even in divergence from all those whom he most valued and trusted, his system was unable to sustain the shock. They may not have realised it, but he suddenly saw it very clearly, and it nearly killed him. Without doubt, Bash had no idea that his very moderate requirement of the charismatics in his officers' room would have such a devastating effect on one of them. Indeed, how could he? Even with hindsight, it is strange to tell. Yet from this moment on, David was subject to outbreaks of crippling asthma when under stress, and since he persisted in working far beyond his natural strength, and in undertaking projects which would have daunted a much stronger man, it is not surprising that he was a great sufferer as well as a great leader. Perhaps his leadership would not have been so great, if his suffering had not been so also.

A man whose personal sense of security was as weak as was David's might well have cracked under the onslaught, but back at Cambridge he went on with his work at the Round, leading Children's Church which he increasingly enjoyed, preaching in the normal services and pastoring among the people. He stayed 'utterly loyal' to Mark and to the ministry as he directed it, avoiding any mention of tongues or any of the other controversial gifts, but he longed to be able to share something of the renewing work of the Spirit which he had experienced.

In the midst of all this controversy, he was suddenly and unexpectedly overtaken by romance.

10

Marriage

DAVID WAS NOT REALLY A GOOD CANDIDATE for marriage.

Although his mother's stalwart and devoted care in the face of great difficulties cannot be faulted, his own home had not given him much example of married life. His father's absence, both on army service and through his early death, meant that a relationship between his parents scarcely existed. He saw his mother's lonely struggles to bring him up, her comparatively unsuccessful second marriage, and very little evidence of true partnership between a man and his wife. The Collins' home at Gillingham was the first, and just about the only family home in which he lived. Perhaps he was somewhat blinded to the significance of the married partnership by their gracious inclusion in their home of much of the parish staff. It became a wonderful community of friends over which Diana Collins presided as a cross between an older sister and a benevolent matriarch. Everything else he knew was almost exclusively male.

He and David MacInnes had discussed the problems raised by the possible onset of matrimony, and had agreed together not to fall into the trap. This is perhaps not as surprising as it might seem. Both had been products of Camp and greatly influenced by Bash, who appeared to them, and especially to David, as a marvellous example of a Christian minister, not only in doctrine and method, but also in personal style. Bash was a bachelor. So were a number of his leading colleagues and ex-colleagues, including John Stott. After Gillingham, each of the two Davids went to work with an ex-Iwerne man who was a bachelor, Watson with Mark Ruston, and MacInnes with Dick Lucas. Without doubt there was some sort of an emphasis towards celibacy in the Camp fraternity, though it is very hard to quantify it.

Bash was utterly dedicated to working among boys and young men, not only to bring them to faith in Christ, but also to train them to become Christian leaders in British society. When he took up this work in the early Thirties, the leadership of society was very largely male. Moreover, the source from which that leadership was produced was in the main the boys' public schools and the two senior universities of Oxford and Cambridge, which were still very predominantly male. In Bash's world, therefore, women were only upon the fringe of society. Anyway, he was not a very social person. Some of his closer friends knew that Bash had at one time seriously considered marriage, but had deliberately chosen to remain single. He opted for celibacy because he knew that he was called to a ministry which would make it difficult, if not impossible, to establish and maintain any abiding married relationship. He knew that his would be a travelling ministry, continually taking him away from his home. He preferred to be free from family responsibilities in order to devote himself to the pursuit of his calling the more wholeheartedly. He accepted St Paul's advice to live as one whose undivided attention could be given to 'the affairs of the Lord, how to please the Lord'.[1]

Contrary to popular misconception, Bash did not disapprove of marriage and never spoke against it. He had a natural inclination towards celibacy because that had been his choice, but he sometimes advised men to get married. On one or two occasions he even allowed himself to suggest a particular person as a bride, though he was not usually a success as a matchmaker. Yet because of his own choice of style, several followed his example and found much happiness in the single state. At Camp there was virtually no preparation or training offered to those for whom marriage would follow, the male ethos of the work making this inevitable. It is therefore not surprising that David Watson's almost obsessional desire to 'please the Lord' and his in-built need for the approval of his peers, and especially of Bash, made him consider the unmarried state with favour.

Then David MacInnes got engaged to be married. Another green bottle fell off the wall! David Watson 'felt almost betrayed', but was nevertheless happy for his friend, and very pleased to accept the invitation to be his Best Man. His own attitude towards marriage soon changed as he saw for himself the happiness it brought into the lives of David and Clare MacInnes. He was also finding himself inordinately lonely in Cambridge. The pressure of standing alone against the general tide of opinion, often expressed quite intemperately, required more of him than he had expected. What is more, he began to wish for something a little more domestic to be added to his life.

David records Christmas Day 1963:

The Christmas morning service had just finished, and I was standing with Mark Ruston at the Norman porch of the Round Church saying 'Happy Christmas' to all the members of the congregation. A very attractive girl suddenly caught my eye. 'Have we met before?' I asked. 'I don't think so,' she replied with a trace of a Scottish accent. 'My name is Anne MacEwan Smith, and I'm nursing at the Maternity Hospital in Mill Lane.'

I had always mistrusted the romantic sentiment of 'love at first sight', but the 'vibes' were undoubtedly there.[2]

Anne obviously had almost exactly the same reaction. She wrote later: 'I had read about electric shocks going through people when they meet, but always dismissed it as romantic fantasy. Fact is certainly stranger than fiction! The experience left me rather out of breath.'[3]

Elizabeth Anne MacEwan Smith was born in Burma in 1941, the first child of Cecil William Smith and his wife, Jean. When she was one year old the Japanese invaded, and Mrs Smith took Anne out to India, covering the first seventy miles or so by air and the rest on foot – quite an adventure. Mr Smith, who worked for British Petroleum, stayed on for a while to try to maintain the supply of petrol to China. However, the Japanese advance was so rapid that the oil installations had to be demolished, and the BP personnel crossed the mountains into Assam, arriving some three months after their families. After a brief reunion in South India, Anne's father was sent to Abadan in Persia/Iran where he spent the rest of the war. Jean and Anne Smith were evacuated by ship from Bombay round the Cape, but landed at Durban when their convoy was attacked. They waited in a cold Cape Town winter for another ship to carry them home, spending four or five weeks there while Anne developed a serious bout of pneumonia and her mother, pregnant with her second child, kept herself busy nursing her. Eventually they came home to Scotland and settled for the duration of the war at Jean's mother's cottage in Kinrosshire. Anne's brother, Kelvin, was born in Edinburgh in 1943.

As soon as possible after the war the family was reunited in Abadan where they stayed for the next nine years, though Anne came home to a boarding school in Crieff when she was eight. Owing to political upheaval, her parents had to leave Iran in 1954 and were posted by BP to Ellesmere Port in Cheshire. Anne came south to day school in Chester, a small private school called Hollybank where, in her own words, 'the academic standards were not too high'. This gave her the opportunity to gain confidence and to develop an appetite for reading and for the use of the mind without being put under pressure. She responded by achieving considerable success, gaining excellent results in her 'O' Level exams. She started her 'A' Levels at the Queen's School in Chester, but then, at eighteen, began nursing training at Guy's Hospital in London, where her mother had also trained. She spent four years there on the SRN course and the Guy's badge for nursing, carrying off some prizes in her year.

During those four years she began to read her Bible with the help of

Scripture Union notes, provoked into this action by her room-mate's habit of doing the same. She persisted with it, but could make little sense out of what she read. 'I might just as well have been reading a German Bible.' Then one day a lively and presentable young doctor invited her to go with him to the hospital Christian Union meeting, and afterwards for a meal in an Italian restaurant under the London Bridge railway arches. They talked somewhat of the Christian religion, and John 3:16 cropped up. It suddenly struck Anne that if God had so loved the world that he had given his Son for it, she had never thanked him for doing so. Back in her room she did just that, very deliberately and quite sincerely. When she looked up she saw the Lord standing across the room, smiling at her. Next morning her old Bible seemed to be in beautiful, plain English. It had a clarity that shone with new light. She was utterly amazed at what she read, and began to tell everyone about it, even the hospital boilermen and the patients. Some of them came to faith in Christ. She says she never had any problems with evangelism until David started to tell her how it should really be done!

Now a believing Christian, Anne, with typical good sense, began to pray about her future and decided she was called to become a missionary. She was not without experience of the world overseas and this seemed the way in which she could most usefully be occupied in building the kingdom of God. To be a good missionary meant to be really well qualified, and that implied being a midwife as well as a nurse. She got a place in 1963 at the Mill Lane Hospital in Cambridge to study midwifery. Anne was a bright, attractive and intelligent young lady with a practical bent and an enthusiasm for the simple but beautiful things in life. Her Christian faith was real and practical and it meant everything to her. Moreover, it was not institutionalised and dependent only upon what was taught in church and experienced by other Christians. It contained the freshness of supernatural happenings which excited her, but which retained a practical reality.

Soon after coming to Cambridge she read a magazine which invited readers to contribute towards some needy children whose pictures were on the back. This she did, but when a letter of acknowledgment came she found herself deeply moved and excited even before she read it. In the envelope was an article about how faith could move mountains, and she knew at once that she did not have that quality. She went to the window and looked out, but there was no convenient mountain to be moved. There was, however, a tree in the garden which she commanded to move across the lawn but she knew that she did not believe.

Humbly she recognised that it was impossible to please God without faith and, down on her knees, she said, 'Lord, I'm sorry but you'll just have to give me faith because I can't please you. I don't have any. I don't even have a mustard seed's worth and I can't move a tree.' Then she knew the presence and love of God powerfully upon her, embracing her and sanctifying her. Very fearful, a great sense of awe compelled her to say, 'Please put me down, Lord.' The intensity of the experience passed, but not the sense of fulfilment or the new level of faith it engendered. She found herself making strange noises to God which surprised her because she had no knowledge of the gift of tongues, but it did not worry her because she knew she was just loving him. He was truly now her heavenly Father.

Not long before Christmas 1963, she heard what seemed like an audible voice saying, 'Anne, get confirmed into the Church of England.' The Presbyterian lass replied, 'Not likely, Lord, I'm a member of the Church of Scotland.' There was silence. Then the same voice spoke the same words very clearly and quietly. 'But Lord, I've only recently been confirmed into the Church of Scotland.' Again the short silence. Then a little more firmly came the voice again, 'Anne, get confirmed into the Church of England.' This time she said, 'All right, Lord, if you say so.' Because there was no Church of Scotland church that she could discover in Cambridge she had been going, like so many others, to the Round Church. So, after the morning service on Christmas Day, she went up to Mark Ruston, the Vicar, and asked to be confirmed into the Church of England. He told her that he was just about to begin a three-month sabbatical leave and that she must see David about it. She crossed the path to talk to him, told him her name, and the romance began. David records:

I had in fact already started the confirmation classes, and since we were covering a carefully planned syllabus, it was necessary for Anne to catch up on the classes she had missed. Whether it was appropriate or not, I arranged to give her one or two private classes before she could join the rest. At our first session I handed her an Anglican Prayer Book and asked her to turn to the Confirmation Service. Following my usual practice, I commented, 'You will find it just before the Marriage Service!' A word of prophecy indeed![4]

David naturally wanted to check up on this potential wife as soon as he could and characteristically it was her spiritual condition which was his first interest. He discovered that she had been converted at Guy's, although she had been a lifelong churchgoer before that. What was more, she had very recently had a spiritual experience of some depth which she could not easily describe, but which sounded promising. He gave her a booklet by Michael Harper to clarify the issue. When she brought it back the following Sunday morning after church, she told him exuberantly in the churchyard, 'David, I do speak with tongues.' Since tongues were taboo at the Round, he was embarrassed by her outspokenness and tucked the booklet away under his surplice, hushing her up as best he could.

There followed a cloak and dagger courtship, called by David, 'an essential subterfuge'. He decided his friendship with Anne must, if possible, not be known in Cambridge, and they went to extraordinary lengths to avoid this. It is not easy for a clergyman to undertake such a thing in any parish, and the Round, with its bachelor vicar and eligible young curate, may perhaps have had more than the usual quota of hopeful ladies. Some of the anxiety and the need that David felt for secrecy was probably due as much to the difficulty under which he lived in trying not to speak of his charismatic leanings and practices, as to his own lack of confidence. He undoubtedly exaggerated the caution needed, and he could write humorously about it later. At the time he shared his hopes only with a few friends.

In March 1964, David wrote to John and Diana Collins about Anne:

Just a note to you and Diana, in *strict* confidence please, because I have recently been thunderstruck by a super Scots lass called Anne MacEwan Smith! I am proceeding cautiously (as far as possible) because:

a) It is spring.
b) I'm in a most vulnerable position here, all on my own and feeling quite lonely at times.
c) I have not known her for long and have not yet met her parents.

But she is really splendid spiritually, is being used by the Lord, prays such heart-warming prayers, and has been filled (baptised) with the Holy Spirit (entirely on her own, not knowing what had happened until several weeks later). She is also intelligent, full of life and ideas, shrewd and has a gift of leadership (could be a good speaker too, I should say). I've thought and prayed *very* much over the last two weeks, and all the time I have increasing confidence, 'This is it'!

In April they got engaged, but as the whole period of courtship had taken place while Mark Ruston had been away from the parish on his sabbatical, David insisted that any announcement must await his return. More secrecy! At the end of the month he wrote again to John and Diana to bring them up to date:

Just a note to say that I am now definitely though unofficially engaged. Wow – what a responsibility! The final encouragement came when my mother was thrilled to bits with Anne, and now she cannot stop talking about her. In fact, she virtually proposed on my behalf. We shall probably wait till mid-May before we announce it, so as to leave it till Mark gets back; and I think we *may* get married sometime in September. It seems the most obvious time.

That programme was to be fulfilled.

Anne finished her course at Mill Lane in May and postponed the second part of it until after the wedding. Her mother whisked her home for a three weeks' crash course on cooking and to get properly ready for everything. In Cambridge, they hunted together for a small flat, which was all they could hope to afford on his curate's stipend, and they knew Anne must go back to work to swell their income. Of course, if their future missionary work was to be in England, there was not the same need for Anne to qualify as a midwife and they now needed every penny she could earn. They found a little flat in Park Parade. It was too small really – just two rooms, kitchen and bathroom – but they could not manage more, and it was near the Round.

David was getting more confident about the charismatic dimension in spite of the increasingly vocal and literary opposition to it, but he felt alone and vulnerable in the cockpit of Cambridge. Anne was a tremendous encouragement to him because, although she was not terribly inclined to discuss theological issues, there was no doubting the validity of her experience to put beside his own. Moreover, the personal affirmation that David always needed she could most certainly supply. When the incident with Bash in the officers' room at Camp occurred that summer, it was Anne who was quickly sent for and drove David away from his last Camp to her home in Cheshire where, despite her mother's skilled nursing, recovery was very slow. There seemed to be little relief available from drugs and not much hope in the long process of chasing an allergy.

His departure from Iwerne, coughing all the way to Cheshire, took place just three weeks before the date fixed for the wedding, and Anne soon began to wonder whether he would be fit enough to get to the church. On the night before the wedding, he was very ill and quite breathless. She went upstairs and sat on his bed, trying to find a way of voicing her anxieties. When she asked at length whether he thought it would be better to postpone the wedding, he went quite wild. 'No! No! No!' he cried. 'Promise me you will never do that to me.' When she arrived at the Round next day, her first question was, 'Is David here?' He was and the service duly proceeded, attended by many of David's old friends, Bash included, of course. John Collins took the service and preached. David MacInnes was Best Man. The honeymoon was spent at Trebarwith Sands in North Cornwall where they had a delightful hotel all to themselves, beautiful weather and rolling surf. But David could not breathe, especially at night, which he spent sitting up in an armchair, coughing. When they got back to Cambridge, the asthmatic condition continued.

There was a good sitting-room in the new flat, besides a bedroom, a bathroom and a kitchen. Anne was spared the necessity of going back to work by a generous gift from a friend. In any case, David's health would have prevented her. He could only just climb the stairs to the first floor flat and on bad days could not go out at all. He would cough all night and sleep a bit during the afternoon. Nevertheless, he continued working to his very tight schedule – one visit after another, Bible readings in the colleges, sermons in the church, endless preparation and study. Anne was awake all night with him and could not rest during the day because of the constant need to answer the doorbell downstairs. When he was studying, sleeping or interviewing, she could not use the sitting-room and had only a kitchen stool or her bed upon which to sit. When friends came to stay, she would have to move all their own things out of the bedroom up into the attic, where they shared a single bed while their guests occupied theirs.

Then she found that she was pregnant, much to David's consternation. He could not see the end to their present circumstances, into which it was hard to see where a baby could be fitted. In her exhaustion and frustration, she had a miscarriage and, shortly afterwards, a nervous breakdown. There were days when she could not face life at all. The slightest problem would make her cry and often she stayed in bed all day. David had no idea how to cope with this. When she broke down and cried over her hoovering, he did not offer to do it for her, but suggested they should pray about it together. These were grim, dark days for Anne. She went home to Cheshire for a brief rest, and told her mother she couldn't face going back. 'Anne, you've made your bed and you must lie on it,' said the inexorable, but not unsympathetic, Jean Smith. She struggled back to Cambridge to her no less relentless husband.

Asthma or no asthma, wife or no wife, David was set upon the service of the Lord. His daily schedule was demanding, to say the least. He almost seemed to say to Anne, 'Wist ye not that I must be about my Father's business?'[5] Of course, when the asthma was bad he would not rush around so much, but was shackled to the flat. He might find time to instruct Anne in the proper way to have a Quiet Time, or how to lead someone to Christ. She could not understand why his way was the right one, and eventually learned to do it her own way. Gradually the asthma improved, partly because his doctor, Stanley Gould, found drugs that seemed to give him some relief, but that only gave him opportunity to work to an even heavier schedule. They went down to Gillingham on one of their days off to meet Edgar Trout, a Methodist lay preacher, who laid hands on David and prayed for him. The asthma was in total remission for three weeks.

Because both David and Anne have always been very open about their difficulties within marriage, many people have supposed that their relationship was far worse than it really was. In fact, they loved one another deeply and their marriage, though beset with circumstantial difficulties, proved to be able to stand the test of time and to reward them both immeasurably. They had complementary personalities, each with different gifts for different ministries, and it took them a long time to understand this, and to work it through. Anne believes that David did not really learn the true pattern of family life until after they left York and settled in London, when he found a model for it in another couple.

In the early days, the difficulties were not made any easier by the fact that David was a workaholic, and something of a perfectionist too. 'The ministry was the whole of David's life, particularly the evangelistic ministry,' wrote Anne.[6] His wife, apparently, was a most useful, indeed delightful, adjunct to his life but, of course, her role was domestic. Since she loved the same Jesus and was filled with the same Spirit, she should know that she must not interfere with his work, which was paramount. She existed, presumably, to promote it. If he had to have the sitting-room, of course she could not have it, however desirable it might be for her to have somewhere to sit down.

All this was clearly wrong, but it was not malicious or even selfish. He longed to have more suitable quarters for them, because he loved her dearly and hated her frustration and misery in the circumstances imposed upon them by the size of their flat. It never seems to have occurred to him that it would be right to modify the intensity of his programme to allow more room for her. He simply had to 'please the Lord'. On the other hand Anne, a very determined lady, was not particularly easy to please in the very difficult circumstances in which they found themselves.

Meanwhile, David was in great demand in the colleges and there was plenty to do in the parish. He was beginning to be asked to take part in university missions as his reputation as an evangelist grew. Although Inter-Varsity Fellowship circles were strongly opposed in those early days to anything connected with 'speaking in tongues', there was never any embargo on David as a speaker for evangelistic meetings or services, and he was always careful to avoid saying anything which might cause divisions. The same care had to be exercised daily within the pastoral ministry in Cambridge, where Mark's continued disapproval and David's determination to maintain his loyalty to him made the situation a little tense. Nevertheless, Mark considered that David's sermons at the Round Church were completely acceptable and uncontroversial and that his evangelistic preaching was outstanding. Moreover, such was the power and clarity with which he spoke, that those converted through his preaching seemed to be more stable and to have fewer subsequent doubts than others. But there were also many people in Cambridge wanting to learn more about the Holy Spirit, and David and Anne used to meet regularly with several groups for prayer and fellowship, stretching the limits of his licence from Mark.

He longed to be rid of all such restriction and to be able freely to teach people the joy of living in the Spirit and with the power of his gifts. It is probable that he did not fully realise how hard he had found it in Cambridge until after he had actually left. He had begun to look for God's leading for his next move before the wedding in September 1964, and from the New Year the search intensified.

The flat was to be Anne's despair for only ten months.

11

St Cuthbert's, York

David was becoming quite an enigma.

His reputation as an evangelistic preacher, especially in the student world, was growing fast, and the evangelical establishment was impressed. On the other hand, he was also known to be associated with charismatic renewal, which was considered a somewhat eccentric excess of holiness only practised by the not very intelligent and the easily misled. No one was happy to put David in either of the latter categories. He was balanced and intelligent. Moreover, he preached extremely well in that centre for sane and traditional evangelicalism, the Round Church in Cambridge. He was a most valuable teacher and adviser to the CICCU, and was in considerable demand for university missions and conferences. But he made no secret of the fact that he belonged as much with the charismatics as he did with the evangelicals. He emphasised the importance of being filled with the Spirit, and connected with this the use of the spiritual gifts.

When it became known that he would very soon be ready for a new appointment, there were several parishes suggested. One prestigious and significant parish was offered to him provided he would undertake no longer to speak with tongues or to teach about it, but David would never have dreamed of accepting something with such 'strings attached'. Anyway, one of his hopes was to escape the restrictions applied to him in Cambridge. He was very firm in declining the offer. Three others were offered in turn, one in the East End of London which reminded him of the potential of Gillingham, but which was, he thought, made unworkable by being joined with another parish across a major railway line.

Eventually, he was approached by Derek Wooldridge, a Curate of Heworth at York, with whom he had recently worked on a mission to Loughborough College. David had discussed his future with him, expressing the hope that he might be able to continue to work among students. David believed that many of the modern universities springing up all over the country would need to rely upon local churches for spiritual care, since they were not often supplied with chaplains. Cambridge and Oxford, in comparison, were richly endowed in this respect, as well as in their Christian foundations and long traditions. Derek wrote to suggest that David might take over the nearly redundant church of St Cuthbert's in York and use it especially for students, as well as for others in the parish and city.

St Cuthbert's was a small medieval church in Peasholme Green, just within the ancient walls of York, with the parish extending outside them. It was on the right side for the new university recently built in Heslington, which was at that stage chaplainless. The congregation of St Cuthbert's had been declining for some time, together with the health of their much-loved Rector, R. V. Bainton, who had served the parish faithfully for twenty-four years. His sight had been failing steadily, and by the time of his death early in 1964 he was completely blind. The Diocese of York had set up a committee to look at the future of the many churches in the city which had been founded long ago to provide pastoral care for parishioners living in crowded accommodation, both within the city walls and outside them. Many of the old houses were now being converted into shops and offices and the parishioners were moving out to new areas on the fringe. In Peasholme Green, the little old houses had deteriorated and been demolished, leaving the parish very largely denuded of dwellings and ready for the new light industries which were springing up. Very few of St Cuthbert's parishioners remained.

On the death of the old Rector, the diocese decided to put the church under the charge of the incumbent of the nearest parish church outside the walls, which happened to be Holy Trinity, Heworth, of which the Vicar was Basil Brown. Heworth had three churches, and therefore two curates to assist the Vicar. When they were also required to look after St Cuthbert's, they discussed the matter at a staff meeting. Ian Bull, the second Curate, suggested that they look for a man who might be able to use St Cuthbert's to reach the students at the new university. Basil Brown liked the idea. Derek Wooldridge suggested David Watson's name, and was asked to contact him to sound him out.

So it fell that David and Anne came up to York to see the situation, and to talk and pray about it. That first visit might well have been enough to put them off completely. It was a very foggy day, which brought on a severe attack of David's asthma, and neither the damp and somewhat run-down church nor the vast, unheated, fourteen-roomed rectory, where they would be expected to live, seemed very attractive. They discovered too that David's stipend as a curate in York would be little over £600, whereas in Cambridge he had been receiving £900. Of course they would not have to pay rent for their house, but neither would they still be receiving the gift from a generous friend which had just about kept them solvent. It scarcely seemed a very sensible move. That night, in the Wooldridges' house, David's asthma was so bad that sleep in bed was impossible. He had to spend the whole night sitting up in a chair. Next day he learned that St Cuthbert's was heated only by two old coke stoves, which were liable to give off very unpleasant fumes.

Yet David and Anne both had a growing sense that God wanted them in York. While David was talking to the churchwardens, Anne found herself counting the chairs in the church. They had been told that the largest congregation at present would only be twelve, but there were exactly 120 chairs. She sensed the Holy Spirit reminding her that 120 was also the number of believers who gathered on the first day of Pentecost, who subsequently turned the world upside down. During the next few weeks, as they prayed together, they were given a verse from Haggai to claim as a promise: 'I will fill this house with glory.'[1] They wrote to tell the Vicar and churchwardens that they would come. The letter was sent in March 1965, and they offered to start work in York on 1 July.

By secular standards of course, this was a preposterous decision, yet in *You Are My God* David makes it clear that the growth of a sense of call and the given promise were more than sufficient reason. Nevertheless, it may have been a decision influenced partly by his own lack of self worth, the insecurity which remained with him all his life. At St Cuthbert's he would not have the ultimate responsibility, which would remain with Basil Brown, his Vicar. He would not be taking over a large congregation, set in certain ways and moulded to many prejudices. He would not have to compete in the rather arid North East of England (judged by evangelical standards) with the flourishing churches in the South. In York and with Anne's help, he could make a new start away from the intellectualism of Cambridge, and be free to develop his own church as he saw God's Spirit guide him. Basil had agreed to give him his head.

All these things would be true, of course, and some of them at least he had carefully considered, but for them both the sense of call was what counted most. They faced poverty in a much too large and ill-equipped house, for which they had very little furniture, in order to minister in a small, old-fashioned church with almost no people and therefore no money. Without any question they chose to do it because the Lord told them to, whatever may have been the subconscious attitudes which also encouraged the decision.

In June they drove up to Scotland for a holiday and called at their new rectory on the way. Meeting a diocesan surveyor, they learned that since the diocese did not expect St Cuthbert's to survive the next year, no money would be spent upon the house, except to make it safe. With this in view, it would be re-wired and some windows secured, but nothing else. Anne had been looking forward to taking David to Scotland, but the weather could not have been worse. It rained night and day for a fortnight. They did nothing, saw no scenic views, and had no romantic picnics. They got back to Cambridge more depressed than when they set out.

They had begun shopping for furniture. Using David's mother's home as a base, they tried Eastbourne and found two wardrobes, two chairs, a Belgian cotton carpet and various small items, all of which cost them £73. David thought they had spent enough. But it would make little impression on fourteen rooms. Then Peggy, David's mother, decided to move into a small flat in Andover where her daughter Diana was working as a solicitor, and gave them some of her spare furniture. Mrs Ruston, Mark's mother, produced some more. Then a hostel in Cambridge closed down and David and Anne were given some of the beds and chairs. Some of their Cambridge friends very kindly stored these in their garages against the removal date, when the van found itself touring the neighbourhood picking up odds and ends from different places. But the major breakthrough came when Cecil and Jean Smith, Anne's parents, met them in York one day and offered to 'advance their will' to provide carpets, curtains and some furniture for them. The whole furnishing project began to look possible.

Moving in to their new home became quite an event. Seeing the van off from Cambridge in the late afternoon, David and Anne drove through the night to York, arriving at 3 a.m. Trying to gain access to the rectory, they inadvertently disturbed their neighbours. Anne suddenly saw a burly Yorkshireman, armed with a rubber torch and a big stick, bearing down on David, supposing him to be a thief who was breaking in. When peace was restored, they got inside and stretched out on a mattress for a few hours' sleep, grateful that some Smith furniture had arrived the day before. Daylight revealed a complete mess. The electrician had done his re-wiring, plastering over the various holes he had made in the walls, so that there were lumps of dried plaster and builder's dust everywhere. The kitchen especially was filthy. Later they learned from the lady who cleaned the church that some of the congregation had wanted to clean the house, but had never previously been allowed in. Anne hoovered all over the bare boards before carpets could be laid. Clearly this was going to be true missionary work.

The first job was to do some decorating and to their great joy John Freeth, their old Iwerne friend from Ridley Hall, came to give them two weeks of his time and his practical gifts and experience. Rather typically,

David decreed that a sitting-room should be done first and then his study. The big front bedroom upstairs was chosen for the sitting-room and the old morning room downstairs near the front door became David's study. Anne loved it all. In spite of the dust and the hard labour involved, the large roomy house delighted her, and the large garden at the back was a special joy. They lived for that fortnight off fish and chips, which could be obtained from either end of the street, and a rich harvest of raspberries from the garden, so that she did not have any cooking to do. David too was enjoying himself. With the pressures of Cambridge left behind and only a tiny congregation to meet and minister to, for once in his life he didn't have enough work to do. He became the fish and chip fetcher, this suiting his skills rather better than the manual work. He quite shocked the purveyors when one day he went shopping in his clerical collar, and they discovered who he was.

His asthma was definitely better at this stage, still the aftermath of Edgar Trout's ministry to him, and it was to remain better, though not cured, for another six months or so. Even the experience of meeting the Chairman of the Church Redundancy Commission and all its members in St Cuthbert's on his second day in York did not bring on an attack. He roundly and piously told them that, 'If anyone comes to this church and preaches the simple Gospel of Christ, believes in the power of prayer, and trusts in the Holy Spirit, this building will be full in no time.' No record remains of what they said about that then or later, but they gave him, 'one year's grace before, regretfully, they would have to close St Cuthbert's down'.[2]

He wrote to introduce himself to the people of St Cuthbert's in the Parish Newsletter:

What do we aim to do? Quite simply, to proclaim Christ. We never cease to wonder at his mercy and compassion, his forgiveness and peace. How perfectly he understands us! How faithfully he meets all our needs! Our greatest desire is that others too may increasingly experience 'the unsearchable riches of Christ'. What do we hope to find? A fellowship of Christians, marked by love, full of faith, and pressing on to know the Lord more and more.

Just what the little group of members made of this, it is difficult to say. They were so few that David could list their names from memory, writing eighteen years later. The early Communion attracted about four of them, Morning Prayer about the same, and the Evening Service ten or twelve. One family, the Linfoots, dominated the membership with eight, and provided the leader and churchwarden in the person of Dan, who had attended St Cuthbert's for over fifty years. He started as a bell-ringer when he was ten years old, and later he earned a shilling for blowing the organ. He used to get a lot out of the services in those early days and his faith always meant a great deal to him, so it had been a great sadness to him to see the congregations getting smaller.

Not knowing quite what else to do, David soon started visiting in the parish, hoping to get to know more of the people living near the church. If there seemed to be any interest in spiritual things he would leave a copy of *Journey into Life*,[3] and he would always pray with and for the people in each home before he left. He was never aware of anyone joining the church as a result of these visits, but he felt he made personal contact in a way that showed he cared; he was not just asking for money. But the unfruitfulness of this parish visiting convinced David and Anne of the need for a warm and vibrant church fellowship to stand behind and be involved in any outreach to unbelievers. Increasingly, they came to see the poverty of any witness to Christ being offered by an unsupported individual. Far more penetrating was the impact made by the Body of Christ on earth, living and loving, praying and giving. The greater the unity within the body, the greater their influence upon the world around them.

It is a long-standing and popular misconception that the clergyman's role is to visit in the parish to seek out the lost and the erring. David was a gifted and experienced evangelist whose reputation in this field was already well established, yet he found that systematic visiting from door to door was comparatively unproductive. It was not without any value, for it produced good relations with the church's neighbours and corrected some false impressions. As far as it went, that was good, but if David had concentrated on this it would have taken years to build up much of a church in St Cuthbert's.

He sought a better way. He and Anne decided to keep Wednesday in each week as a day of prayer and fasting. Instead of breakfast, they would have only some coffee and instead of lunch, a glass of orange juice. They would draw the day to a close with supper in the evening. In between, they prayed. It was not their day off, although that became a rare and virtually non-existent fixture, but they tried, without being rigid, to keep Wednesdays free from all other work in order to have this time for prayer. It was largely worship in which, with their Bibles open, they praised God for his goodness, his faithfulness to his promises and his characteristic love poured into them by his Spirit. They found this could take up quite a long time. Then they interceded systematically for everyone and everything, connected with St Cuthbert's and unconnected. Then they praised him again in prospect for the answers he would be giving to the prayers they had just offered. They might read a psalm together or consider some other passage of Scripture. They might remind each other of past experiences or of some story of the experiences of others. They certainly laughed together in God's presence. It was a day spent with God, spent for God. It worked wonders for their spiritual lives and confidence, and also in their ministry.

Secondly, they did what David had declared to the Redundancy Commission he would do: preach the gospel and trust in the Holy Spirit. They concentrated whatever effort they could upon the church, the Body of Christ. David found the services, and especially the sermons, quite hard going. The little band at St Cuthbert's were not unappreciative, but they were clearly not used to listening to sermons in order to receive the word of God. Something had to be done to change that, so David and Anne opened their home to them. David announced that there would be a prayer meeting for all the congregation in the rectory at 7.45 p.m. every Thursday evening. He wanted this to be a priority for every member of St Cuthbert's, and for many years there were no other mid-week meetings so that no one had an excuse for not coming. He resisted the formation of any specialist groups, such as a women's fellowship, as alternatives to this all-important event.

Yet the first prayer meeting did not give the impression of being very important or very successful for, as Anne recalls, the total attendance was five, including themselves and a woman with a dog. After a short Bible reading, David invited each to pray a short simple prayer: David prayed ... silence ... Anne prayed ... silence ... David prayed ... silence ... Anne prayed ... silence ... the dog barked ... they said the grace together and went home. But they had made a start, and gradually over the months more and more people started to come to the rectory on Thursday evenings.

As the numbers grew and overflowed into other rooms and upstairs Noel Pallier, a GPO engineer who had recently joined St Cuthbert's with his wife, installed loudspeakers in each of the rooms. When it was time for prayer, each room became a separate prayer group. The steady growth in attendance of the Thursday evening meetings was mainly because people from other churches in the city started coming for David's Bible readings, though many still went to their own church on a Sunday. This trend was to continue for several years.

David's Bible expositions were crucial to the health of the prayer meetings. They were not only a time for prayer. They became a way in which David could awake in his people a sensitivity to the word of God. His short, punchy style of teaching, always by exposition of the Scriptures and always heavily laced with illustrations, was irresistible even to those unused to listening. In the informality of the rectory it was very effective, and helped to educate St Cuthbert's into understanding the Bible and living by the Bible. But the prayer meeting was also an occasion for fellowship. As David taught about the Holy Spirit, the people, crammed higgledy-piggledy into the various rooms, began to experience an overwhelming love being poured into their hearts. All sorts of barriers were broken down between them, and the great oneness in Christ, which is in principle true for all churches, became actual in experience. More and more, St Cuthbert's became a church where the relations between the members were almost more significant than what they believed. 'By this all men will know that you are my disciples, if you have love for one another.'[4] Beliefs build relationships, but good relationships command attention to the validity of those beliefs.

On Sundays he preached as never before. Having to win the attention of the congregation, he knew he had to work harder than ever at his preparation. He began to study more carefully the science of communication. He observed the way in which great speakers (both Christian and secular) held the attention of their audience. He knew that it was important to make proper use of stories or illustrations to throw light on what the Bible was teaching. He described a sermon without illustrations as like a building without windows, and he developed a carefully indexed file of sermon illustrations, on appropriate-sized paper to be clipped into his Filofax. It was no good teaching any truth, however important, if it was not applied to everyday situations in everyday language. That was the difficult thing to do. He had learnt much here from Dick Lucas, Rector of St Helen's, Bishopsgate, in the City of London, whose skill in application is remarkable.

He was always concerned to prepare a structure for his sermons, taking to heart the words of John Stott in his book *I Believe in Preaching*: 'No sermon is really strong which is not strong in structure too. Just as bones without flesh make a skeleton, so flesh without bones make a jelly-fish; and neither bony skeletons nor jelly-fish make good sermons.'[5]

David realised that the opening moments of each sermon were vital in either capturing the attention of his congregation or in sending them off on some day-dream of their own. He would often start with an arresting story, an amusing incident or a topical allusion, but he was also quick to show how it was relevant to the theme and message of the sermon. He learnt too that the ending was of great importance, carefully preparing the actual words with which he would close. He built upon the foundation of what he had learned about speaking to boys at Iwerne and during the days at Gillingham when the science of preaching and communicating was carefully debated. But it was the detailed, hard work which paid the dividends. Word upon word, line upon line, he built in the sanctity of his study. 'You did not disturb my husband when he was preparing his sermon,' said Anne.

Furthermore, he believed strongly in the power of expository preaching. He never stopped learning what the message of the Bible was, and he knew that the word of God was the essential spiritual food without which no Christian can grow in faith. It was Christ centred and Christ revealing, 'living and active, sharper than any two-edged sword'.[6] He believed it to be a privilege and a responsibility to expound God's word, and was encouraged by the inscription on a plaque on the wall of the church, in memory of a former rector: 'I determined not to know any thing among you, save Jesus Christ, and him crucified.'[7] Someone else had done it in St Cuthbert's before him.

Realising the need to build up the faith and expectation of his congregation, David started a series of sermons teaching the principle of faith through the experience of Abraham, just as St Paul presents it in Romans 4. Nevertheless, he knew that he was preaching as much to himself and to Anne as to the rest of the congregation. The story of Abraham kept coming back to the subject of faith, even some of the more obscure passages. Harvey Dean, who was to become David's first Reader at St Cuthbert's and an important figure in those early days, recalls that when he and his wife Valerie first attended a service there, David's subject was 'Abraham at the Oaks of Mamre (Genesis 18:14): "Is anything too hard for the Lord?"' David also preached a series on the Prayer Book Canticles, believing that the very familiarity of words sung every Sunday could all too easily blind the congregation to the meaning and significance of what they were singing.

Each sermon was part of a short series based upon a book in the Bible, or a biblical theme or character, but each was always a complete entity in itself. The series was announced on a long poster board outside the church, clearly visible to anyone driving along Peasholme Green. In the early days David and Anne put up the posters themselves, Anne leaning over from the back to hold the paper in place while David wielded the long-handled glue brush from in front. She found this a little difficult when she became pregnant.

The sermons were not only announced but recorded, David switching on the tape recorder as he climbed into the pulpit. Later, Noel Pallier fitted up a more sophisticated recording system and organised a tape library to enable people who missed a sermon to catch up on the series. This was to become a regular feature of David's ministry as listening to recorded sermons and other teachings became a very popular activity, especially for Christians whose regular minister was not a particularly gifted teacher. David's clear, resonant voice and outstanding ability to make known the revealed Christian religion made his tapes very easy to listen to and understand.

Soon the Parochial Church Council, or PCC ('We were all on the PCC,' said Anne, 'there were so few of us') was meeting in the vestry for a practical demonstration of another of David's new ideas. Most of them were rather sceptical about having Family Services, but were completely converted to them by what they saw and heard in the demonstration. They voted to have a Family Service once a month in place of Mattins, but very soon it became every Sunday, and remained so throughout David's time in York. John Collins' insistence at Gillingham that David overcome his unease about leading Family Services was now to bear fruit. It became the focus of the church's outreach. The very first Family Service, in December 1965, brought one new family into church membership, which just about doubled the congregation. Gradually, other families and single people started coming too. Even students from the university and other colleges in York seemed to appreciate the simplicity and relevance of this type of service, though more students came in the evening. More than anything else, it was the Family Services which attracted new members to the congregation.

The Family Service was not a Children's Church such as David had run in Cambridge. They used the CPAS special form of service put together by Michael Botting for the very purpose of a Family Service. To this were added hymns and songs which children could sing with meaning and adults could join in with conviction. Eventually, it was based on the *Alternative Service Book* Morning Prayer. But the key to the success of the Family Service was that it aimed to reach the children through the parents, and not the other way round. Most churches make the mistake of having the service appropriate for the children, hoping that some of it will rub off on the parents. It becomes a children's service, often inspired by teachers in the congregation whose skill lies in communicating with children. The parents know it is not for them and only some of them find it to be personally helpful, rather than merely enjoyable for their children. Few families join the church through such services and often they become bored with what they find to be rather amateur religious entertainment.

Instead David aimed the service at the parents, presenting his message in a way which would also communicate with the children. Each address was to last ten or at the most fifteen minutes, and would be in terms appropriate for adults. It would have only one point, not three, and it would be very well illustrated by a memorable visual aid. David and Anne would work this out together, for Anne had an artistic talent which she used to create excellent and exciting visual aids. It involved hours of hard work as they would not allow themselves to treat the service and the sermon as less important and easier than others. If it was to be real outreach, it must be word perfect, and the visual aid must serve the talk exactly as they wanted it to.

They had started doing this in Cambridge, and on one occasion when trying to get a cardboard camel through the very small 'needle's eye' of a gate in the wall of Jerusalem (also cardboard, but quite extensive), the son of a very distinguished professor called out, 'Cut its hump off!' By this method, many families learned about the Christian faith and came to join St Cuthbert's. Children found themselves nurtured by Christian parents as well as welcomed into a Christian church. A London vicar, hearing of St Cuthbert's Family Service, suggested to his curate that they might adopt this system and was rewarded by the comment, 'Yes, but they have Watson to do the teaching.'

One member who joined St Cuthbert's as a result of a Family Service was Peter Hodgson, who came with his eight-year-old son. Peter had been a Reader in York, but his licence lapsed when he moved away in 1959. Now back in the area, he and his family soon became regular worshippers at St Cuthbert's, and later he became the full-time lay pastor and played an important role in the subsequent growth and development of the church.

Another area of church life which began to change perceptively was finance. When David came to St Cuthbert's, the weekly collections totalled about £2 and other costs had been covered by jumble sales, whist drives and the usual money raising events. Consequently, they had never had any money for strategic advance. When David wanted to issue a parish newsletter and other information, he had to buy an old duplicator out of his own pocket. By August 1965 the collections reached £8 a week, and by November this had doubled. A new central heating system was installed in memory of the old rector.

When a gift day was proposed, it was expected that David would sit at the gate of the church, as his predecessor had done, inviting contributions from the passing public. This he refused to do, causing quite a row in the PCC. He insisted that he would sit in the vestry, inviting people to come in and make a gift and to pray with him. This shifted the giving from outsiders to members, to God's people, who would give because they wished to build the kingdom. Instead of the paltry sum of £13, which was the highest ever raised at the gate, the members were astonished to find they had given £81. In succeeding years the totals at the annual Gift Day grew dramatically: £214, £300, £411, £925, £1,037, £2,115, £3,701,

£4,154, £5,109, and so on. All these were specifically for missionary support, not for the work in York. Of course, they reflect the growth in the congregation as well as in generosity, but the weekly giving was going up rapidly as well.

From the beginning, David emphasised the link between giving and prayer, and that giving in response to the love of God is part of the gospel. Having received salvation as a free gift, the Christian gives everything he is and has back to God in thanksgiving. Thus Christian giving is simply an act of worship in response to God's love. It follows that to David it was not only inappropriate to go to unbelievers to ask for money but positively dangerous lest they suppose that they are earning something by their giving. On the other hand he loved to teach his believing members to give, for every act of loving response to God's love brought blessing in its train. He believed it as important to teach Christians to give as to teach them to pray. The application of this principle left room for much flexibility, but the principle was clear enough.

It was a matter of some surprise to him that when the Church of England 'discovered' the biblical principle known as 'stewardship', it was the Board of Finance who recommended it as a system for raising money and galvanising parishes into action. It was not the bishops who promoted it because they saw it as a spiritual principle within the message of the gospel. Stewardship campaigns were rather better than what had gone before, but how much better still to make the gospel in the parishes so well understood that the Holy Spirit could bring the great joy of giving to every member of the church. At St Cuthbert's, the principle of giving to a loving God was not only well taught, it paid every bill and sent very large sums to missions and charities.

Meanwhile, back at the rectory, the home was gradually becoming more complete. They bought three night storage heaters, one for the sitting-room, one for the study and one for the hall. At least they hoped not to be frozen out in their first winter. David also wanted to get three students from the university to lodge in their top bedrooms. Anne was not keen because she would have to give them part board, but she had to agree they needed the money. So they scraped together the necessary furniture, and for a year and a term they had three Christian girls lodging with them. But before the end of that time they gained another and much more welcome member of the household, for Fiona was born in August 1966. David was almost as thrilled as Anne but he was no good with babies and hardly paused in his endeavours to contribute much to her happiness. From time to time his asthma would return, sometimes very seriously, and his depressions continued intermittently.

By now Anne was beginning to develop an unusually acute prophetic ministry, and her remarkable insights would soon be balancing David's precise and prayerful studies of the Scriptures. They were learning to use their complementary gifts for the edification of the whole church. Once when Anne, having had a disturbed night feeding Fiona, was hard at work washing the nappies in the kitchen sink, she recalled the promise that the Holy Spirit would bring all things to a believer's remembrance (John 14:26). 'Go on, Holy Spirit,' she prayed, with arms deep in the suds, 'bring something back to my memory.' Almost immediately a particular passage from one of the Gospels came to mind. As she thought about it, she found herself understanding why it had happened and receiving several insights into the story. Rather excited, she hurried into David's study to tell him. He was sitting behind his desk, surrounded by large, open commentaries. He listened patiently but was obviously not enthusiastic.

At lunchtime she apologised for interrupting him and asked why he had not been pleased with her revelations. A slow smile came over his face. 'I get up early to start on my sermons. I work very hard in my preparation and study all the best commentaries, but I was still struggling with it when you came in. You don't get up for a quiet time, don't do any serious Bible study, and yet the Holy Spirit reveals to you in a moment all the things which were puzzling me in the very same passage.' It proved to be quite a happy lunch.

These, then, were the foundations upon which St Cuthbert's was being built. Some people from other churches started coming when they heard about David's preaching, or when the Family Service started. Some transferred their membership with the blessing of their own vicars, to encourage and support David. In addition, while most of the growth was through transfer, the Family Service, as it developed, also brought in some non-churchgoing families. David and Anne's early months in York may have seemed to them like a struggle against unkindly odds but, through their struggle, the Lord God was building a great future. By Easter 1966 there was a reasonably well-attended Family Service every Sunday morning and the evening congregation was growing too. The *Yorkshire Evening Press* quoted a report from the Archbishop of York's Commission on Redundant Churches, stating that there was a reasonable chance that St Cuthbert's would continue. This prompted David to write in the Parish Newsletter: 'We praise God that if the Redundancy Commission came to our church on some Sunday nights, they would be hard pressed to find a seat. As long as Christ is preached and worshipped in the power of the Spirit, St Cuthbert's will never become redundant.'

12

Growth at St Cuthbert's

NO CONSIDERATION OF DAVID AND ANNE'S LIFE in York would be accurate which did not give proper place to the great scourge of his asthma. Writing in *You Are My God* of his temporary healing after Edgar Trout's ministry to him in Gillingham, David says, 'Thus healed, I was able to enter into all the strenuous work at York without the affliction of asthma.'[1] It sums up his attitude to life. Work came first because that was his calling, and because he loved it, and because he was good at it. Nothing else was quite in the same league. If he was healed, to him it was obviously for the work which he was to do. It did not seem to occur to him that he was ill because he overdid the work and that if only he could live under less pressure his asthma might well abate.

After Fiona was born in August 1966 Anne had to endure many broken nights as every, or nearly every, mother does in the natural process of feeding and nursing her new baby. But by this time David's asthma was beginning to break into his sleep patterns again and Anne became involved in caring for his coughing as well as feeding Fiona. She was soon showing signs of exhaustion once more, and this placed both of them under further stress, which exacerbated his asthma. The situation was aggravated by the continual flow of visitors to the rectory, which was the parish headquarters and office as well as the only space available for all the activities often undertaken in a church hall. There was therefore no time or opportunity for Anne to rest. Fiona was often woken by the comings and goings, and David worked on without respite. Years later he could look back on it with rather more realism:

'First things first' had always been my unspoken motto; and for me, at that time and for many years to come, the work of the church came unquestionably before my responsibility to my family . . . I understood little about fatherhood, and I fear I have frequently been a poor husband and a worse father . . . I had much to learn about God's priorities in life. The apostle Paul wrote that the quality of a man's relationship at home is a major factor in his qualification for Christian ministry.[2]

The American evangelist, Billy Graham, conducted another London Crusade at Earl's Court in 1966, and there were land-line relays to many centres around the country. David threw himself into the planning and organisation of relays to York. It was the first real contact the clergy in York and their congregations had with this dynamic young evangelical and they became aware that David Watson, though technically still a curate, was a man of considerable ability. He undertook the training of the counsellors, and many evangelical Christians from other churches were left wondering whether this gifted teacher might not be a man to follow. The drift of members from other churches to St Cuthbert's accelerated.

During the previous few years, David had been invited to help in a number of evangelical missions organised by Christian Unions at universities in different parts of the country. In January 1966, he was asked for the first time to be the main speaker at a mission. It was the first mission that the Christian Union at Reading University had ever held and it had been arranged at rather short notice and with some trepidation. The mission was planned to last for a week, with David speaking each evening. It was a remarkable occasion. The Christian Union numbered only fifty members, but they had optimistically put out 120 chairs and ordered 150 cups of coffee for the first meeting. Gavin Reid, one of the assistant missioners who was later to be Secretary for Evangelism of the Church Pastoral Aid Society and Director of Mission England, wrote, 'fortunately, the caterers let them down, sparing them the embarrassment of having to make 150 cups spread over twice that number of people. In a university renowned at that time for its apathy we never had less than 200 students attending each night, and sometimes twice that number.' Twelve people gave their lives to Christ that first evening and during the week at least sixty students found a real faith for the first time.

It was the first of many university missions David led. They were to play a big part in his life during the next few years. The PCC agreed to release him for fourteen weeks each year so that his undoubted gifts as an evangelist could be fully used. In all he led over eighty missions during the next eighteen years.

The cost to his own health and to Anne's happiness can only be estimated. After Christmas 1966 David went to Switzerland to give a series of addresses and Bible readings during a two-week winter sports houseparty organised by the Officers' Christian Union (for commissioned officers in all the armed services). David looked forward to it tremendously, although Anne and Fiona were not to accompany him. For them it was to be yet another painful separation. It was a splendid evangelistic opportunity and began very well, but by the end of the first week he had to stop skiing when his asthma attacked him once again. As it got progressively worse he had to stay in bed and conduct what ministry he could from his bedroom. Eventually he had to be sent home one or two days before the end of the houseparty, and when Anne met him at York station he was so ill that she had to push him up the platform on a luggage trolley.

'Like a madman', as he later wrote, he was off again a month later to Trinity College, Dublin, to lead a mission, but again could not complete the course. He wanted to fulfil his next engagement, a mission at Durham University, but Anne and his doctor, Walter Stockdale, insisted that he withdraw from it, and reluctantly and at short notice, he did so. He was in fact very ill. The difficulty in breathing, and subsequent oxygen deficiency, would sometimes make him semi-delirious, and at about 3 a.m. one night he was under the impression that Anne was his optician. It took two injections by his doctor to bring him some relief. Soon the doctor was back, bringing with him a consultant who wanted to take him into hospital, but agreed to leave him at home when he discovered that Anne was a nurse. However, he insisted that David needed three months' total rest, away from all the pressures in York.

David was characteristically devastated by this decision. How could he abandon his work when so much was happening? Would he ever be able to cope again? Already he had been forced to pull out of one university mission and abandon another completely. Would any university or college ever risk inviting him to lead a mission again? He felt he was a total failure, not only in his ministry but also as a husband and father, and a bad period of depression settled on him. The turning point came when he realised that he had come to love the Lord's work more than the Lord himself. He came slowly back into the experience of renewal, confessing his pride and 'nestling' into the Lord's arms.

That's what renewal had always meant to him, a deep and loving trust in God, intimate and personal. It inspired him to believe again in the Jesus who said, 'Abide in me, and I in you.'[3] St Paul had to learn the same lesson. Possessing the same sort of restless, obsessional temperament, he describes how God had said to him, 'I am with you; that is all you need. My power shows up best in weak people.' Paul was able to affirm, 'Now I am glad to boast about how weak I am; I am glad to be a living demonstration of Christ's power, instead of showing off my own power and abilities.'[4] For David this was a hard lesson to learn, and it was one he tended to forget when he was fit. He never learned it fully. Perhaps no one ever does.

The enforced holiday gave David plenty of time with Anne and Fiona and he began to enjoy having a little daughter. He found he no longer saw her just as an additional burden in an already overfull life, or as a threat to his liberty to fulfil his calling. He was able to appreciate her antics as she started to crawl and he entered fully into the fun of seeing her develop a personality of her own. This was a God-given therapy which helped him relax, and the absence of stress brought a welcome relief from asthma. Both David and Anne did some much-needed catching up on sleep. Physical recovery which David experienced at this time was assisted and accompanied by renewal of his spiritual life. His thoughts thus turned to the need for revival in the churches, and he announced in the May 1967 Newsletter that he planned to preach a series of sermons entitled 'Ruin or Revival – Which?'

The following month he wrote about the importance of prayer if the church was to be prepared for revival. He urged more people to come to the Thursday evening Parish Fellowship:

It should be a true 'family affair' – a fellowship for all ages where we can learn more of God's plan for our lives and where we can share together our personal needs and problems. God intends that every Christian should belong to a living, caring fellowship like this, where we don't have to pretend we're all super-saints. Far from it, we are ordinary folk with ordinary needs that ought to be shared. And if we don't share them with other Christians, we shall no doubt have to put up with far heavier burdens than the Lord ever meant us to bear.

He was contrasting the normal way that men and women conduct their lives in Western society – largely in isolation from each other and bearing their own burdens as best they can – with the freedom which is available to believers within the fellowship of the Church. 'Bear one another's burdens,' said St Paul.[5] It became an essential plank of David's platform that Christians belong to one another and have a mutual responsibility. More and more he asked his people to show their love in practical terms, to value others as much as themselves, and to look at every decision in the light of the personal interests of other people. 'It is essential that the members of a church develop a strong love for each other ... True Christian love begins with commitment and issues in practical service.'[6]

St Cuthbert's was to become a 'relationships church'. He was not saying this was unique for a church, or even new, but he had come increasingly to believe that this basic Christian attitude had become blurred by the use of the word 'fellowship' to describe membership of a warm friendly community, which was satisfied to be no more than that. The New Testament use of the word 'love', in whatever form, includes that element of commitment distinctive to Christianity, and 'fellowship' should not be devalued to something less. He determined to lay emphasis upon this doctrine of Christian love and unity.

He saw the Church in terms of what God had intended to achieve both by creation and redemption. The Garden of Eden, in which God used to walk 'in the cool of the day' looking for fellowship with Adam and Eve, presents a picture of peace, order and beauty where love operated unspoiled, and where God's purposes were fulfilled. If they were frustrated by the Fall of Man in flagrant disobedience, 'God was pleased to have all his fullness dwell in him [Christ] and through him to reconcile to himself all things ... by making peace through his blood, shed on the cross.'[7] God so loved us all that we ought, by the command of our Lord, to love one another even as he has loved us. 'All men will know that you are my disciples, if you love one another.'[8] David realised that those who believe themselves to be reconciled to God by the blood of Christ should practise and enjoy reconciliation with each other at all costs:

As the body of Christ, the church should be a powerful testimony of the reality of the risen Christ today. And that will be true only when individual Christians, or groups of Christians, lose their independence and learn again what it means to belong to one another and to share together their common life in Christ as members of his own body.[9]

He determined to build St Cuthbert's upon this principle. Everything was done to build relationships between people. He saw the teaching and preaching in this light. The people were not only to believe truth, as though the more true the teaching, the better the Christians they would become: they were to learn so to relate to one another that they could actually become God's family in practice. A family does not simply accept each of its members, but is responsible for their health and happiness, making sacrifices for each other and delighting in each other, whatever the cost. The family of God is also the Body of Christ, made up of many limbs and organs, each interdependent and mutually responsible. This David began to teach firmly and continually. He showed it was the whole purpose of the gospel to reconcile us to God and to one another; 'the Father's good pleasure' for us to be so reconciled to him that we love him and our neighbour. But for this to be real it must be given a structure.

Thursday evening Parish Fellowships in the rectory were hopelessly overcrowded. Not only was the church growing as the Family Service drew in more people and they responded to the gospel, but the quality of teaching at the Bible studies was attracting members from other churches who didn't worship at St Cuthbert's. In April 1970, the opportunity arose to rent a building belonging to the University of York which was adjacent to the church and which would be ideal both for overflow services on Sundays and for the Thursday evening meetings. Although David was a little reluctant to leave the informality and family atmosphere of the rectory, Anne was quite adamant that she could not bear the noise and disturbance of Thursday evenings a day longer than she had to. The meeting moved into 'the Annexe' and made this the centre for the social life and the prayer life of the church. Suddenly, they seemed to have come of age. The relationships between members began to mature into real Christian love. David encouraged church members to see their houses as places where Christians could gather to study the Bible together informally, to listen to talks on tapes, or just discuss Christian living. He wanted Christian homes to become 'household churches' within the fellowship of St Cuthbert's.

The steady increase in numbers made David feel the need for a full-time colleague in the parish. He was himself still, technically, only a curate, under the vicar of Holy Trinity, Heworth, and so there was no possibility of him having another curate under him. So in 1967 he invited Ross Patterson, a graduate in Law and Theology from Cambridge, to consider the possibility of coming to work at St Cuthbert's as a layman. Although Ross had undergone a full theological training at Ridley Hall, and was qualified for ordination, the Archbishop of York was unable to ordain him because there was no post for a curate. Ross, who believed that God was calling him to work in China, was looking for a suitable sphere of experience to equip him for his life's work. Knowing the renewing work of the Holy Spirit in his life, Ross wanted to work in a church where he would learn to minister in the power of the Spirit. St Cuthbert's was only able to supply a modest living allowance and the diocese could not contribute anything, so David and Anne housed him in the rectory. He did a few hours' teaching every week to earn a little money but relied on prayer and faith to meet the rest of his needs.

David tended to lead by example and rather expected those on his staff to get on with their work without being told what to do or how to do it. He was still far too busy with his own work to be able to spend the sort of time on others that John Collins had spent on him. Ross was therefore not given any clear schedule of tasks to be done. There was, however, a sentence in the Parish Newsletter to remind people that 'Ross Patterson has now arrived. Make use of him!' He shared in the preaching and teaching ministry and was aware of the great responsibility of doing this with David, whom he describes as a 'gifted and anointed man'. But David's anointing kept him in his own study, praying by himself and preparing both his sermons and his many evangelistic talks. It was some months before he found time to pray with Ross about what he was doing in the parish.

Ross knew that many lives were being changed through David's prayers and ministry, and that the City of York had in some way been prepared for David's work by the Holy Spirit, and he accepted his role gratefully, accompanying David on some of his evangelistic missions and becoming a significant part of the scene at St Cuthbert's. At the end of 1968, the Lord reminded him that he should not be putting down roots in York as his work was to be among the Chinese people. In 1969, when he left for Taiwan, his support both then and subsequently came almost entirely through the harvest weekend Gift Day offerings at St Cuthbert's, which that year amounted to £925 (more than double the 1968 total). It topped the £1,000 mark in 1970, and reached over £3,000 by 1975.

In April of 1969 Anne was expecting her second child. Having worked out that it should be born on about 8 April, David had willingly agreed to preach in London on 15, 22 and 29 April. The invitation had come from the Rev. Dick Lucas, Vicar of St Helen's, Bishopsgate, whose Tuesday lunch-hour services were attracting large numbers of city businessmen. April 15 and 22 came and went, and still no sign of the baby's arrival. Then, early on the morning of the 29th, Anne went into labour. David hastily summoned the midwife before rushing off to catch his train to London.

As soon as he arrived at St Helen's Church he rang to find out the news. The nurse who answered told him to ring off as the birth was imminent, and so David waited nervously until just before the service was due to start before ringing again. This time he heard the good news that he had a son, and that all was well. The subject of David's address at St Helen's had been advertised in advance as 'The New Birth'. He started: 'Ten minutes ago my son was born in York.' He then spoke of the fact that Anne was, according to their calculations, three weeks overdue, adding, 'had it gone on much longer, it would have been dangerous for her. Some of you, spiritually speaking, are not just three weeks overdue. You are thirty to forty years overdue. If you go on much longer, it may be dangerous for you.' It was an effective illustration, ably used by a skilful evangelist; but the question of whether he should have been with Anne in York rather than preaching in Bishopsgate did not enter his mind until much later on.

David and Anne were thrilled to have a son, Guy, as well as Fiona, who was just over two and a half years old. However, his arrival meant a return to disturbed nights, with more frequent asthma attacks and all the strain and tension that these caused.

Meanwhile, growth in the church was coming on apace. When in October 1969 they decided to hold two identical Sunday morning services at 10 a.m. and 11 a.m., the *Yorkshire Evening Press* took note. Their reporter, John Blunt, wrote:

Four years ago St Cuthbert's, Peasholme Green, York's smallest surviving church, was a potential candidate for redundancy. It was given a year of grace to prove itself; a year of reprieve won by the then new minister, the Rev. David Watson, a 36-year-old curate belonging to Heworth Church. Today St Cuthbert's is trying to fathom how to cope with 'full house' notices. Already they have two identical Sunday morning services, and evening services are relayed fifty yards up the road.

David Watson has worked a minor miracle in a city church which was fast losing its roots as areas of old terrace houses in Layerthorpe came down. He has done it at a time when congregations in many churches worship in handfuls. St Cuthbert's is packing them in. People arrive three-quarters of an hour before a service to make sure of a seat. Everything is alive and vibrant.

I sat among 150 worshippers at one of the relayed services – the church itself was full. The physical link may have been a slender thread of wire, but the spiritual link was real and compelling. People sang as if they meant it. They said their prayers knowing and believing in what they said. Church to them has long since ceased to be a Sunday chore.

David's ministry to a wider public was also on the increase, aided not a little by a number of BBC Radio broadcasts which were made of St Cuthbert's services. As the pressures on David grew he decided to appoint six pastoral elders to share some of the burdens of leadership, and to oversee the life of the church. At that time this was a very unusual concept within the Church of England, where the tasks given to lay people were more generally concerned with financial and material, rather than spiritual matters.

The eldership did not in any way replace or supersede the officially elected PCC, but inevitably there was overlap between the two bodies. David believed that this overlap was important in order to reduce the possibility of tension between the two groups. By its constitution, the PCC dealt with financial and administrative matters, whereas the eldership was entrusted with responsibility for the pastoral side of the work, and it seemed right that not all of the elders need also be members of the PCC. In time, one of the elders, Peter Hodgson, was appointed as a full-time lay pastor. A lay reader for twenty years and a worshipper at St Cuthbert's since 1965, Peter felt called to full-time Christian ministry, but lacked the academic qualifications required to train for ordination. He was to play an important part, along with others (including Harvey Dean and Walter Stockdale), in holding together and coordinating the work at St Cuthbert's and subsequently at St Michael-le-Belfrey, during David's ever-increasing commitments outside the parish.

Perhaps partly because of David's frequent absences, executive responsibility gradually settled more and more upon the elders. They were spiritually competent to lead and became a warm and supportive forum for David to share his thoughts as the task he was undertaking became ever greater. Authority to lead moved imperceptibly from David, the anointed leader, to the group over which he presided and whom he had appointed initially only for pastoral oversight.

At this stage there was no question in David's mind, nor in the minds of most members of the church, that there could or should be women elders. That question did not arise for several more years. In fact, at the time, St Cuthbert's was a very male-dominated church, the only 'spiritual' role exercised by women being that of prophecy. One result of the appointment of pastoral elders was that Anne, who had worked very closely with David in the early days and who had a genuinely deep spiritual insight, was now further removed from the spiritual leadership of St Cuthbert's. Previously she had been able to discuss with David her vision for the future and leave him to consider it in the light of biblical principles. Now she had to channel her thoughts to the eldership through David, but he was often away on missions elsewhere, and she was increasingly tied to the house with two young children. He did, however, respect her undoubted gift of prophecy and authorise her to speak out in church from time to time as the Spirit gave her a word. This became a greatly valued experience for the church and a ministry she found increasingly satisfying.

As 1972 drew to a close, two exciting possibilities had presented themselves. David had become concerned about the evangelistic Guest Services, which were attracting ever larger numbers, with the result that once the church, annexe, and overflow hall were all filled, people were having to be turned away. David discussed the problem with Canon David Galliford, the Treasurer of York Minster, whose daughter was a member of St Cuthbert's, and enquired about the possibility of borrowing the Minster after normal services were over. Canon David discussed the matter with the Dean and Chapter, and it was agreed that the Minster could be used for a Guest Service on the evening of Sunday 3 December 1972. In addition to the normal publicity arranged by St Cuthbert's, the media considered it newsworthy that a curate should have to borrow York Minster to accommodate his congregation. About 2,600 people turned up for that first Minster service, and subsequently the Dean and Chapter invited David to use the Minster for all his planned Guest Services in 1973. David Galliford recalls:

It was a wonderful sight to see the nave of that huge church packed with people. They had come from far and wide by train, by coaches, and by private car and it was a thrilling occasion to have these great services which ran through 1972, 1973 and 1974. By this time David had set up a team of counsellors and advisers and after the service there was always a great deal of coming and going at the east end of the Minster where his counsellors and advisers had their positions. I believe a great number of people sought help and found it in this way. The whole thing was very exciting for those of us on the staff of the Minster. It was lovely to see the Minster used in this way as the vehicle of evangelism and outreach.

Five Guest Services were held in the Minster during 1973, attracting an average congregation of around 2,000, and these continued until 1977. They were appreciated by many, especially by some of the smaller churches outside York who closed their own evening service and brought a coachload to the Minster instead. Some of the services were also broadcast in York by the Hospital Broadcasting Service. But over the years David wondered whether they were really serving their purpose as an evangelistic opportunity to which his members could bring their friends. He decided to use the Minster only for occasional special Festivals of Praise, and for his annual Carol Service, but to hold evangelistic Guest Services at St Michael-le-Belfrey, of which David became Vicar in 1973 (see Chapter 14).

The former Dean of York (the Very Rev. Ronald Jasper) recalls that the only occasion that they had to say 'no' to David was in connection with a carol service, which David wanted to make 'Carols by Candlelight', with thousands of candles all over the Minster. The fire risk made the Minster authorities adamant that this was not possible.

The typical form of a Minster Guest Service was that, following an introductory song, David would welcome the congregation, explain the theme of the service, and give out any notices (including some 'domestic' notices for regular members of his congregation). There would then be a hymn, followed by prayers and a Scripture reading, sometimes in dramatic form. Another well-known hymn followed, during which an offering would be taken up on behalf of Tear Fund or some similar mission or relief agency. There would then usually be a dramatic sketch closely related to the theme of David's sermon. He would preach for about forty minutes and his sermon would, as always, be solidly based on Scripture, liberally illustrated with relevant stories, full of appropriate quotations from newspapers and from well-known writers, and spiced with humour. But it would demand a definite response from his hearers and at the end, after a song, he would speak again for five minutes or so, making very clear the steps by which anyone could come to know Christ personally, usually by four simple, easy to remember steps, for example, Turn, Trust, Take, Thank. He would then lead a prayer which anyone could make their own if they wanted to take these steps. After a closing hymn and blessing, there would be an opportunity for anyone to receive personal counselling from himself, or one of the elders. The whole service would normally last about ninety minutes.

The other exciting prospect at the end of 1972 was the suggestion that the entire congregation of St Cuthbert's might permanently 'take over' a much larger church across the road from the Minster, which was itself threatened with being declared redundant. It was called St Michael-le-Belfrey.

13

University Missions

DAVID WATSON WAS BECOMING VERY WELL KNOWN. Obviously in St Cuthbert's, but also in York as a whole, he was something of a figure, perhaps more than he realised. But in addition, his reputation as an evangelist and leader within the wider Church was spreading rapidly. At first it was limited to two areas in particular: the charismatic movement, both in the traditional churches and among the emerging house churches; and the world of students in the increasing universities and colleges.

After the 1966 mission in Reading University, David became one of the recognised missioners sought by the Evangelical Christian Unions in the universities. The Christian students who had imbibed not only the New Testament doctrines of salvation by grace through faith, but also the zeal to proclaim these, generally sponsored a mission to their contemporaries every three years. In this way, they aimed to span the length of the degree course and to provide an opportunity for each undergraduate to hear the gospel message clearly proclaimed during his or her time at university.

These missions involved considerable effort and not a little sacrifice on the part of the sponsoring members. They provided most of the workforce and also met much of the expense. Since the same students were also sponsoring the usual weekly programme of evangelism and Bible instruction, and since they usually received no help, material or spiritual, from the universities themselves, the degree of commitment involved was very great. It followed that they were extremely anxious to recruit a missioner whom they could trust, and who was manifestly effective as an evangelist.

The field was not wide. A good local minister is not necessarily also gifted as an evangelist, particularly among students. Some of the older men such as John Stott, who had proved most effective in the Fifties and early Sixties, were beginning to move out of the student age range and into wider and heavier responsibilities. The evangelical strand within the churches was then very small, and in fact is still a minority in spite of growing influence and authority. Only from among the Evangelicals could the students expect to find an evangelist with the necessary cutting edge to satisfy their need in a mission. Furthermore, they needed someone with both the intellectual and spiritual qualifications, as well as the calling and experience for evangelism. During his time at the Round, David had clearly demonstrated his gifts as an evangelist in a university setting and as he matured he realised this potential more and more.

Having himself come to faith in Christ as a student at Cambridge, David knew that the three years or so at college presented a unique opportunity for reaching men and women at a particularly formative period of their lives. In some universities the Christian Union was one of the larger student organisations, perhaps numbering nearly 10 per cent of the student body. In others it was very small, and the task of arranging a large mission seemed a daunting one. David felt that it was very important for him to meet the whole Christian Union, or as many members as possible, for a long weekend conference before term started, to prepare the Christian students for the mission. He wanted to awaken in them a sense of urgency and expectancy. It was essential for them to recognise that no amount of human effort and organisation could achieve anything worthwhile for God. They had to turn to God in earnest prayer and ask for the power of the Holy Spirit.

At Cambridge, Dr Donald Barnhouse from the USA had led the missions in 1946 and 1949, followed by the Rev. John Stott in 1952, and then Dr Billy Graham in 1955, when David was a student. David had worked as an assistant missioner in his old college, St John's, during the 1965 mission led by the Rev. Dick Lucas, but he felt it a great privilege to be invited by the CICCU to lead the university mission in February 1968. Although no two missions are ever quite the same, it is worth looking at this particular one in some detail to see what it involved for David.

In February 1967, twelve months before the mission was due to take place, the CICCU Executive Committee, who had by then decided on the date of the mission and invited David to lead it, set up a Mission Committee which had the responsibility for making all the detailed arrangements. The Chairman of the Mission Committee was Stephen Travis (now Director of Studies at St John's College, Nottingham). His committee included six other people, all graduates, who had some previous experience of a mission when undergraduates at either Cambridge or Oxford. The President of the CICCU also served on the Mission Committee, which held nineteen two-hour meetings during the next twelve months. A new President and Executive Committee were elected after the initial decisions had been taken. The newly elected President was Stephen Bowen, now Vicar of Felbridge.

After the initial invitation to lead the mission, all the correspondence with David Watson was undertaken by Stephen Travis. Twenty-six assistant missioners were required, one for each college, plus one for sportsmen and one for overseas students. More than half of these were ordained clergymen, but among the laity were women assistant missioners for the women's colleges. The first invitations to serve as assistant missioners were sent out more than a year before the start of the mission and it was several months before the list was completed. The role of the assistant missioners was vitally important for the success of the mission. David also saw it as valuable training in evangelism for anyone going into full-time Christian ministry, and he would suggest names of people whom he considered suitable. On this occasion he suggested Ross Patterson, who was then on the staff of St Cuthbert's, and he was accepted and allocated to Trinity Hall.

David knew that it was important for him to be in touch with all that was going on in the university, so that he could include topical allusions in his addresses. To help him in this, Stephen Travis would send him a copy of the university newspaper *Varsity* each week from the beginning of the Michaelmas Term.

For many years it had been customary to hold the main mission meetings in a church (usually Great St Mary's, the university church), but more recently it had been felt that a secular building was preferable. The Mission Committee decided on the Guildhall, which was 'central, acoustically adequate, large, reasonably well-lit and comfortable', with some provision for smaller after-meetings or for counselling when necessary. It was booked twelve months ahead for the eight-day mission, starting and ending on a Sunday (4–11 February 1968). David Watson was also invited to give the Saturday evening CICCU Bible Reading on the day before the start of the mission. This was a final preparation for the CICCU members, on whom lay the main responsibility for inviting their friends to attend the mission meetings, to complement the pre-mission conference held at Herne Bay in January 1968.

The agreed overall title for the mission was 'My God is Real', and David was asked to give eight main mission addresses in the Guildhall, starting at 8.30 each evening. In addition to these main meetings, David agreed to speak at a breakfast meeting in his old college, St John's, and also at a special meeting for theological students and ordinands, for which he chose the title 'Preaching and the Holy Spirit'. It was decided that

David should live in Darwin College during the mission, and be available there for private interviews each afternoon from 2 p.m. to 6 p.m.

Considerable thought was given to the publicity. Five hundred posters were printed, 13,500 cards giving details of all the main addresses were distributed, personally wherever possible, to every member of the university. In addition, there was another card for each undergraduate with information about the assistant missioner in his college, and special invitations to meetings for special interest groups. Advertisements and announcements were also placed in *Varsity*. In addition, table slips were placed on college dining room tables with brief details of the meeting that day. It was hoped that these would give Christian Union members a talking point and an opportunity to invite people. With all this publicity no one in the university should be unaware that there was a special mission taking place. Much, however, depended on individual Christians praying, and some 8,000 prayer cards were sent out, as well as three prayer letters to between 1,500 and 2,000 supporters.

Immediately after meeting CICCU members at their pre-mission conference, David wrote a letter to all the assistant missioners:

During the pre-mission conference at Herne Bay (a good time with over 150 present and a clear sense of unity and purpose) I felt that a number in the CU needed considerable encouragement: a little frightened by the size of the task, somewhat nervous of visiting fellow students, and rather conscious of the 'foolishness' of the Gospel. All this is understandable, but I would suggest that our immediate task on arrival may be to encourage the college groups.

Recently I have been made more aware than ever of the spiritual battle which rages in the heavenlies. In a delightful university setting it is easy to pay lip service to this truth. But clearly we are contending against 'all the various powers of evil that hold sway in the darkness around us' (as one translation puts it). May I urge you to press this point with your college group, to claim the authority of the name of Jesus, and to demonstrate the power of prayer.

He then alluded to an evening during a recent mission where God had manifested his presence in an unmistakable way. He quoted Arthur Pont, one of the assistant missioners, who had written later: 'I had a truly exceptional time of prayer all the time you were speaking, on my own in Committee Room No. 1 . . . I mention this, because I would like to suggest that in other missions, you should invite one of the other missioners to be similarly "at war with the enemy" while you are speaking.' David continued:

I have quoted this as I believe that here is where our confidence must be. If you feel God prompting you during the week to share in the battle in this particular way, I am convinced that we shall see the control of Satan broken in many lives.

'This kind cannot be driven out by anything but prayer' said Christ to the disciples, shamefaced with their impotence.

The format of the main mission meetings in the Guildhall was very simple. The President of the CICCU, Stephen Bowen, chaired the meeting and gave a welcome to those who had come. After brief announcements there was a Scripture reading, followed immediately by David's address. There were no hymns, no songs, no drama; in stark contrast, of course, to David's later missions. On two evenings David incorporated brief testimonies from undergraduates into his address to press home the practical relevance of his message. One of these testimonies was given by Priscilla Chadwick (the daughter of Professor Henry Chadwick) who, as the Rag Queen that year, was well-known in the university. David's addresses were always quiet, straightforward expositions of the gospel, full of relevant quotations, illustrations and humour.

There were between 650 and 700 people in the Guildhall on the first Sunday evening, so the hall, which could seat 720 (with room for another 100 on the stage behind the speaker) was well filled. The attendance dropped to 600 on the Monday evening, but otherwise remained fairly constant, rising to 720 on the Friday and filling every available seat on the final Sunday. At the close of each address, David invited people to stay on for a short after-meeting, and a high proportion of the audience did so. At the close of the after-meeting he asked anyone who had made any sort of commitment to come forward so that, with their agreement, their names could be passed on to their college CICCU representative and to the assistant missioner in the college. Some 150 people professed faith in Christ during those eight days, and CICCU members were still in contact with the great majority of these several weeks later, though inevitably a few had lapsed.

Don Humphries (now Vicar of Holy Trinity, Cambridge), who had first stayed with David and Anne on a parish placement as a student at theological college in 1967, worked with David as an assistant missioner on many missions between 1967 and 1974. He recalls that the missions at places like Oxford and Cambridge were always well attended because so many zealous Christian Union members came along to the meetings, which were always held in a respectable, neutral venue. On the other hand, the mission at places like Keele University, where David knew it was likely to be hard going, seemed to be more effective in reaching a high proportion of non-Christians. The mission meetings there took place in the main Union building, where undergraduates normally gathered to socialise and drink. Each day there would be special prayer that God would be glorified in a place where his name was, at other times, only used as a swear-word.

One thoughtful touch by the Cambridge Mission Committee was to send Anne a box of chocolates during the week, to show that she had not been forgotten and to thank her for letting David come to Cambridge.

David's talks at Cambridge were subsequently edited and published in 1970 by Kingsway with the same title, *My God is Real*.[1] It has proved a valuable evangelistic tool, and was supplemented later by *In Search of God*,[2] based on David's addresses to the Oxford University Mission in 1973, and by *Is Anyone There?*[3]

Nine days' non-stop ministry, during which David gave thirteen talks and addresses and spent many hours in personal conversation, in prayer, and in detailed preparation of his talks, was a heavy workload. But the next few days back in York did not allow much time for rest and relaxation. David was due to give Bible studies on evangelism at the Thursday Fellowship on 15 and 22 February, to preach at the Guest Service on Sunday 18 February, and then he was off to Sussex University for another mission on 26 February.

The pattern was repeated in the autumn. In September David took a team from St Cuthbert's, most of whom were students, on a nine-day parish mission at a church in St Helen's, Merseyside, where the vicar was a former curate of Heworth. Apart from the main mission meetings there were also house-meetings, meetings for teenagers, children's meetings, Guest Services on the Sundays, and widespread visiting in the parish. Then, in November, there were two more university missions, at Manchester (nine days), and a shorter 'mini-mission' (three days) at Leeds.

David knew that God had called him and equipped him to be an evangelist, but he never found it an easy task. 'Even after a simple evangelistic service, the effort of preaching Christ and seeking to convince men about Christ has frequently left me drained and exhausted. I can think of few activities that are more demanding.'[4] He also knew that Satan would attack him in various ways whenever he was engaged in evangelism. Sometimes the attack would be on Anne and the children at home, but very often it would take the form of a severe bout of depression: 'I am never more vulnerable to attacks of depression than when just after preaching or speaking to those who desperately need Christ but who remain totally unconcerned.'[5]

David was also, of course, still prone to attacks of crippling asthma, and he dreaded the possibility of one of these attacks during an important mission away from home. He had a special fear of damp beds, and whenever he went away from home on a mission he used to take with him his 'survival kit for damp beds'. One essential item was a small mirror, which

David would put between the sheets to test the bed for dampness whenever he was put into a spare room which might not have been used for some time. If the mirror misted up he knew the bed was damp, and the rest of the survival kit came into action. Over his pyjamas he would put on a black nylon mackintosh, and he wore thick woollen socks on his feet. Once, when he was staying in a vicarage, the vicar brought him up an early morning cup of tea, and was surprised to see David sitting up in bed in this rather unusual attire!

Each of David's missions brings back special memories to different people, but there are many now serving God in the ordained ministry who can look back with gratitude to God for speaking to them in their college years through David Watson. Chris Edmonson, the Bishop's Officer for Evangelism in the Diocese of Carlisle, was a student at Durham University when David led the mission there in February 1970. Although he had been brought up in a loving Christian home, he knew that there was something missing in his experience of God. Somewhat reluctantly he went along to hear David, expecting it to be a rather extreme, emotional type of meeting. He was surprised to hear a very unemotional presentation of the gospel by a compelling speaker who made you want to listen. When David affirmed (quoting the Pentecostal leader, David du Plessis) that 'God has no grandchildren – he only has children', Chris realised that his own faith was derived from his parents and that it had to become first-hand. He knew then that God was calling him to the ministry and he was ordained in 1973.

At Sussex University in 1971 open opposition to the gospel had been expected, but nearly 200 people turned up on the opening night of the mission for an evening led by the actor Nigel Goodwin. There were between 70 and 150 people present to hear each of David's four evening addresses, and among the people who committed their lives to Christ was Simon Holloway, Captain of Tennis at the University, now a vicar in Sparkbrook, Birmingham. Simon had been interested in Christianity for some time, and had even purchased and read a copy of Michael Green's book *Runaway World*[6] at a Christian Union Book Week. He had several friends who were members of the forty-strong Christian Union, including one or two in the tennis team. He was aware too that his much respected maths lecturer, Dr John Weir, was a committed Christian, and he wanted to find out more about the Christian faith which clearly meant so much to his friends. As he went to the mission meetings each evening, he soon realised that he had never before heard the gospel so clearly and simply explained. Shortly after the Wednesday evening meeting he was challenged by a personal question put to him by one of the assistant missioners,

Phil Vogel, and committed his life to Christ. About fifteen months later, through reading David Watson's book *God's Freedom Fighters* (later reprinted as *Hidden Warfare*)[7] he heard God's call to the ordained ministry.

A young man who came to faith in Christ during the mission at Birmingham University was Frank Hung, now a vicar in New Cross. Frank, who had already obtained a first-class degree and was working for a PhD, considered himself an atheist. Nevertheless he came along to the mission meetings, and Don Humphries recalls that he was always arguing or asking difficult questions of David or one of the assistant missioners. But during that week Frank, much to their surprise and joy, committed his life to Christ. Frank himself describes what happened:

I must admit that up to the time of my conversion, I hadn't found him [David Watson], *humanly* speaking, particularly impressive as a speaker. I had been a nominal 'Christian' in my youth, and it seemed to me at first that I hadn't heard anything from David which I hadn't already heard before, although he struck me as being, unlike some clergymen that I had heard, someone who honestly and passionately believed in the divinity of Christ, the resurrection etc. But it was very much a surprise to me that after one of his meetings, at which he invited the listeners to pray that God would come into their lives as a real living presence (or words to that effect), that this was what actually happened to me!

It has always seemed to me since that David Watson was so clearly a man who, though he perhaps had little personal 'charisma' (secular use of the term), had tremendous spiritual charisma because, far more than the great majority even of committed Christians, he was a man who was truly 'filled with the Spirit', and whose life and ministry was so open to the power and leading of the Holy Spirit, that God could accomplish great miracles through him and his ministry. He was truly a man of and for God who, because of his quiet and undemonstrative nature, probably managed to reach a great many people such as myself who would have been put off by a more flamboyant style of evangelist.

Thus, released by his PCC, David gave priority between 1966 and 1975 to university missions. He was usually away from York for several weeks in February and March and again in October and November each year. Moreover, university missions were not the only evangelistic engagements that David undertook during this period. There was, for example, a visit to army units in Germany in November 1969, a parish mission back to St Mark's, Gillingham in April 1970 (to which he took a team of eight people from St Cuthbert's), and a United Church Mission in Belfast in September 1970.

The support and patience of the parish back in York, left as they were without their leader for much of the time, cannot be underestimated.

David was fortunate to have several Readers at his disposal who took over many of his duties, including the preaching, when he was away and the Heworth clergy also lent their support. Moreover, David knew that whatever difficulties he was facing in the mission field, he could always rely on the congregation of St Cuthbert's to pray. Whenever he was away, he could be sure that the Thursday evening Parish Fellowship would be praying especially for him, and claiming the victory of God over the opposition of Satan. Their contribution should be recognised when one considers the hundreds of men and women whose faith in Christ began as a student during a mission led by David Watson.

14

St Michael-le-Belfrey

OVERCROWDING IN ST CUTHBERT'S had been a problem for several years. There was no further room for expansion and it was not even certain that the Annexe next door would be available much longer for use as an overflow. David and the elders of St Cuthbert's had been praying that God would show them what to do. Moreover, the diocese was disappointingly slow to address the problem and to take proper responsibility for the future of this expanding Anglican congregation. Ironically, of course, the growth of St Cuthbert's had taken place at a time when the large number of ancient churches in the centre of York were suffering a severe dearth of membership, as described in Chapter 11. A scheme was being considered by the Pastoral Committee for the reorganisation of all the parishes in York city into one pastoral entity with a small team of clergy deployed strategically among them. Many churches expected to be declared redundant and closed.

One of the churches with no obvious future before it, no vicar to lead it and not enough people to sustain its life and maintain its fabric, stood immediately beside the great Minster. St Michael-le-Belfrey was a medieval building capable of seating about 800, and one of the largest of the city centre churches. Standing across a narrow street and only a few yards from the south side of the Minster, it was completely dwarfed by it, not only in size but also in spiritual value, for it had tried to offer services which were in a style not very different from those of the cathedral. It had a small and elderly congregation with an average attendance of about seven for the Sunday morning service.

The Rev. Henry Lambert-Smith, already in his seventies, had been appointed Priest-in-Charge in a part-time capacity in order to keep the church open until the diocese could arrange for its redundancy and closure. Although he also helped in the parish of Clifton where the Rev. Robin Fletcher, a contemporary of David Watson at Ridley Hall, was Vicar, Henry had been blessed by David's ministry a few years previously at a clergy conference and he often used to attend the Thursday evening meetings at St Cuthbert's. Another member of St Michael's, Muriel Price, was also such a visitor and these two prayed for St Michael's to grow and become more effective as a church, just as St Cuthbert's had become.

Talking one day with Canon David Galliford, whose support had allowed the Minster Guest Services to take place, David looked across to St Michael-le-Belfrey and said, 'I wish we could use this building here.' David Galliford explained that the PCC of St Michael's had recently asked the diocese to declare the church redundant as they could no longer be responsible for its upkeep. The Dean and Chapter of the Minster were now officially the Lay Rectors responsible for St Michael-le-Belfrey. David Watson asked Canon Galliford if he could suggest to the Dean and Chapter that, instead of declaring the church redundant, the congregation of St Cuthbert's be allowed to use the larger building. The Pastoral Committee was reluctant to unscramble their plans at such a late stage, and there was some fear that other surrounding parishes, which had already lost some of their members to St Cuthbert's, might object if David Watson took over St Michael-le-Belfrey. But the new Archdeacon of York, the Ven. Leslie Stanbridge, supported by the Bishop of Selby, the Rt Rev. Morris Maddocks, and the Archbishop of York, the Most Rev. Donald Coggan, persuaded them to halt the Redundancy Scheme and let St Cuthbert's move in.

Before this could happen, the PCC of St Michael-le-Belfrey had to give their consent. Peter Gibson, a churchwarden of St Michael's, remembers being invited to a meeting at Bishopsthorpe where the Archbishop asked him what would be the reaction of the tiny residual congregation if another, unnamed clergyman came to St Michael-le-Belfrey, complete with his own congregation, which had outgrown their own church building. He replied that he was sure that they would all agree that any alternative was preferable to the complete closure of St Michael's. Peter Gibson did not actually meet David Watson until he and his fellow-warden were invited by the Archdeacon to discuss the proposal with David and the church-wardens from St Cuthbert's. Peter recalls that it was a very amicable meeting at which David was extremely sensitive to the feelings of the St Michael's representatives. It was agreed that almost two years' work on the St Michael's Redundancy Scheme should be suspended, and in record time for the Church of England (under two months) a new provisional scheme was approved whereby the entire congregation of St Cuthbert's would move to St Michael-le-Belfrey. The Anglican leadership could certainly move when it wanted to.

David Watson was licensed as Priest-in-Charge at a special evening service conducted by the Bishop of Selby on Thursday 4 January 1973. Ten days later the church was packed for David's first Sunday evening service in St Michael's. The original members of the congregation were amazed as more and more people of all ages flocked in. They had been expecting about 200, which was all that St Cuthbert's could hold, but had forgotten that St Cuthbert's also had another 200 in its overflow congregation. The person who was reading the lesson was so over-awed by the sea of faces in front of him that he lost his place in the Bible. The members of St Michael's, used to a quiet Prayer Book Evensong, not unnaturally found it rather traumatic to have their church taken over and filled by a strange congregation, a strange clergyman, and what seemed a strange form of service with unfamiliar hymns and songs.

Peter Gibson was somewhat apprehensive about the future, though he very much wanted to be part of any new life for St Michael's, which had been his parish church all his life. He was reassured that, throughout the negotiations, David frequently consulted him to get the feelings of the St Michael's members. It was agreed that there should be an initial experimental period of one year to see how it would work out, but in fact the changeover went extremely smoothly and the scheme was made permanent in less than nine months.

Most of the St Cuthbert's members were of course delighted to be together under one roof. It was also a relief to be sure of getting a seat for the evening service without having to get there an hour early. Nevertheless the contrast in size between St Michael's and the Minster disguised an equally sharp contrast between it and St Cuthbert's, and not all of the people from St Cuthbert's were completely happy with the move. Their old church was a small, cosy and well ordered building with a simple beauty and was very attractive to some who had been worshipping in it for years – even before David's arrival.

St Michael's, on the other hand, was further away, was in the city where parking would be a problem, was in a general state of dilapidation through years of neglect, and was not a particularly attractive building. Moreover, it lacked some important facilities. The heating system did not work (it was mid-winter at the time) and the wiring was condemned. There were piles of rubbish in the gallery and plenty of clearing up was needed everywhere. Considerable amounts of money and a lot of hard work were called for. It was decided that the morning Family Service would continue to be held at St Cuthbert's for a few more months as the smaller church provided a more intimate and friendly atmosphere. This meant, of course, that they would have to go on running two identical morning services, one after the other, as St Cuthbert's could not accommodate the numbers wishing to attend. It was not until 8 July 1973 that the Family Service was transferred to St Michael's.

ITV televised the Family Service on 22 July, which was a great success although one of David's visual aids did not go quite as planned. He was illustrating the story of the Rich Fool[1] using balloons, one of which he burst to prove his point. Unfortunately the gas cylinder which he was using to inflate the balloons failed to work, and he had to blow them up himself in front of the TV cameras. For an asthmatic, it was quite a feat.

Some of the original congregation of St Michael's found the changes more than they could manage. Although at first they tried to be faithful, they found that the Minster services were more to their taste, and gradually transferred their allegiance across the street. Peter Gibson also found it difficult at first, but David asked him to stay on as churchwarden and he agreed to do so. He has continued to serve St Michael-le-Belfrey in that capacity ever since. As Superintendent of Glaziers at the Minster (and a leading authority on stained glass), Peter knew all the Minster clergy and was a great help to David in cementing the links between St Michael-le-Belfrey and the Minster. Only one other couple remain of the original St Michael's congregation, Donald and Muriel Price, who subsequently managed the Church Bookstall. The Rev. Henry Lambert-Smith agreed to stay on as an honorary curate, and fitted in remarkably well in a mainly pastoral role. He was much loved, but sadly he was killed in a road accident in 1982 while travelling to visit his daughter in Leeds.

The move to St Michael-le-Belfrey heralded a new phase of growth in the size of the congregation. Numbers had remained fairly static for the past three years at St Cuthbert's, having reached the limit imposed by the size of the building. Also, as St Michael's was a city centre church, its services attracted a good number of tourists and visitors to York, something which had seldom happened at St Cuthbert's, situated as it was much further from the city centre. David quickly realised the evangelistic opportunities provided by St Michael's strategic position, and in the summer evenings there would be singing and dancing, or dramatic sketches, on the forecourt outside the church.

The number of Easter communicants, which had remained at around 175 from 1969 to 1972, rose to over 250 in 1973, 400 in 1975, and over 800 in 1976. Electoral roll figures show a less dramatic increase: 234 at St Cuthbert's (plus 35 at St Michael's) prior to the move in 1972, to 297 in 1974 and 367 in 1976. This is, perhaps, some indication of the larger proportion of visitors attending services at St Michael's. David once estimated that tourists and visitors accounted for as many as 80 per cent of the evening congregation on one Sunday in August when many church members were away on holiday.

In order to make St Michael-le-Belfrey more suitable for worship, allowing flexibility for a music group and choir and for dance and drama when appropriate, David asked for certain structural changes. The nineteenth century choir stalls and the large, cumbersome minister's stall were removed to provide more space in the chancel area and later the rather forbidding pulpit was replaced. All these changes required time, as it is always necessary to obtain legal permission (a 'faculty') to make alterations inside an Anglican church building.

David's attitude towards his own role began to change also. As an apparently perpetual curate in a nearly redundant little church, he had struggled against heavy odds to fulfil his ministry. Because he was away so much on his missions, and worked so hard when he was at home, he had become rather isolated from other clergy in York and tended to feel himself suffering from a lack of care by those responsible for him. This in turn bred a spirit of independence, and even rebellion, in his heart. He sat rather lightly to his loyalty to the Church of England, which had been characteristic of the ministry at Gillingham and at Cambridge. In spite of all his labours, why had he been left a curate for fourteen years? Why, with all those people in St Cuthbert's and his services to the Church in missions elsewhere, was he without the help of a curate of his own? When he looked around him at other clergy, at the work they did and the success they achieved, was he actually so much less significant than they? His own boss, the Vicar of Heworth, was younger than he was and had been ordained later. It is not surprising that David had to hold his frustrations in check.

Of course, the real Church of Christ is not just the Church of England but includes the great company of believers from every denomination. No denomination is perfect, and no expression of the Church at any level will escape without blemish and weakness. Yet the Church of England has remained an historic fellowship of believers down through the centuries. It is the 'one holy, catholic and apostolic Church', reformed and for ever reforming. David belonged to it because he had begun in it, believed in it, and had learned to love it. Others might leave it to find freedom from its disciplines, but David rejoiced in its biblical formularies and flexible structures. Yet at St Cuthbert's his loyalty had wavered because of his loneliness. The warmth of fellowship he enjoyed in the charismatic movement, which embraced every type and tradition of Christian, was in sharp contrast to the enfeebled churches in York. And the diocese seemed to ignore him.

Suddenly everything changed. On 19 September 1973, after serving for fourteen years as an assistant curate, David became for the first time the Vicar of a parish. The Archbishop of York, Donald Coggan, preached the sermon, and the Institution was conducted by the Archdeacon of York, Leslie Stanbridge. In the twinkling of an eye, it seemed, the great machinery of diocesan decision-making, under its Archbishop, had made him a vicar, given him a large and roomy church right in the centre of things, and was counting him worthy of its trust and care. The pendulum swung back and he was once again an enthusiastic Anglican. He was as warmly embraced by the charismatic fellowship as ever, and as firmly rooted in the evangelical gospel, but at St Michael's he adhered more closely and more gladly to the new *Series 3* forms of service which had recently been approved by the General Synod. He found these services provided him with a considerable degree of liturgical freedom, but the Anglican discipline and structure for worship were there. Even his Family Service was based on this, and upon the 1980 *Alternative Service Book* which replaced *Series 3*.

As soon as David knew that he was to be appointed Vicar of St Michael's, he realised that there was at last the possibility that he would be allowed to have a curate working under him. David's request received a favourable response from the Archbishop, and arrangements were put in train for Andrew Cornes to start working at St Michael-le-Belfrey immediately after his ordination in York Minster on 22 September 1973.

Andrew had come to faith in Christ during a three day 'mini-mission' which David Watson had conducted at Oxford University in 1967. After three years at Oxford, reading modern languages, Andrew went to theological college (Wycliffe Hall, Oxford and then Cranmer Hall, Durham). His final student placement, at Easter 1973, had been with David Watson. On the last night of his stay in the rectory there had been guarded talk, on both sides, about the possibility of working together sometime. The next day, on the way to the station, Andrew asked David if he had been serious and told him he was still looking for a place for his curacy. David said that he would be delighted to have Andrew as his curate if the Archbishop agreed, and soon sent a definite invitation for him to come.

Something which Andrew was a little concerned about was the fact that he was not charismatic, and he wrote to David setting out various areas on which they might not agree. After discussing Andrew's letter with the elders, David wrote to confirm the invitation, saying that they had taken note of everything that Andrew had said, but that it was still the unanimous wish of the elders that he should come as a curate. Although David himself was fully committed to the charismatic movement, he never suggested that a person who did not emphasise the supernatural gifts was a 'second class' Christian or minister. David's understanding of 'being filled with the Spirit' was wider and more generous than that of many charismatics at that time. He recognised the Spirit-given gifts of preaching and teaching as perhaps even more important than speaking with tongues or prophecy.

Andrew lived in the rectory with David and Anne for the first few months, which gave him a valuable opportunity to get to know David as a friend, and not just as his boss. They were able to spend time together in prayer and fellowship, and they both enjoyed this greatly. David did not try to introduce Andrew to every aspect of the work of a minister, but gave him a fairly free hand to develop his work in the way that seemed best. Andrew had, in fact, been in York for over six months before he was asked to visit someone in the hospital, and he then had to admit to David that he didn't even know where the hospital was.

Andrew had a first-class mind and brought a very valuable gift of teaching to St Michael's. He complemented David's gift and during his time the team at St Michael's was at its strongest, presenting a balanced gospel. If David's emphasis was upon evangelism and upon seeking a response to Christ in the heart and will, Andrew's was upon building a measure of understanding about the cross, the resurrection and the person of Christ. Where David found his message in the Gospels and the Acts, Andrew dwelt upon St Paul's expositions of Christian doctrine. He was suspicious about the charismatic movement, particularly where it related to young people. He feared that they might be carried away emotionally and lack a firm doctrinal base. He believed that any church experiencing renewal had a vital need for a strong teaching ministry, without which there is no backbone, and the Church risks an unhealthy over-emphasis on the exercising of the gifts of the Spirit. These are, of course, perfectly valid fears which David recognised as such.

Andrew's three years at St Michael's were as revolutionary as David's, in a way. He began a youth group from nothing and when he left it had a membership of over 100, of whom 80 used to meet weekly for Bible study and prayer. He ran a week-long evangelistic outreach for them every year, and four houseparties a year. The group became known as Eureka and its success was due to Andrew's ability to train leaders and weld them into an effective and committed team. Eureka met after the evening service and finished around 10 p.m. Many of the members owe a thorough grounding in the Christian faith to his single-minded approach from the very beginning of his curacy.

He shared in David's general preaching and teaching ministry and David showed complete trust in him and would often seek his help with matters about which he was not sure himself. Many fruitful discussions took place between them. There were occasions when their opinions differed; for instance, when Andrew's interpretation of the word 'elders' in 1 Timothy did not fit with what David had been teaching and the Thursday Fellowship were confused by this. David merely asked him to point out that other interpretations were possible. So marked was the value of Andrew's teaching gift, especially during David's many absences, that it is perhaps no coincidence that some of the difficulties experienced later owed something to the lack of his able mind after he had moved on. David had always stressed the importance of sound teaching and the early days were proof of this, but latterly his commitments elsewhere prevented him from covering as much ground as he would have liked with his own congregation.

Relationships between St Michael's and the Minster were generally very good. There were even occasions when the Minster wanted to borrow St Michael's. When, in 1980, the Diocese of York arranged a major celebration for the launching of the *Alternative Service Book* (with which the Dean, Ronald Jasper, had been very closely involved), St Michael-le-Belfrey took a very active part in it. The only occasion when there seemed to be a lack of cooperation was when the Minster arranged a special series of evening services in August with VIP preachers. With the Archbishop's blessing, all the churches in York were asked to close down their evening services and join together in the Minster. David Watson and the elders of St Michael-le-Belfrey decided that they could not shut down their evening service, which normally attracted some 800 people from far and wide, and so two services were held simultaneously on either side of the street.

Despite this, relationships between the Minster and St Michael's remained, according to Ronald Jasper:

... most harmonious. We catered for different kinds of congregations, and since we never had services on Sunday evenings there was no rivalry. We were packed out on a Sunday morning and they were packed out on a Sunday evening. I think it is true to say that the sight of the Minster and St Michael's side by side and doing such different things was a remarkable demonstration of Anglican comprehensiveness. The Minster, of course, had no parish of its own – we were all St Michael's parishioners and for legal purposes we had to be regarded as such; but it never created problems.

David Galliford said:

I met people who came enormous distances to York on a Sunday who would come to choral services in the Minster, to which they were attracted because of the music, the ritual, the sense of the numinous or whatever, and who would finish their day in York by going to the service in 'the Belfrey' for some good strong Christian teaching. It seems to me that David's ministry in the centre of York was something that matched the other side of Anglicanism represented by the Minster. There we had all the beauty and solemnity of worship very well done, but in which the congregation had to take their part silently; whilst across the road in 'the Belfrey', we had the kind of worship in which everybody took their full part vocally and at the same time benefited from the great input of teaching ministry. From time to time this was combined, so for example in Lent 1972 and 1973 we had a series of lunchtime services in the Minster when the preaching was organised and sometimes done by David himself and the music and so on was run by the Minster. These services attracted a very considerable number of people from the city, and at the same time brought in many visitors who come to York from all over the world around the year.

If relationships with the Minster were good, relationships with other churches in and around York were not always so. Although St Michael's had a parish of its own, it was not looked on as a normal parish church. In fact, only eight members of the church lived within the parish area, which had a population of about 600. Thus, St Michael's penetration of its parish was far less than that of a typical English middle-class suburban church, and was much more akin to that of a large urban working-class church. So, if the people making up the congregation at St Michael-le-Belfrey did not come from within St Michael's parish they must have lived in the parishes of other churches, and some clergy (not only Anglicans) were not too happy about it. It was said that the biggest congregation of Methodists in York was to be found at St Michael's.

Parish boundaries exist to ensure that every family in England is in the 'cure' or care of some church and its clergyman, who is licensed by the bishop to discharge this responsibility. However, some clergy seem to believe that their licence gives them the right almost to possess their parishioners, whereas the rights of the parishioners include those of attending whichever church they wish. The system needs revision to prevent the enterprise of another clergyman being excluded from a parish which, for one reason or another, is unable to cater for the needs of its people.

The creation, in October 1973, of St Michael-le-Belfrey Area Groups all over York, meeting in almost every parish except St Michael's own, was another area of tension. Initially there were eighteen groups, but in 1977 this increased to twenty as a result of six new groups and four closures or amalgamations. In some ways, they were a natural development from the Thursday evening Bible studies, though there was obviously a difference between being taught in a large group by David and gathering together in groups which averaged nineteen initially and later rose to twenty-five or so. They were organised on the basis of geographical locations so that whoever lived in a certain street or district attended the local group and became entirely the pastoral responsibility of that group. The care for the needs of each became the practical and necessary task of that local group.

When the Rev. Robin Fletcher (now Rural Dean of York) was appointed as Vicar of Clifton in York in 1971, he discovered that quite a number of Clifton parishioners had joined St Cuthbert's during the last few years; some had even been advised to go there by a Clifton curate. There was always a tendency amongst Christians in York to pay occasional visits to St Cuthbert's/St Michael's to see what was going on, particularly when they heard of new developments, in order to taste 'the charismatic flavour of the month'. There were thus some unhappy feelings within the Deanery, mainly in the clergy Chapter, which were not helped by David's rather infrequent attendance at Deanery meetings. It is a pattern repeated in many other towns and cities where a big, flourishing, eclectic church draws its congregation from a wide area, and then naturally feels a responsibility for its members, even if they live outside the parish.

The parish of Heworth, of which St Cuthbert's was originally a part, had probably been affected more than any other parish in York, and St Michael's had more Area Groups meeting in Heworth parish than in any other. The Rev. Dick Rayner, who was Vicar of Heworth from 1972 to 1981, and so had David as one of his four curates for a short part of that time, says that the relationship between them could have been difficult because:

I was the incumbent and yet naturally all attention was being focused on David's remarkable and growing ministry. That the relationship did not prove difficult was due to David's sensitivity and true humility. When various legal or pastoral problems arose, he would phone and ask for advice even though I sometimes guessed he knew the answer as well as I did – but he wanted to involve me.

Dick Rayner did, however, pick up some of the feelings of other clergy: 'David's ministry in York sometimes provoked criticism from some clergy based, I fear, upon jealousy. Once or twice the telephone would ring and I knew what was coming when I heard the opening words, "That curate of yours . . ."'

15

St Michael's under
the Microscope

THE CONGREGATION AT ST MICHAEL'S doubled and redoubled. Many of the new members had come to faith through experience of the obviously genuine life which they found when they met the church at worship, at home or at work. It was compellingly attractive. Others wandered in to see what it was all about and were convinced by the proclamation of the gospel. Offered the chance to make a decision some accepted Christ then and there, while others came back again and again until the truth crystallised within them. The growth in membership increased both the numbers and the responsibilities of the elders. It also made the church a national sensation.

This reputation aroused the interest and hopes of many Christians from other churches throughout the country and elsewhere. A flood of requests came in to visit St Michael's to learn from it and hopefully to capture the secret of its success. Many of those who did, particularly clergy and ministers, wanted to stay for a week or so in order to find out all they could. Their genuine and proper desire to make progress in their own church spurred David and his people to satisfy their curiosity if it was at all possible. However, St Michael's was already a hard-working church with a full programme to fulfil and with a finite number of hours in which to do so. It was impossible to have observers constantly popping up and asking questions during a normally hectic day. If David was at home he would be glad to spend time with any of the visitors, but often he was not in York. Even when he was he couldn't reasonably spend more than a morning talking to them. Furthermore, someone had to arrange accommodation and meals and a programme of hosts to enlighten each visitor on each subject. It soon became completely unworkable.

It was actually a visitor who suggested a practical solution to the problem. In January 1976, during a long weekend visit by three carloads of clergy and laity from Wales, Canon Saunders Davies, Canon Missioner in Bangor Diocese, suggested to David that St Michael-le-Belfrey find some way of making its experience of spiritual renewal available to other churches by a deliberate and systematic means. Shortly after this, a member of the dance group produced the idea of holding a special week once or twice a year when all the visitors came together and St Michael's geared itself to meet their needs. Accommodation could be arranged in the houses of church members so that visitors would share fully in the life of the fellowship and see for themselves its strengths and weaknesses. At the same time, a properly planned programme of lectures and seminars on all aspects of the church could be provided for them during the daytime. David discussed it with the elders and their decision to proceed was later confirmed by a prophecy that God would use St Michael's as a resource for the encouragement and renewal of other churches. Douglas Greenfield, an elder who became invaluable to David in managing his various missions in Britain and overseas, agreed to organise these weeks, which were called Renewal Weeks. The first was held in April 1977.

It was decided not to accept more than four people from any one church, with priority given to clergy and their wives, church workers and group leaders. In spite of these limitations, 150 visitors attended the first week, which is an indication of the number of churches eager to learn from St Michael's. The costs were kept very low. Since accommodation was provided in private homes, it was possible to charge only £17 a head for a full week, including all meals. There was a wide range of seminars available, including:

Ministry – leadership, elders, development of gifts and ministries within the body, lay training and discipleship, counselling, healing, house groups and community living.
Evangelism – Guest Services, Family Services, house meetings, personal work, follow-up, communication skills, open-air work and spiritual warfare.
Music – music in worship, the function of music in the body, practical and spiritual issues, corporate music-making and sharing.
Dance – biblical basis, the value of dance in worship and evangelism, the formation of a dance group, interpretive movement and dance.
Drama – use of drama in worship and evangelism, in church and on the streets and elsewhere, an aid to teaching and preaching, use of the Bible, starting a group and developing techniques.
Youth Work – in schools, clubs and church, evangelism and fellowship, integration with congregation, discipling, training of leaders.
Children's Work – serving the church, teaching, inculcating right relationships, use of dance, drama and banners.
Creative Arts – teaching aids, banners, flower arranging, etc.

Nearly all the workshops and seminars were led by the people from St Michael's who were most closely involved with that particular department.

The most notable exception was the workshop on healing which was led for several years by the Bishop of Selby, Morris Maddocks, whose ministry, friendship and encouragement were greatly appreciated by David and Anne and by many others at St Michael's. He left York in 1983 to become the Advisor for the ministry of health and healing to the Archbishops of Canterbury and York. The fact that St Michael's provided no leader for the healing seminars from within its own ranks is indicative of the undeveloped use of the supernatural gifts there in those days.

Christians came from all over Britain and from many other countries to attend the twelve Renewal Weeks held from 1977 to 1982. Altogether, 1,500 or so came from many different countries and fellowships and from many backgrounds and traditions. The then Archbishop of York, Stuart Blanch, has commented that the Renewal Weeks 'generated considerable ecumenical support, and contributed in no small measure to ecumenism in the diocese as a whole. For example, it startled the Roman Catholic hierarchy to hear of priests from Malta and Italy attending the residential conferences organised for them in York.'

Among those who attended one of the early weeks was the Rev. Brian Mayne, then Rector of Belvoir in the Diocese of Down and Dromore, Northern Ireland. He describes the week:

A choice of two seminars was open to each member of the course (each seminar consisting of more than one session). The majority of visitors opted for seminars on Ministry and Evangelism and were given plenty to think about as the full-time leaders described the way in which the idea of shared leadership within the Body of Christ had been applied. Many participants found the week a time of personal spiritual renewal, without which no renewal can be expected in any local church. Even those in whose minds questions were raised, and perhaps not resolved, appreciated the warmth of the love and acceptance they received.

The value of a course like this lies chiefly in the encouragement and stimulus it gives. People coming from local situations, which seem fairly hopeless, can return home and weigh the biblical principles to see how they can be applied in their own churches. If God can do in such unpromising soil what he has manifestly done in 'redundant' churches in York, he can do new things in any place if his people open up to him and in the power of the Holy Spirit respond where they can.

An important part of the Renewal Weeks was the degree of openness in the relationships in the church. No attempt was made to hide any mistakes which had been made or the weaknesses that caused them. This willingness to give expression to the whole truth about the church was a powerful factor in all the teaching given. Some of those who came undoubtedly entered into a new and deeper experience of the Holy Spirit and sometimes through this the life of their church was transformed. Nearly all found something of value to take back with them. Several churches in different parts of the country have subsequently followed the example of St Michael's and started to offer similar courses, which is a testimony to the value of what was pioneered in York.

An example of the effect of the Renewal Weeks can be seen in the emergence of renewal in the churches in Wales. It was said that in Wales, 'Persons were more distinguished if they had the letters B.Y. (Been to York) after their names than if they had B.A.' Frivolous as this comment was, there is some substance in it. Renewal became a subject for discussion on committees and at conferences throughout Wales and every diocese of the Church of Wales now has its own renewal group. Days of renewal have been held in various places regularly, notably in Brecon Cathedral, and a quarterly newsletter keeps people in touch with each other.

Canon Saunders Davies has written:

David Watson gave a great deal of personal encouragement to the steady growth of spiritual renewal in Wales. He paid several visits to North and South Wales. After one night's celebration at St Mary's Church, Swansea, David was invited to spend a whole week in the city. After prayer and consultation he agreed, and 8th–15th September, 1979 was one of the most memorable events in the life of the churches in Swansea in the second half of this century.

David's humility and warmth of personality attracted Welsh people, but the effectiveness of his communication lay in his personal conviction and sincerity of faith in God, alive and active within his own experience. That living experience rang true and still resounds in the hearts of many Christians in Wales who thank God for the new vision of what the Body of Christ can be in the power of the Holy Spirit.

In the midst of his full and over-busy life, David managed to write five more books during the years at St Michael's. He would write late at night or early in the morning, only occasionally being able to set aside a complete day or two for writing. Much of it was done whilst continuing his normal routine, in his own words, 'Half a day here; then two or three weeks later, half a day there.' Once, when Peter Hodgson, the lay pastor, asked David why he worked at such a pressure and how he managed to get so many different things done, he had replied that he did not expect to live a long life. He tried, therefore, to squeeze as much as possible into his allotted span, believing there were so many urgent things needing to be done for the kingdom of God. It is not possible to know whether this was some form of premonition or whether it was an attempt to justify the inexcusable pace at which he chose to live. Only a man with great self-discipline could work under such pressure, and it is more than possible that the schedule which David set himself shortened his life.

I Believe in the Church was David's second contribution to the 'I Believe' series, as he had already written *I Believe in Evangelism*. It was completed in 1978 and dedicated 'To the members of St Michael-le-Belfrey, York, whose love, support, encouragement, patience and forgiveness have made both the title and content of this book true for me.' It is by far David's longest book (368 pages) and shows evidence of his wide reading. A study guide for the book was published in 1982.[1] The book is written in three parts:

Part I, 'A Look at the Church', includes a brief survey of Church history, and a survey of Christ's plan for the Church as revealed in his great prayer in John 17.

Part II is entitled 'The Nature of the Church' and looks at it under the headings of various pictures of the Church in the New Testament – The Kingdom of God, The Church of God, The People of God, The Body of Christ, The Building of God, The Bride of Christ, The Army of God, and The Spirit in the Church.

Part III describes 'The Life of the Church' and deals with Worship, Preaching, Sacraments, Ministry and Leadership, The Mission of the Church, The Unity of the Church and The Mark of the Church.

David's thinking about the ministry of women and the place for the ordination of women developed as he was writing the book and continued to develop for another year or so afterwards. Nevertheless, the issue remained unresolved and the first women elders were not appointed until after the book had been published.

In his Editor's Preface to this book, Michael Green wrote:

This is not a major theological treatise: its author is not an academic theologian, and in any case, most theological libraries positively groan with the weight of heavy tomes on the nature of the Church. But it is that much rarer contribution to the Christian reading public: a thoughtful, intelligent and above all 'earthed' presentation of what, according to the Bible, God intends his church to be like. 'Earthed' is an inadequate word. The reader will find this book more like a bridge than an earth wire. For one end is firmly rooted in faith in the presence and vitality of God's Holy Spirit in the midst of his people, while the other end is rooted in the practical and effective expression of these principles at ground level. It is a book that could point the way to renewal for many a church that has lost confidence and even credibility.[2]

In November 1977, St Michael's received a visit from a team from the Archbishops' Council on Evangelism, or ACE, a body who among other things visited individual parishes in order to study them and then to publish a report of their findings. Strictly the name ACE referred to the quarterly bulletin which the Council published, but the Council itself was also usually referred to as ACE. It had no real official status, and received no more than a nominal grant from Church funds. The Rev. John Poulton was its Executive Officer and for some time the only full-time member of the staff, but as the value of his work was recognised so the calls upon ACE for parish consultancy, workshops, etc., led to the appointment of additional staff. At the time of the St Michael's survey, ACE was at its zenith. David wrote in his Parish Newsletter:

If you haven't come across ACE yet, you soon will! Nine of them are coming to St Michael's during the period Nov 17–23 to do a detailed study of what is actually going on in this church. In some respects, I'm very nervous of the thought of it. It is rather like asking Rentokil to have a thorough look at your house. In fact, when Rentokil *did* come to the house in which I live, they found my study was just full of dry rot – an illustration with a possible spiritual truth too near for comfort. Seriously, I am quite certain that the whole approach of ACE will be totally positive. Not that they will hide any dry rot or paper over the cracks; but they are trying to see the lessons that we feel God is teaching us, in order to share with the wider church. I am sure we shall learn a lot ourselves; but if we can be of any encouragement to others, praise God for that.

Five years had elapsed and many developments had taken place since an earlier ACE Parish Study on St Cuthbert's, and David now felt it right to invite them to make an in-depth study of all aspects of the life and ministry of St Michael's and to submit a report to the elders. There was now so much media attention and publicity focused on David Watson and the rejuvenation of St Michael-le-Belfrey and St Cuthbert's that help was needed to ensure that what they were doing was soundly structured and capable of bearing the scrutiny to which it was being subjected. The original idea of the ACE Parish Study on St Cuthbert's had come from within ACE itself and was one in a series of studies which they carried out, but this time the initiative came from David with the backing of the elders. What was requested was a fuller and much deeper report. The Newsletter continued:

Much has happened since 1972. In fact, many of the most significant developments have come since then: area groups, mission teams, renewal weeks, households, creative arts, the Mustard Seed [see chapter 16],[3] greatly increased full-time workers and so on. Hence the need for a fuller and much deeper study – which we pray will be invaluable for us all. Fortunately, I know most of those who are coming, and I am sure you will love them in the Lord, make them feel quickly at home, and co-operate in every way possible. It is one small way in which we can serve not only them, but also the wider church.

The team, which was led by the Rev. John Poulton, certainly received every possible help and cooperation from David and Anne and from the elders, who provided hospitality, and from many members of the congregation. The visit even attracted the attention of the *Yorkshire Evening Press*, which reported:

A nine-strong team from the Archbishops' Council on Evangelism will attempt to establish what lessons can be learned from St Michael's unorthodox forms of worship and its other methods of Christian outreach. They will be interviewing members of the congregation and the clergy of other York churches. The team will look into every aspect of the church and its effect on the community, including statistics, finance and work with children and youth.

It became clear to John Poulton at an early stage in the study of St Michael's that both the church and David himself were suffering from David's steadily increasing commitments away from York. Although David had a curate, Patrick Whitworth, another very able and delightful man who had followed Andrew Cornes in the role, as well as an experienced lay pastor in Peter Hodgson, and a team of pastoral elders, there were always a number of important matters which required the attention of the vicar.

The normal method of operation for a Church of England parish was for everything to pass through the hands of the vicar. Even if he delegated much of his responsibility and activity, there remained a sense of neglect if the leader was himself preoccupied with extraneous affairs. No doubt much of the reason for this rested with the clergyman's own desire to keep control of his church, sometimes because he was soon threatened by lay ambition if he didn't. The Church of England gives its vicars a freehold right to their office so that they might minister 'without fear or favour', and this was and is a great strength. If, however, a vicar is unable to exercise his ministry to the full, either because he has an inadequate understanding of it or because he chooses, as in this case, to be ever more committed beyond his parish boundaries, the church finds itself lacking in proper leadership.

John Poulton, after discussion with the rest of the team, suggested to David that the most sensible thing to do was for him to become Rector of the church and to appoint another clergyman as Vicar, with responsibility for the day-to-day running of the parish. This pattern of working had been pioneered at All Souls, Langham Place, when John Stott, needing to expand his worldwide teaching ministry, had become Rector and, with the Bishop's approval, had appointed Michael Baughen to be Vicar. On that occasion, a firm understanding had been reached that, at a suitable moment, John Stott would resign and Michael Baughen would succeed him. The idea of doing this at St Michael's immediately appealed to David.

He and Anne felt that the obvious man to become Vicar was already in the congregation. The Rev. Graham Cray had been living in York for some time as the Northern Co-ordinator of the Youth Department of the Church Pastoral Aid Society and for the past two years had worshipped at St Michael's whenever his duties permitted. He had recently been appointed an elder. While he had had no previous experience as a vicar of a parish, he was already well known, and he would have the confidence of the other elders. David immediately discussed the possibility with Graham and then with the Archbishop of York.

The Archbishop at the time, Dr Stuart Blanch, was full of admiration for David's wider ministry and wanted to do all he could to facilitate it. He has since commented:

His ministry in and from York was a phenomenon – and was accepted as such by the diocesan authorities who recognised the value of his ministry at home and abroad and were ready to make special provisions to enable him to sustain it. That does not always happen. It was a work of the Spirit – unplanned, unexpected and unprecedented.

Certainly the Archbishop and the diocesan authorities worked fast on this occasion and gave official approval within a month. With the agreement of the elders and the PCC, Graham Cray was appointed Vicar and started his work in that capacity in July 1978. To him David delegated full responsibility for the leadership of St Michael's and all the details of its life, subject only to David's overall authority. Since he had already delegated so much of his leadership to the elders and had clearly imprinted upon them and the church his vision and methods, what Graham in fact inherited was no easy task. The very size of the fellowship and the intensity of the aims which it pursued made for considerable diversity of understanding within the body. Graham could not assume that the love with which David was supported would automatically be extended to him, but bravely he accepted the commission and won the respect of the leaders and members. He also was required to attempt to re-establish the relationships between St Michael's and the other churches, Anglican and otherwise, within York. His success in this over the next few years was shown by his election in 1985 by his fellow-clergy to the General Synod of the Church of England, coming top of the poll.

The ACE team produced a full report, of which a lengthy summary was published in their quarterly bulletin. John Poulton had asked each member to investigate a particular aspect of St Michael's and received also from one of them, the Rev. David Wasdell, Director of the Urban Church Project, a much wider and more detailed document which overlapped those of the other members. Wasdell was a sociologist with an able, prob-ing mind and had been asked to examine the statistics of the parish at every level, but had gone much further than this. When John Poulton had been able to collate the work of his team into one report, of which he called the summary 'It's Far From Being a Myth' (Appendix 1), he discussed this first with David Watson and the elders at a residential weekend.

Although the report affirmed and commended much of what was being done at St Michael's, it also asked a number of searching questions and exposed some areas of weakness. The main points of positive approval referred to the place of prayer in the church, the power of 'living worship', and the way in which music, drama and dance were integrated with the sermons into a full-orbed proclamation of Christ. Some might think this to be rather thin praise for a church whose overwhelming success was so widely known that it had prompted the survey in the first place. It also identified areas of weakness: the lack of involvement of church members in secular organisations; the failure of the church to attract or hold working-class people; the level of financial giving, which was seen to be going down when corrected for inflation. Of course, these are old chest-nuts within the English Church, representing the greatest difficulties fac-ing any church at a local level.

However, more specific problems were identified in two particular areas. The first was the Area Groups, which were seen as being too big to be effective and not always well led. The second was the whole question of shared leadership, which denied any leadership role to women. All in all, many of the elders remember that weekend as a traumatic and threatening time, and David himself suffered an attack of asthma.

David believed strongly in the principle of shared leadership, and the appointment of pastoral elders in 1970 has already been described. John Poulton has made two important comments about this:

Firstly, what was happening was not so much 'shared leadership' as 'group leader-ship' in the sense that the members of the congregation did not themselves 'share' in decision-making. This was the business of the elders group.

Secondly, David's own position is not what is implied in the phrase 'primus inter pares'. Although in a superficial way his role might have looked like that of one elder among others, he had the sole right of appointing and dismissing them, however much he might consult along the way. He was thus verbally committed, by his understanding of the pastoral epistles in particular, to a systemic or shared leadership, while events (and perhaps his own personality as well) moved in an opposite direction. I have used the word 'authority', but that word and 'power' were avoided at St Michael's, being substituted by 'serving and caring roles'. Semantics do not, however, alter facts.

I can illustrate what I mean in an apparently simple matter like the raising of agenda in elders meetings. David would come to these meetings with a list of points he had accumulated during the week. As a result, there was seldom time for others to raise their own agenda after he had finished his. This is a form of leadership which in other organisations is used in directive patterns rather than in enabling or facilitating styles of leadership. There are limits therefore to the extent to which we may really call David's style a shared pattern of leadership.

Thirdly – and this is really an Anglican footnote – once the eldership system had come into operation, the PCC became much more a routine administrative group, deprived of the opportunity to comment creatively upon matters of strategy. The PCC and Standing Committee (the elected and representative organ of the local church under Synodical Government in the Church of England) took on a subsidiary role. It was probably significant that the electoral figures for the church did not seem to have been kept adequately, and very little importance was placed upon electoral roll membership. In other words, the voting rights of the laity at annual meetings were simply not significant. A parish development that seemed to be one of 'shared leadership' proved to be at the expense of member-responsibility.[4]

David Wasdell had come to the firm conclusion that David Watson's leadership style was the direct result of his childhood experiences:

The use of and response of authority are intuitively patterned on the experience of the father and mother roles in early childhood. Now it is common knowledge that David Watson's father died when David was 10, as a result of refusing a blood transfusion, a decision taken because of his own religious convictions. His teenage life therefore represented a steady process of levelling with the mother, while the image of the father was fixated in relationship to the 10 year old, possessing virtually unlimited authority, yet profoundly absent. An authority figure held in the mind and yet unchallenged. There was no experience of growing up in relationship to authority, or of the struggle that that involves, or of the mature man to man adult relationship of father and son, nor was there experience in the teens of examining the relationship between father and mother within the home. The mother's significance was reduced with David's growth, the fantasy father maintained in absent omnipotence.[5]

David Wasdell's report goes on to draw various conclusions which David Watson found insensitive and intrusive. The above paragraph, as a socio-psychological analysis of the possible effects of losing a father at the age of ten, is no doubt valid. However, it is more questionable whether it can be used as a basis for the consideration of St Michael's and its leadership structure, which owed at least as much to an attempted adherence to biblical principles as it did to David's psychology. Whatever else may be thought of it, this report, which had not actually been commissioned, was a great shock to David and contributed to his continuing but unnecessary sense of failure.

David Wasdell visited York in May 1978 to discuss this with David and Anne Watson, and to try to help David to work through it. He also shared his views with some of the elders so that they could give David and Anne all the pastoral support which they would need. There is no doubt that David felt somewhat battered, both by the ACE Report on the whole life of the church and particularly by David Wasdell's probings into his own childhood background. John Poulton has commented: 'David suffered, I know, from our turning the microscope upon him and his work. It never was an easy thing to let yourself appear in public "warts and all". It is no small tribute to the size of the man that he welcomed and encouraged the exercise.'[6]

David may well have 'encouraged the exercise' but in the event he did not actually welcome the report, and certainly not the findings about him personally. He was very deeply hurt. On the other hand, the question might be asked, what else did David expect? Was he expecting nothing but praise and affirmation? Perhaps herein lay the problem. In his News-letter, David wrote that ACE were 'trying to see the lessons that we feel God is teaching us, in order to share with the wider church'. Whereas the introduction to the report asks the questions: 'Can [St Michael's] successes teach the rest of us anything useful? Or are the more important lessons the ones that come from weakness and failure?' There is a subtle but important difference in these two aims. What David is describing is really what the Renewal Weeks were for, whereas the specialist team from ACE were not wanting to be taught lessons but to do an in-depth study so as to uncover things which perhaps St Michael's itself was not fully aware of.

The positive side of St Michael's was plain to see and was already being described and taught by David and others. ACE did not deny any of this. 'St Michael's is not a myth. It is an extraordinary example of growth in a congregation within the charismatic renewal.' In fact, the report is surpris-ingly positive for an academic sociological study which, almost by defi-nition of being analytical, will be critical. It is saying, 'Everything they say is true, but there is still room for improvement and anyone else trying this should be aware of the following pitfalls.' Furthermore, the aspect of someone else attempting to emulate St Michael's success is significant. The introduction also asks the questions: 'Is it all to do with David Wat-son's personality? What happens when he goes?'

ACE's assessment that the shared leadership was a rose by any other name, that the leadership was actually still fully dependent on the authority of David, was lent some weight as he was increasingly absent from the parish and the leadership structure fell into difficulties. Moreover, many of the problems which were to arise later had their roots in the Area Groups and their leadership, and in particular in the unresolved, and even ignored, issue of the leadership and position of women. Thus, however hurtful the main ACE Report undoubtedly was to David, the subsequent history of St Michael's went a long way towards proving the validity of many of its conclusions. Certainly, it seems doubtful if the concept of shared leadership ever fully recovered from the analysis, and indeed David came later to change his mind radically on this subject.

16

Community Living and
the Mustard Seed

IT WAS FREQUENTLY ANNE who first saw in what directions the church might develop, and the idea of having an extended family living in the rectory came to her as a result of a vision about the Body of Christ during a Communion Service at St Michael's. Contact with the Fisherfolk, and with the Rev. Graham Pulkingham, Rector of the Church of the Redeemer, Houston, USA, had shown her the value of community living and made her realise that a community household could be a living demonstration of what the Body of Christ really meant. David was not so keen on the idea at first, especially if it meant opening his home to others on a permanent basis, not as short-term lodgers but as members of the family. As always, David went back to the Bible and the example of the early Church in Acts 2:44–45. Andrew Cornes recalls that David preached one or two sermons on the subject but seemed to find little positive response from others in the fellowship.

It was David's firm belief that the vicar of a church must always be just one step ahead of his congregation if he is to be an effective leader, so he and Anne decided to invite one or two others to come and live with them, and Fiona and Guy, in the rectory. At first those who came were people with obvious need of a home, but gradually the idea developed that the household could be a means of setting people free for full-time ministry within the church. The household operated a 'common purse' whereby all income and expenses were pooled, and each member of the household received a small amount of 'pocket money' (£3 per week in 1975) for his/her own personal use. It meant shopping for second-hand clothes, but in this way one or two salary earners were able to support several others.

Everything was shared, but David insisted that his study remained sacrosanct. He was *not* amused when he returned from one of his missions to find that someone, as a prank, was pretending to have taken up residence in the study. However, Anne was much freer from domestic responsibilities since all those duties were shared and she was able to devote more time to a creative ministry amongst the children in the church.

David outlined three important principles for household living:

First, everyone must support the ministry of the house, which in our case included several growing ministries in St Michael's, as well as my own wider work. Second, everyone must support the children, and see them as young but vital members of the household. Third, everyone must support one another, expressing this by serving each other in practical and specific ways. Then, if there was any energy left, they could look after their own interests![1]

Other members of the household would often play with Fiona and Guy, read to them in the evenings, and help put them to bed. Fiona, in particular, sometimes found people who could help her with her school work, and she also learned some musical skills from members of the household. She and Guy certainly gained from acquiring a number of older 'brothers and sisters' or 'aunts and uncles', but there were also times when they wondered why they could not have Mummy and Daddy to themselves a bit more. None of the grandparents found it easy when they came to see the family. There was one occasion when Guy's grandfather saw him putting away his small amount of pocket money in a savings box. 'What are you saving up for?' asked grandfather. Guy replied, 'I'm saving up enough money so that we can buy a house where Mummy, Daddy, Fiona and I can live by ourselves.'

There were at one time no less than seven communities or households in York, living more or less according to the three principles David outlined. In addition, there were eight 'lesser' households, where people lived together or where a nuclear family shared their home with others. These extended families would not consider themselves to be mainstream communities, but the common factors were commitment to each other, mutual support, both emotionally and financially, and general support for the church by this means. These common factors were not limited to the households, but became prevalent in the whole church. Already attempting to be a church where relationships between members were the motivating characteristic of the Body, St Michael's now deepened its understanding of this to include a more simple lifestyle and a greater sharing of resources. Many individuals and families were learning to use their homes in new, more open ways – holding meetings and prayer groups and providing hospitality to visitors to the church.

The whole worshipping fellowship accepted the challenge of this as David preached and taught on the subject of simple living on many occasions. He had been very impressed by the book *Rich Christians in an*

Age of Hunger by Ronald Sider, and indeed wrote the foreword to the English edition. In it he said:

We [Christians] have accepted a lifestyle which is so similar to the covetous world around us as to be indistinguishable from it. We have accepted a largely middle-class culture, with its worldly values and selfish ambitions, and have conveniently ignored the utterly radical teaching of Jesus concerning money, possessions and social standing within the kingdom of God. Most serious of all, perhaps, our lifestyle, both individual and corporate, is astonishingly different from the lifestyle of our Master whom we profess to follow and serve.[2]

Thus the concept of simple living was underpinned by David from the pulpit and the households represented, if not an answer to the problem, at least a willingness and a commitment to address it. Bonds were created which produced that indefinable attitude of 'having all things in common', which is much greater than the material activity sometimes supposed to be meant by the phrase. All this manifested itself in the togetherness at the Sunday services.

Community living, therefore, must not be seen as separate from the life of the fellowship but an integral part of it. The spirituality of the whole church was challenged by the households. Deeply entrenched positions were changed as striving for success yielded to mutual interdependence, and status gave way to service and submission. The concept of possessions changed dramatically. Peter Hodgson, a tireless worker on the staff at that time, remembers: 'My salary could in no way meet basic family demands, but we were short of nothing. The experience was both exciting and frightening at the same time. I once wore David's trousers – a bit big, but OK. He had another pair.' There grew a very genuine brother–sister love from which sprang innumerable expressions of generosity and self-giving. Nevertheless, such experiences cannot but attract difficulties and David would quote William Blake, 'Joy and pain are woven fine.' He was right to do so, and fully experienced the two extremes himself.

Temperamentally, David found all this more difficult than many. His upper-middle-class, public school image, with children at private schooling, was for a time not consistent with what he was teaching. Although the children's education was being paid for by their grandparents, he went through a considerable cultural change in deciding to send them to the local state schools and found this very difficult to come to terms with. His position in the rectory was not an easy one. Anne became absorbed by community living, finding a new role and fulfilment in its demands. She was always eager for change as one project after another appealed to her, received her considerable and energetic support and then, having been promoted, was passed to others to be fulfilled. She was not an evangelist and had no part in David's missions, which seemed to grow ever more frequent, but she was a great builder of faith in the developing church. David, on the contrary, remained rather on the periphery of the household. He even had a partition erected in the rectory hall, cutting off his study and the office from the rest of the house, and retreated behind it to live his life on the other side.

The truth is that community living is very difficult to achieve without strong leadership and clear rules of life. David could not really offer this since he was involved with so much else and Anne could not do it without challenging his views on male headship. The York households differed from each other considerably but the effect was the same in each – major benefits on the one hand and mistakes on the other. The benefits are to be seen in the remarkable progress in some areas of church life, progress which was most unlikely to have been achieved without the households. Most obvious were the developments in worship, in drama, in dance, in a distinctive children's work and in banner production. Some of these were Anne's projects, sometimes received in a vision or message from God, thought through and undertaken very practically, and woven into the fabric of the church. Without the households to share her commitments and her vision, it is doubtful if she could have carried them out. That is the real point. The household set her free to do them and then helped her in the doing. Sharing resources in simple living enables people to do far more than they could otherwise.

Andrew Maries (now Director of Music at St Andrew's Church, Cullompton) came to York as a music student. Returning later to become Director of Music, he combined life in the rectory household with some part-time teaching. He became that rare being, a professional and sophisticated musician who understands and loves worship as much as music. Under his leadership the music at St Michael's was of great importance, always adapting to new insights and new methods. It has had an influence far beyond York. He looks back to Anne's spiritual ministry to him, relentless and unequivocal, as the most formative influence on him. Without the household, this could not have been. Andrew, who married another member of the household, continued to lead the music at St Michael's until 1991. One of the rooms at the rectory became known as 'the music room', and was used by Andrew and others for practice, rehearsal and composition.

Paul Burbridge met David at a mission to Oxford University. David invited him and his friend and colleague Murray Watts to come to York and use St Cuthbert's, now rather underused, as a base for religious drama. Paul joined the rectory household and began to travel with David on his missions. Together they recruited a number of others to form a team of singers, dancers and actors to travel with David to illustrate and supplement his addresses. Since these had to be available to go anywhere at any date for long or short periods, it was impossible for them to hold down normal jobs, and the households provided the answer. The considerable contribution made to David's ministry by his teams was only made possible in the first instance by the households. Eventually, some of his original team formed the Riding Lights Theatre Company, which has made a significant breakthrough in religious drama, and other team members took their place in David's ministry.

Eventually the households overstretched themselves and gradually disintegrated. They tended to take in too many problem people with whom they were ill-equipped to deal. It was taught that Christian love demanded this for those for whom society had no answer. But the households were not professional institutions catering for emotionally needy people. They existed for another purpose altogether, which they found difficult enough to fulfil – the building of a Christian church in an unbelieving society. Their emotional energies were already taxed by loving each other, and working out together a social structure to enable them to do this truly. One person with deep problems might have been absorbed successfully, and perhaps should have been, but more than one endangered the whole relationship.

Secondly, they tried to delve deeper than they knew into matters which they did not understand well enough. Anne, faced with the plethora of reactions stimulated by the confines of community living, encouraged them to 'walk in the light' with each other (as preached by the East African Revival described in Chapter 6), and to 'speak the truth in love'. They should be open about their likes and dislikes of each other, and, under the influence of a book by Ruth Carter-Stapleton, to seek to minister 'inner healing' to each other although they had little or no experience of or qualification for this. These are means by which human hurts and relationships are deeply affected and great permanent healings can result. They need, however, both a level of love which is difficult to achieve, and of integrity which is rarely experienced.

It is clear that the households, and in particular that in the rectory, went a long way towards achieving these, but there was never any intention of real permanence for the households, and when they had served their purpose they were allowed to fade away gradually without too many regrets. While they were in existence, no less than thirty-four people were supported by them and thus released for service in the church in one capacity or another. This availability of workers for the work as a whole was a very major factor in enabling St Michael's to emerge from being a somewhat amateur effort into a well-organised and structured unit where high standards could be achieved and staff properly employed. No longer was the burden carried on the backs of a very few. Now the system was made to work and the love and power of God was 'serviced' by an adequate human programme.

It was during this time that David wrote what many believe, and he himself considered, to be his most important and lasting book. *Discipleship* was published by Hodder & Stoughton in 1981. In the USA it was entitled *Called and Committed*. Recognising that the tendency in the West is to seek converts and not disciples, David points out that it is to discipleship that Christians are called. In the Introduction, he says:

Christians in the West have largely neglected what it means to be a *disciple of Christ*. The vast majority of western Christians are church members, pew-fillers, hymn-singers, sermon-tasters, Bible-readers, even born-again-believers or Spirit-filled-charismatics – but not true disciples of Jesus.[3]

And again:

Discipleship sums up Christ's plan for the world. Yet for all its brilliant simplicity, it is the one approach that most western churches have neglected. Instead we have had reports, commissions, conferences, seminars, missions, crusades, reunion schemes, liturgical reforms – the lot. But very little attention has been given to the meaning of discipleship.[4]

The book was born out of the household experience – David's own understanding of discipleship was sharpened by community life with its stresses and challenges. As always when he received fresh insights, he began to submit these to the scrutiny of Scripture and to try to express them in realistic and practical terms for the benefit of others. His great gift of communication was brought to bear upon a remarkably wide spectrum of issues which the serious and sincere Christian must face. The table of contents itself covers no less than five pages. It is a handbook for true Christianity presented with characteristic simplicity and compelling power. As Dr Jim Packer says in his Foreword, 'You do not have to agree with every single statement to appreciate the authority and power of his vision for life in Christ, and to be made most uncomfortable as the searchlight of Watsonian simplicity swings your way.'[5]

For instance, Catholics are unlikely to be satisfied by David's eucharistic theology,[6] but few will feel that his short paragraphs on the subject do not present them with a challenge to face before they can go on to 'higher things'. Similarly, those who are anxious about surprising happenings in church will sympathise with the lady who said to her minister: 'I hope nothing supernatural will happen in our church,' but will surely agree with David's comment that 'The trouble is that, through fear, it may not!'[7] Some churches, ten years after publication, are still using *Discipleship* as a text book for study purposes and for spiritual growth. The value of this book will far outlast its availability.

David wrote *Discipleship* during a very difficult time for him and Anne, probably the most difficult of their marriage. David was not temperamentally a suitable candidate for community life, and was propelled into it by Anne's persuasion. As *Discipleship* shows, he valued its lessons and he submitted as best he could to its demands but his calling, as he saw it, was to be an evangelist and communicator. He could build a church by proclaiming the gospel, which again, as *Discipleship* shows, began with the message of salvation and went on to include and enrich every area of human life. In order to fulfil his ministry he needed time – time to be away, but also to be alone in prayer and in study and writing, uninterrupted by community stresses. Anne, on the other hand, was in her element in community life. Just as David was very frequently away on his missions, sometimes for quite long periods as invitations from overseas began to come in, so Anne was automatically always in York with her children and her home. The building up of the church, rather than evangelism, was her particular interest and joy. Within the household she found room for the expression of her prophetic gifting and her pastoral skills. To her most things were very clear and were expressed in definite terms.

So they drifted away from each other – Anne within her household with all its problems, and with her prophetic spirituality towards the affairs of St Michael's; David with his team (some from the rectory household) travelling the world to evangelise and to reconcile, leaving behind the tensions in the rectory to taste the sweetness of public appreciation and acclaim. For each it was enormously exacting, and yet tremendously rewarding. But in spite of so much common ground they were on different paths for a time and the marriage was stretched quite painfully. Once, at least, it nearly reached breaking point, but not quite.

One particular household had a more spectacular identity and purpose than the others. The vision for it had been given by God gradually and not to any one person in the first instance. Anne had advocated several years earlier that, 'What this fellowship needs is a shop.' Later she read Isaiah 58:12 and understood it to say that the restored city streets were for people to live in. Before long, God was also speaking to another family on what seemed to be a slightly different line, and in June 1976 'The Mustard Seed' was opened in High Petergate.

Philip and Elizabeth (Wendy) Wharton lived in Escrick, a few miles from York. Philip was an engineer with the National Coal Board in Doncaster, and Wendy was manageress of Marshall and Snelgrove's fashion store in York. Their daughter Judith, a nurse, felt God calling her to give up her nursing and join the rectory household to help Anne. She became one of the leaders of the dance group at St Michael's. Wendy, too, in response to a sense of call, gave up her job and found peace of mind in having more time to share her faith with others. The challenge of community living as a means to serve God began to reach them. Wendy had a mental picture, which she believed was a message from God, of a long, narrow house in York. One day Judith came home to say there was a vacant shop close to the church which David and Anne would like them to come and see. Wendy was horrified by what she saw. Both the shop itself and the accommodation above it were in a terrible condition with filth everywhere, some ceilings were down and there was even a dead rat in the bathroom. Her own home in Escrick was spotless and elegant to a fault, but despite all the dirt, she immediately recognised the shop as the house she had seen in her vision. She stood on the stairs and prayed, 'Lord, if this is really your will, I'll do it.'

The Escrick house was sold to provide the capital for the repairs and the refitting of the shop, and Philip continued with his work to provide the rent and rates and to meet personal family costs. Staff was provided for them, after much prayer, by volunteers from the church who gave up their jobs to live in community with Philip, Wendy and Judith in the flat above the shop. A multi-talented young American, Geoffrey Stevenson (who later joined the Riding Lights Theatre Company with Paul Burbridge, and eventually married Judith) came to be their chef. Each day opened with prayers in the Wharton household, and the staff worked at 'community rates' of £3 a week.

The Mustard Seed soon became a popular meeting place for Christians of all denominations. A cup of coffee or a light meal was available and customers could purchase high quality gifts and other goods. It was convenient and easy for members of St Michael's to meet others and to bring their friends. David often used it for this purpose. Many tourists came into the Mustard Seed after visiting the Minster and sometimes conversations on spiritual subjects would open up with them. Occasionally, Wendy would organise evening evangelistic parties where David or another speaker would address invited guests. Always the witness to Christ was implicit in the community's attitudes and the warmth of the welcome given to all who came. Wendy had a mural painted in the shop showing a mustard tree standing before the cross with the words 'The Kingdom of God is among us.'

David found it to be a jewel in the crown of St Michael's. It brought the church out from behind its stone walls to present itself publicly before the gaze of the city. It was a significant and powerful witness to all he had been doing and, without being perfect, he believed it demonstrated by its very existence the validity of the gospel itself. True, it had been set up by the Whartons rather than by St Michael's, but the vision had always been that the work should be part of the life and ministry of the whole of St Michael's. It was therefore a devastating blow to him that, while he was on an extended and much-needed holiday in Cornwall in 1979, the decision was taken to close it down. He returned in time only to attend a meeting between Philip and Wendy and the elders at which the final decision was made. He felt he had reluctantly to concur.

Why should so promising a project end in such failure? The truth was that between human beings, even Christian ones, good relationships are very hard to maintain. They are based upon trust and love. Where these get worn away by the passage of time and the emphasis on one set of values over another, good intentions crumble if they are not very firmly founded. Of the good intentions of each party in this case there can be no doubt. Philip and Wendy had made considerable sacrifices to set up the Mustard Seed, and had submitted themselves and their project to David, and through him to the church. They built their community on Christian love, trying to treat their staff as members of their own family and to value their contributions as from the Lord himself. Those who came to serve at the Mustard Seed similarly made their sacrifices of careers and of salaries and submitted themselves to Wendy as 'head' of the project. The church elders, whether or not they agreed with David in his vision for the Mustard Seed, without question were dedicated to the cause for which it stood and wanted wholeheartedly to honour Christ through it. Indeed, it was closed precisely because, in their judgment, it was now failing to honour him. Some of the elders saw it as evidence that God's plans did not include the headship of women over Christian projects.

The truth is unlikely to seem the same to each, but it lies in failure to fulfil the original vision. Wendy was given the vision and tried to keep it safe. Did she succeed in sharing it adequately with her staff, or did she think of it as hers? Could she really expect her staff, living at community rates, to be wholly satisfied under her dominance, however benevolent? Was her vision fully shared by the church members and the elders? Was the standard of excellence in everything carried to such an extreme that the Mustard Seed became too expensive for church members to patronise? Why did David and Anne not foresee the direction in which things were moving and arrange for proper support and pastoral care for Wendy and her staff? Why did the staff not demand this from the church much earlier? Why did the elders not have more experience of the Mustard Seed themselves and, above all, why did they allow such fundamental decisions to be made in David's absence?

These questions are now but idle and only succeed in showing how difficult it can be to do God's work. Most Christians will recognise in the Mustard Seed something which bears relation to some failure of their own. Answers to the questions are no doubt available from anyone to whom they may be asked, but, as so often, it would be a futile attempt. It is sufficient to say that, for David, it was a deep and lasting sadness which showed him that his own influence in St Michael's was not as strong as it had been. It also brought home to him that grievous set-backs could still occur whenever the church did anything, even with good intentions and careful spiritual precautions. The demise of the Mustard Seed was the first of a number of disasters which were to help weaken his determination to continue his work in York.

17

Worship and Evangelism

IN MANY OUTBREAKS OF REVIVAL or renewal in the Church, notably the Welsh Revival and the Wesleyan Revivals, there has been a spontaneous explosion of contemporary worship in 'psalms and hymns and spiritual songs'. Usually this has been accompanied by indignant protest from reputable musicians who have become the self-appointed guardians of God's good taste, preserving him as best they could from having his ears insulted by the insipid, the vacuous, the sentimental, or the just plain bad music which his enthusiastic new worshippers wished to offer him.

David Watson was not particularly musical himself and not a performer or an expert, though he enjoyed music and could certainly make choices and give opinions. He used music, as the Church has always done, as a vehicle for worship and for lifting the heart to God and inspiring the will to obey him.

David had been brought up in an age when music from other cultures began to invade western civilisation, bringing a new freedom and vitality to rhythm, melody and form. At Iwerne he had become used to choruses as an invaluable aid to worship and teaching for the young. When first ordained he found himself confronted by new Christian songs, to a more syncopated rhythm, being produced by the youth culture of the Fifties and Sixties which challenged many of the attitudes of the older generation. David had been glad of them, although they were still didactic and objective in character as, of course, Church worship in general tended to be. They were the product of the burgeoning work among young people and students which the evangelicals undertook to great effect in parishes such as St Mark's, Gillingham, and were not associated with the charismatics at that time. In particular, this movement for the composition of new hymns and songs became greatly accelerated by the leadership, amongst others, of Michael Baughen, now Bishop of Chester, when he succeeded John Stott as Rector of All Souls, Langham Place, and many churches, not all evangelical, have contributed to it and benefited from it.

The beginning of the Charismatic Movement, however, in which David played so significant a role, saw a dramatic surge in the use of new worship songs of a slightly different character. Often imported from America, but reflecting a variety of musical cultures – especially African, Caribbean and Israeli, they were enthusiastically received and widely used. Their distinctive characteristic was that they were much more subjective in style, very simple and singable in melody and given to much repetition. Without question, many were naive, short-term compositions which were wide open to deprecation; perhaps especially from the evangelicals, with their growing interest and expertise in modern hymnody.

The trouble with subjective worship is that it is exclusive. When expected to sing 'I love you, Lord', only those who feel that they really do, and are comfortable saying it so many times, will be included in the experience. It is much easier to sing out some great objective truth which expresses what ought to be believed by the Christian, even if his life is not being lived in obedience to it at that time. Unfortunately, this can lead to a dryness and formality of worship which, of course, ignores its very essence. After all, 'I love you, Lord' is the appropriate and essential response of faith and dedication to the Christian truth upon which every-thing rests. Without it there are only dry bones, and no amount of ortho-doxy can compensate for that. The Psalms show a proper balance between the two extremes by continually worshipping the great and loving God, extolling his mighty deeds and wonderful love, while at the same time applying this to the believer and allowing him to respond personally to it. Traditional Church worship, with its respectable objectivism, can be seriously unbalanced.

David was never very happy with the weaker songs which seemed to say little and say it too often. But many of the charismatic worship songs sounded out the greatness of God and gave clear expression to the wor-shippers' personal dedication. These he believed to be of great importance, and selections of them were made for use in York and on his missions. He wanted them sung a little slower than the musicians tended to want to play them, in order to avoid insincerity of purpose by the easy tripping-off-the-tongue which could so often happen, and a little more quietly to avoid triumphalism and mere musical performance. He believed repetition was essential to enable the worshipping mind to grasp the significance of what it was trying to do, but not so much repetition that the mind eventually wandered from the point and got lost. Without implying any disrespect for great music, which could inspire by the very quality of its sound, he believed that simple melody was needed, unsophisticated and in the modern idiom, so that everyone could join in. Parish church worship in the common or 'vulgar' tongue, which was the aim of the Book of Common Prayer, must strive to keep up to date musically as well as liturgically.

In St Cuthbert's, David had come to see that the atmosphere of worship contributed powerfully to his people's awareness of the presence of God and prepared them for the spoken word. Unhurried use of worship songs, without inhibition or convention, was able to generate a sense of awe which made the congregation receptive to the word of God. Worship and evangelism together were a powerful combination, though worship must never be seen as a tool for evangelism. In *I Believe in Evangelism,* he wrote:

True worship must always be first and foremost God-ward in its direction, even though the expression of worship, certainly in terms of serving and giving, may bring much blessing to other people. But when we are taken up with worship, and when we are unashamed of the fact that we are in love with God and in love with one another, that can be very powerful indeed. The world today is starved of love, suffocated with words, bereft of joy, and lacking in peace. Therefore, 'a praising community preaches to answer questions raised by its praise'.[1]

David had written earlier in the book:

On many occasions I have seen the close link between the praise of God, when marked by the freshness and freedom of the Spirit's presence, and powerful evangelism. Quite often during a Communion service, when both service and sermon were directed almost exclusively to the convinced believer, I have seen men and women brought to faith in Christ, largely through the praise of God's people.[2]

He frequently quoted William Temple's definition of worship, pointing out that it could equally well serve as a definition of evangelism:

Worship is the submission of all our nature to God. It is the quickening of conscience by his holiness; the nourishment of mind with his truth; the purifying of imagination by his beauty; the opening of the heart to his love; the surrender of the will to his purpose – and all this gathered up in adoration, the most selfless emotion of which our nature is capable.[3]

At the International Renewal Conference organised by Michael Harper and his Fountain Trust in Guildford Cathedral in 1971, David had met Merv and Merla Watson from Canada. He commented that they were 'not only brilliant musically; they were able to convey a wonderful sense of worship, leading us into the presence of the Lord and making us deeply aware of his glory and grace.' He invited them to lead two Festivals of Praise in York in 1972, at which they were joined by a large team of singers and dancers. Then in 1973, they went with him on a seven-week tour of New Zealand organised by the New Zealand Inter-Varsity Fellowship involving three student conferences and five student missions as well as a number of public meetings. This tour, which at times attracted considerable opposition, resulted in many students turning to Christ. It was a breakthrough for David.

In the Parish Newsletter for May 1973 he wrote, 'I have never before in student missions worked with singers of the style of Merv and Merla; but I have become increasingly convinced of the power of praise, and I look forward to combining this with the more conventional proclamation of the Gospel.' It was a bold and enlightened step which was to revolutionise his work as an evangelist. He began to work with the Fisherfolk from the Church of the Redeemer, Houston, who came to Britain in 1973 with the Rev. Graham Pulkingham, and who led many Festivals of Praise in cathedrals around the country. He would often give the closing address, and he found that their worship created just the right atmosphere for the subsequent proclamation of God's word.

Unfortunately, this led to accusations of emotionalism from sections of the Church in England who tended to have a more stolid and repressive attitude towards evangelism in general. In the days when evangelicals had their backs to the wall, they had found it almost impossible not to be influenced by such criticism, and so were unwilling to submit all their evangelism to careful scrutiny. Of course, emotionalism is to be strenuously avoided by any teacher or preacher hoping to achieve lasting and healthy results from his work, but evangelism must legitimately employ an appeal to the emotions if it is to reach the whole person. An appeal which does not reach the mind and the will is unlikely to bear good fruit, so that to touch only the emotions is fruitless; but David's message was obviously so much more than an emotional appeal. Moreover, the Parable of the Sower reveals that there is more than one reason why new converts might lapse; and further, that the prospect of a high proportion of listeners not properly receiving an evangelistic message should not deter the Church from evangelism.

David soon recognised the need for a team to travel with him wherever he was invited to go, leading the worship and illuminating his message with drama and dance. In this, of course, he was able to harness the considerable talent within his own church, released in part by the households as described in the previous chapter. Andrew Maries gathered around him a band of skilled instrumentalists and singers, some of whom would travel with David. When he went to a local church, David was of course willing to accept the pattern of worship they preferred, but whenever he was leading a festival or mission, he insisted on his own team leading worship before his address. Paul Burbridge and Murray Watts would write sketches of which David made increasing use to illustrate his message. Thus, a highly talented group of singers, actors and dancers became available to travel regularly with David. It was an original, if not unique, step for an evangelist to take, but David never went back on it and persisted in his determination to take his team with him everywhere. If his hosts were unwilling to make provision for the team, David would make it clear that his own ministry would not be available without them. He came to think of their role as an expression of corporate ministry which enormously enhanced the work.

David's work among young people had not developed since Gillingham and Cambridge, although he was frequently speaking to students. Perhaps his style and his appearance were not helpful to the task of ministering to the youth of the Seventies. In Lent 1976 he spent a week with Paul Burbridge at his old school, Wellington College. Neither the Chaplain nor the Headmaster really approved of an evangelical approach, but an old friend of David's, Peter Waghorn, who was a lay member of staff, had suggested that he be invited for the customary series of Lent talks. Paul recalls that it was very difficult on the first evening in the formal College Chapel with all the staff sitting there in their academic gowns, like great black birds of prey. There was little reaction or response from the boys that night, but for the rest of the week the meeting was held in the Hall and Paul was able to involve some of the boys in the sketches. Gradually more and more understanding of the message was aroused as they both were able to speak in many classes and in small informal groups during the daytime, as well as the big evening meetings. After David's final address at the Communion Service in the Chapel, he invited those boys who had responded to his message to give him their names, and about seventy did so. But it is hard to know how fruitful such missions could ultimately be against official antipathy.

David also conducted a number of Parish Missions. At All Souls, Langham Place, the then Rector, Michael Baughen, comments that David's 'evangelistic gifts were second to none in my opinion and were ideally suited to All Souls. They were splendid missions with considerable grace and blessing.' He took a significant mission in Chorleywood for two parishes, Christchurch and St Andrew's, in October 1971. John Perry, then vicar of St Andrew's and later Warden of Lee Abbey and then Bishop of Southampton, recalls that among those who committed their lives to Christ were 'a number who were later to play a prominent role in positions of responsibility in the church. I remember it as one of the significant milestones in the development of St Andrew's.'

From the mid-Seventies, David began to be involved in City-wide Festivals. They were really missions by another name but they also served the purpose of uniting many churches in a common public witness to their Christian faith in their city. Amongst others he was at Sheffield in November 1975, Leeds in July 1977, Tyneside and then Greater Manchester in May 1978, Merseyside in October 1979, Poole in April 1980, Chelsea in May 1980, Hammersmith and Fulham in April 1981, Birmingham and then Ipswich in October 1981, and Stafford in December 1981. In addition, he led missions of a very different sort in rural areas such as Wensleydale in September 1978 and Cornwall in the following month.

He had not originally wanted to get involved in large-scale events, feeling that a smaller more intimate environment was preferable. However, in 1973, five respected Christian leaders had written to him, apparently quite independently, suggesting that God might be wanting to use him in City-wide Festivals. Quite soon after he had received those letters, invitations to lead bigger events started coming in. David was forced to conclude that God was calling him to launch out into this new area of ministry. The planning and organisation of any large-scale event is quite complex and demanding. When David shared his feelings with the elders in York, one of them, Douglas Greenfield, immediately said that he believed that God wanted him to help with the administration of these festivals. Douglas was a consultant with a pharmaceutical export company, and his pattern of work enabled him to undertake the research required to plan and prepare for these events. Soon after an invitation was received, Douglas would pay a preliminary visit to discuss the proposed plans with the local church leaders in order to determine whether they were ready for a festival. In addition, festival invitations were submitted to the eldership, as indeed were all of David's invitations. If it was agreed that they were ready to go forward, Douglas would be involved in the detailed planning and arrangements in so far as they affected David and his team.

In 1979, a folder of facts and guidelines was drawn up to help those who were considering a large-scale event. It included a commendation from the Archbishop of York (Dr Stuart Blanch). In an introduction, David outlined his thinking behind these festivals:

It is often said that Christians need to belong to three sizes of groups:
    the *cell* of about 12, meeting informally in someone's home
    the *congregation* meeting regularly for worship, teaching and the sacraments
    the *celebration* coming together less frequently to bear witness unitedly to Jesus
    Christ

'If in major cities around the world all true Christians could unite in a "great congregation" joyfully to sing praise to God, hear the word and bear witness, the impact would be incalculable.' (Howard Snyder in *Community of the King*[4])

Having previously been sceptical of the 'big event', I have now seen the truth of that comment. In many united missions over the past few years I have seen these effects amongst others:

1 They have stimulated local church evangelism and life. Some churches were 'born' or 'revived' as a result – to quote the words used by the ministers concerned.
2 They have helped many to find Christ for the first time, and caused others to think carefully about the Christian faith.
3 They have brought spiritual renewal to many Christians and fellowships as people caught a fresh vision of the reality of Christ and experienced a new taste of his love.
4 They have led Christians from different churches, traditions and denominations into a much greater sense of unity in a given place, as they rediscovered that they are all members of the one body of Christ.
5 Partly as a result of this, the whole area has become much more aware of the life of the church, leading to questions being asked about the Christian faith and therefore spontaneous opportunities given for evangelism.

David was anxious that the invitation for a festival should come from as widely a representative group of churches as possible. Often, however, there were one or two churches which would not participate because of fears about the charismatic aspect. Occasionally, there were fundamentalist churches who would not cooperate if Roman Catholic churches were taking part. Each festival was normally preceded (six or more months ahead) by an afternoon or evening Festival of Praise. There was usually also a series of seminars in which David and his team would be able to meet with local church leaders to establish some sort of mutual understanding. During the Festival itself there would be further seminars, for clergy and other leaders, in the mornings.

In some places, local Christians were worried about the use of dance, perhaps because of a residual puritanism among evangelicals. As David himself wrote, 'I knew that the psalmist talked often about praising God's name with dancing ... But such Jewish exuberance in Old Testament days was surely not for respectable Anglicans today.'[5] Nevertheless, when he himself saw dance used in worship for the first time, he was deeply moved. As usual, he turned to the Bible and found nothing to negate the use of dance in church and much to commend it. He recognised the potential dangers of 'unhelpful sexual emotions being stirred by watching pretty girls dance' and advocated that 'the dancers in their dress and their movement must aim for modesty'. Nevertheless, sexuality is God-given, and therefore not to be feared but to be faced, under the influence of his Spirit. He encouraged those who were to dance to meet together to pray and share from the Scriptures, so that 'the quality of their relationships together in Christ would make the dance genuinely an act of worship'.[6] Moreover, just as dramas could be used to provide a visual aspect to the spoken word, so dance could be true Christian worship.

Dance was certainly an issue at Manchester, and was raised when the Chairman of the festival, Val Grieve, a solicitor, visited York to discuss the festival with David. David said that they would leave it out if it was going to cause offence, but Val Grieve wanted the team to operate in their usual way. He recalls that when they came to the Free Trade Hall for the festival, David announced each night that there would be 'movement to music' during one of the songs sung by the group – without ever making any reference to 'dance'. On two days during that festival, Val Grieve managed to hire the Exchange Theatre so that Riding Lights could perform in the lunch-hour. A team of young people visited every office in the city with invitations to come to the theatre at lunchtime. The festival certainly made an impact on the city, the Free Trade Hall being full to capacity for nine nights, with a final closing rally in a football stadium. Val Grieve commented afterwards: 'I have now been working in the City for over 28 years and I can honestly say that there has never been anything like it. One of the outstanding features has been the way in which so many churches have worked together (250 of them).'

During the Leeds Festival in June 1977, a miraculous healing took place in one of the meetings; all the more surprising because there had not been any mention during it of the subject of physical healing. Susan Speight, a former domestic science teacher in Wetherby, had been confined to a wheelchair for four years with a crippling complication of diabetes known as diabetic neuropathy, and had lost all feeling from her waist downwards. Her specialist had told her that it would not come back. During David's talk one night she began to feel her feet getting hot, and eventually complete feeling was restored. She realised that this meant that she ought to be able to walk. When the meeting was over, she called to Andrew Maries and told him what had happened. He helped her to get out of the wheelchair and together they walked right round the Town Hall, without using her sticks. Realising that she could now walk perfectly, she and Andrew went back into the Town Hall to tell David and they spent some time together, praising God for his unexpected healing power.

The 1979 Merseyside Festival (ten nights in the Empire Theatre, Liverpool) was noteworthy for a bomb scare! It was on Friday evening, the third night of the festival, which had been designated as Youth Night. Just before the meeting was due to start, with over 2,000 young and not so young people in the Empire Theatre, a suspicious package was discovered near the electrical wiring. The police ordered an evacuation and cordoned off the area. While the crowd was waiting outside, the Rev. Alan Godson (Vicar of St Mary's, Edgehill) asked the Fire Brigade to erect some temporary lighting so that some sort of meeting could be held on the steps of the nearby St George's. There was some singing, and the team performed a sketch of David and Goliath, with Alan Godson taking the part of Goliath's body with someone sitting on his shoulders. After the sketch, Alan managed to borrow a police car with a loud-hailer so that the Bishop of Liverpool, David Sheppard, and David Watson could sit in it and address the crowd. David Sheppard said a prayer, which was almost inaudible through the distortion, but David Watson managed to get the measure of the loud-hailer and to hold the attention of the crowd. After about an hour the police announced that the 'bomb' was only a hoax, and they were allowed back into the Empire Theatre. Although 2,000 had come out when the 'bomb' was discovered, about 2,500 went back in.

After the 1980 Poole Festival, David Taylor of the Nationwide Initiative in Evangelism undertook an evaluation which showed that 8,900 people, or 2.5 per cent of the population of the area, attended one or more meetings (the total attendance being 14,800), and that one-quarter of these were not regular members of any church. One hundred and twenty-five of them were recommended to join a local church fellowship, and all of them actually did so; six months later, ninety-four were still worshipping regularly. The Rev. Jimmy Hamilton Brown, Rector of Dorchester, who had been the local administrator of the festival, commented in an article in *Tomorrow's Church*:

Who says that mass evangelism does not reach those outside the churches? This Festival reached a far higher percentage than I would have guessed possible. It looks as if the majority of enquirers from outside the church were not just carried away in the heat of the moment. Who says that those influenced by mass evangelism do not last? For those clergy who are still not convinced – let me ask what has happened to your last confirmation class?[7]

The truly remarkable thing about the City-wide Festivals was the comprehensive character of their support. It is extremely unusual for such a wide spectrum of ecclesiastical style and theological opinion to be able to unite behind a single speaker. It has never quite happened, even for Billy Graham, and no Briton other than David Watson has attempted it quite so successfully. He was acceptable to all Christians, from the House Churches to the Roman Catholics. Bishops turned up to support his festivals and the people came to hear him in remarkable numbers. It is true that he tried to avoid using cathedrals because of the restrictions that were often imposed upon him, but on the whole he went anywhere and did whatever he was asked to do. Yet he never weakened his message or dressed it in fancy clothing; and in fact was never asked to do so. It was straight and true and contained all of the revealed Christianity which he had first learned at Iwerne and had continued learning about subsequently. He spoke for God by proclaiming God's word, not his own opinions. The churches were learning that God's word carried its own authority and was still the only source of wisdom, truth and power.

18

The Evangelist

DAVID WATSON HAD MANY FACETS to his ministry. He was a very successful parish priest in York and elsewhere. He wrote many books and recorded many tapes. He was a vital part of the movement for charismatic renewal and later preached powerfully for reconciliation within the churches. However, it is fair to say that first and foremost he was an evangelist. As such, it is appropriate that an examination is made of evangelism and of David engaged in the activity.

For many years, following the Church's failure to take any action on the 1945 report *Towards the Conversion of England*, there was no official recognition of the need for evangelism.[1] Only towards the end of the century has the emptiness of the traditional churches and the weight of evangelical scholarship made evangelism acceptable enough for the 'Decade of Evangelism' to be launched by the general consensus of the traditional churches. David Watson's work, together with that done by others before and beside him, should be seen against the implicit and sometimes explicit rejection of it by the religious leadership, and indeed by the rank and file of worshippers in the vast majority of churches. After Billy Graham's remarkable crusade at Harringay Arena in 1954, which opened up the possibility of the Christian faith being given a good hearing again in the nation, many from the theological establishment appeared to embark upon a campaign of denial and ridicule which more or less killed it off. Only at grass roots, here a little and there a little, with gradual and sometimes imperceptible progress, was evangelism able to make its contribution.

But in 1965 the Archbishops of Canterbury and York set up the Archbishops' Council on Evangelism, under the chairmanship of Cuthbert Bardsley, Bishop of Coventry, with the brief 'to stimulate and encourage evangelism in the Church of England'. Through its quarterly bulletin (*ACE*), and its conferences and workshops, clergy and laity rediscovered evangelism as a task to which the Church is called. As such they wanted to hear from those few who seemed to be able to do it effectively, particularly such people as Cuthbert Bardsley himself, Bryan Green, Michael Green and, of course, David Watson (see Chapter 15). Furthermore, the Nationwide Initiative in Evangelism, chaired by Donald English, Head of the Methodist Home Mission Department and twice President of the Methodist Conference, had the support of most of the churches around 1979–80. Nevertheless, it is surprising how many church leaders and able theologians of the twentieth century have despised evangelism and rejected the work of evangelists, either because their churches seem to them to be threatened by them, or because their theology leaves no room for the intellectual simplicities which the evangelist must proclaim.

So what is evangelism that it can generate such controversy within the Church? One might assume that any organisation would be pleased to have new members and that time and effort would quite naturally be expended to encourage growth. However, evangelism is often misunderstood, even in churches. Many see it as merely an attempt to cram religion down unwilling throats; a straightforward recruiting drive. Surely those who are quite happy as they are and comfortable with their beliefs should be left in peace; it is offensive to impose. Particularly is this seen as true for people of other faiths, who have as much right to believe what they like as Christians have, and especially if they belong within an ancient, time-honoured and culturally respectable religion.

Others equate evangelism with spreading the beliefs, methods and styles of evangelicalism. After all, evangelicals are so called because they believe in and practise evangelism. Thus, people disapprove of evangelism simply because they do not agree with evangelicalism.

Inevitably many of David Watson's books, including his earlier works *My God is Real, In Search of God* and *Is Anyone There?* imply what David thought evangelism was all about. Furthermore, he produced a major work on the subject, *I Believe in Evangelism*. In it David quoted two definitions of evangelism. The first, originally given in an official church report in 1918, was made famous in *Towards the Conversion of England*: 'To evangelise is so to present Jesus Christ in the power of the Holy Spirit that men shall come to put their trust in God through him, to accept him as their Saviour, and serve him as their King in the fellowship of his Church.'[2]

The second, more recent, definition came from the 1974 Lausanne International Congress on World Evangelization: 'To evangelise is to spread the good news that Jesus Christ died for our sins and was raised from the dead according to the Scriptures, and that as the reigning Lord he now offers the forgiveness of sins and the liberating gift of the Spirit to all who repent and believe.'

Another definition which David liked to use, as he had been closely associated in its formulation, came from the Evangelism Group of the Anglican International Conference on Spiritual Renewal held at Canterbury just before the Lambeth Conference in 1978. It stated simply: 'Evangelism is the presentation of the claims of Christ in the power of the Spirit to a world in need by a church in love.'[3]

Thus, evangelism is presenting good news. It is a confident proclamation rather than an insistent demand. The aim is to present a truth rather than to recruit members to one's cause. Since the news is good, the evangelist may properly expect a positive response, but cannot demand it. In the Parable of the Sower the evangelist scatters seed, some of which may germinate but some of which will not. The Sower does not attempt to force each seed to grow (he could not if he tried) and does not even protect the seed from sun, birds and weeds. It is left to God to elicit an appropriate response.[4] Thus, for the evangelist, the use of pressure, manipulation, emotionalism or even excessive argument, is counter-productive. The failure to secure an entirely free and glad acceptance by the will leads to a decision without validity. On the other hand, if the evangelist truly believes that what is being proclaimed is good news, there is no need to argue or manipulate. The only concern is to be absolutely clear what the news is, so as to avoid it being misunderstood as something other than good. Telling people that they have won a prize or been promoted or are going on a holiday in the sun, one does not expect to have to talk them into it. One expects them to be delighted. Thus, the evangelist's message should be as attractive as possible so as not to give a false impression, rather than because it requires a hard sell.

Consequently, evangelism in itself is a wholly appropriate activity of the Church. As with anything, it can be abused and no doubt has been on many occasions; but it is the abuse rather than the evangelism which is invalid. The exposure of error does not invalidate the quest for truth. If, then, it is appropriate, why is it necessary? In the first instance, of course, it is necessary because it is good news. As Michael Green writes in the Introduction to *I Believe in Evangelism*: 'If you have found good news, it is churlish indeed to keep it to yourself. If you are so thrilled about it, why should you not show it?'[5] The other side of the coin is that there are millions who have not heard the gospel. If the news were not good, it would be fortunate that most people had not heard it. If most people had heard the gospel, there would be less need to preach it. Yet, in fact, the Church is the repository of great good news, which has not yet been heard by the bulk of humanity.

In *I Believe in Evangelism* David starts by looking at the urgency of evangelism:

It is worth remembering, as you read this, that within the next hour some 4–500 people in the world will die from starvation, and a further 6,000 will die from other causes. At the same time more than 14,000 babies will be born. This means that according to the present rate of explosion, the world population increases by approximately 8,000 every hour or 200,000 every day, the majority of whom will be born into areas where there is little or no knowledge of Christ.[6]

Of course these figures are now out of date, but his point is equally valid.

As he discusses the motives for evangelism, he quotes the American evangelist Leighton Ford, who wrote: 'It has been estimated that in spite of the combined efforts of all churches and evangelistic and missionary agencies put together, it is taking 1,000 Christians an average of 365 days to win one person to Christ.' The book is not a call for 'mass evangelism', or for bigger and better evangelistic crusades, but for churches and individual Christians to be aware of the needs and the spiritual hunger that exist in the world and so seek every opportunity to share the good news of Jesus Christ with others. There are valuable chapters on personal evangelism, evangelism and the local church, growing up as a Christian, worship and evangelism and the role of the Holy Spirit in evangelism.

In commending *I Believe in Evangelism* Michael Green, editor of the 'I Believe' series, wrote:

David Watson is well equipped to write about evangelism, which he devotes himself to through public preaching and personal conversations, in universities throughout the world, in city-wide campaigns, and in schools. But it should also be apparent that his perspective is very different from the traditional brand image of evangelism. He operates no one man band, no mindless frenzy of decision-making, no emotional challenge. People are coming to faith spontaneously and at times daily in his congregation, not only because of the preaching, but because of the impact of the whole congregation, the quality of its worship, the changes in men's lives, the prayers of that mid-week meeting for praise and intercession which brings some two hundred of the congregation together to beseech God's blessing.

This is, I fancy, the most important book David Watson has yet written. It enshrines principles of evangelism that I have never seen in print before. It is rooted in experience. It is grounded in a remarkable grasp of the New Testament. It is alive with the freshness and power of the Holy Spirit. It will have a very great impact in inspiring congregational-based, worshipful evangelism in many parts of the world.[7]

It is perhaps a little surprising that, as the churches embark in the Nineties upon the Decade of Evangelism, it does not seem that any use is being made of this comprehensive work. Perhaps everyone has read it and forgotten it. The same fate was meted out to *Towards the Conversion of England*.

What then, is the message of the evangelist, and how did David Watson go about proclaiming it? David always emphasised that Jesus must be central to any proclamation of the gospel. The 'good news' is about him, not about the Church, or religion. He would often point out that many people who never go to church, and who are not interested in religion, nevertheless want to know about Jesus. 'Jesus Christ, and him crucified'[8] was always the heart of David's evangelistic message. He insisted that it was a message which demanded a response from the hearer. That response could be summarised in the three words: Repent, Believe and Receive.

Repent. This means a change of mind leading to a change of heart, resulting in a change of direction. With the mind we must acknowledge our sin and guilt before God. However, mental assent is not enough; the heart must feel some sorrow and deep-seated regret that, by our sin, we have offended God and crucified his Son. Yet even the change of mind and heart is not enough. There must also be a change of direction. Repentance means an about-turn. It means being willing, with the help of Christ, to turn away from all that is wrong in our lives, and to go with Jesus instead.

Believe. In the New Testament the call to believe is a call to discipleship. It involves a clear commitment of the will to the person of Jesus Christ. It is far more than intellectual belief in the divinity of Christ or in some doctrine of the atonement. It means a personal and total surrender to Jesus as Saviour and Lord, with all the ethical demands involved in such a discipleship.

Receive. Here is an essential part of the good news: 'You shall receive the gift of the Holy Spirit.' From the moment of commitment to Christ, God sends the Spirit of his Son into our hearts, crying 'Abba! Father!' (Galatians 4:6). It is entirely through the Spirit that we are born again into God's family. And it is through the Spirit's continued indwelling that we enjoy the unfailing presence of Christ in our hearts, and experience the steady transformation of our lives into the likeness of Christ.[9]

Nevertheless, David did not see the content of his addresses as being as important as the activity of the Holy Spirit through them. 'It is useless to attempt to witness to Christ, in obedience to his command, without the power of his Spirit. Anyone can preach words; some can preach convincing and persuasive words; but only God can change lives.'[10] David had begun his Christian experience with the good news of the gospel. To him the revealed nature of the Christian faith was never in question. When it came to ministry, whether in his initial attempts to describe to others what had happened to him or in his later and more sophisticated efforts at student missions and City-wide Festivals, he only had revealed good news to pass on. He found himself dependent upon the activity of the Holy Spirit in every part of his ministerial calling.

Initially, the Spirit had chosen to inspire the Holy Scriptures 'for our instruction'.[11] The Church, under the Spirit's hand, had recognised the divine message of the Scriptures and faithfully preserved them through the centuries as best they could. Later, scholars sought to open up the origins and meanings of the Scriptures, and by submitting their minds to the guidance of the Spirit brought even deeper insights into the revelation. Upon this Christians have discerned by the Spirit's power what is the good news to be proclaimed to the world. They then seek the Spirit's help to do the proclamation effectively, whether it be to a personal friend or to a large audience. Finally, they have looked for the work of the Spirit to bring life through faith to a new believer. If at any stage in this process the evangelist fails to recognise the Spirit's role and allows himself to count upon his own human wisdom he abdicates his great privilege to be God's messenger, and finds his own resources inadequate and therefore ineffective. Evangelism is God at work, actively and distinctively. He does it through men and women, but he does not move over and let them get on with it.

The power of David's evangelism had its source not in his brilliant communication before an invited audience, but in the many hours of Bible reading, study and prayer in the privacy of his home down the years. He was seeking God and his revelation so that he might know it better. He was also seeking grace to enable him to be in submission to the mind of God, not just in principle but in every practical detail. In particular, prayerfulness was the nature of his preparation. Every address, even those given previously on more than one occasion, was prepared afresh over a matter of hours so that it never stood on the ground of its content, already constructed and several times practised, but on the relationship of the preacher with his Lord. Especially after his experience of spiritual renewal, David's determination was to admit the Holy Spirit into every aspect of his ministry and to make his vertical relationship with his Father paramount over every other consideration. This was not difficult, for it was precisely what renewal meant to him, the gift of the Holy Spirit to fill his whole life and to affect his every thought and action, but it needed determination and discipline to maintain it.

Given this position of spiritual strength, David left no other stone unturned. Careful thought was given to content, making it an exposition of the revealed truth of God as set out in the Scriptures. What he found there he brought to his hearers. What he could not find there he discarded, however strong might be the authority for it from other sources. He wanted to let God work his works of love and thought of himself as only a messenger. At the same time, he sought by every means at his disposal to improve his style of address. Mark Slomka, who became the leader of David's team when he moved to London, comments that 'David perceived preaching as a calling from God but behaved as if it was a profession which warranted the pursuit of excellence. He was constantly writing notes, thoughts, quotes and sermon illustrations. He seldom let moments escape him and was never dormant.'

Where humour was introduced, used to change gear, helping people to concentrate and listen and lightening the tension, it was carefully chosen and not overdone. His stories had to be clear, illuminating the message and not distracting from it. They were collected over the years, culled from newspapers, magazines and his own experience, carefully stored in his Filofax, selected for the occasion, trimmed to fit exactly into the address and delivered with skilful simplicity. The entire address had to hang together, each part contributing to the whole and leaving the exact impression intended. Each word was designed to communicate a precise meaning to the hearers and leave no doubt in their minds. Technical terms, jargon and other such obscurities were deemed illegitimate for an evangelist and were banished permanently from David's repertoire. Even the voice had to be kept in good order, as resonant as possible, and with consonants clearly pronounced without eccentricity.

David insisted that the only way to God is through Jesus Christ, but he would point out that there were many different descriptions of the way. Just as Jesus adapted his words and phrases to suit his hearers, teaching immensely profound theological truths in terms of farming, building, fishing, gardening, cooking, sewing, buying and selling, so David varied his presentation to the needs of his audience. He quotes the advice of Michael Green: 'Be totally committed to the biblical Christ, and totally flexible in presentation.'[12]

In his book *To Reach a Nation* Gavin Reid, the Director of Evangelism at the Church Pastoral Aid Society and former National Director of Mission England, makes an interesting comment about David Watson:

A city-wide mission requires the mobilisation of the resources of a high percentage of the city's churches. If this is to happen then there has to be a high degree of trust and respect for the missioner. Very few British evangelists have been given that amount of trust.

In recent years it was beginning to be seen with the remarkable David Watson. An awesomely committed and extremely gracious man, he was able to draw support across a wide spectrum. However, his gentle but unhidden advocacy of charismatic renewal did not please some who would normally support evangelistic enterprises, and his openness to participation alongside Roman Catholics disturbed others.

We shall never know whether David would have graduated to leading ever larger missions and projects. He died when one felt there was more land to be possessed, and many of us still find difficulty in understanding why the Lord took such a gifted and lovely man so early in his life.[13]

Gavin Reid also asks (and answers) the question, 'Why isn't there a British Billy Graham?' He points out that because there are few halls in Britain seating more than 2,000 people, very few British evangelists have much experience of addressing crowds of 5,000, 10,000, or more. Gavin Reid gives three reasons why Billy Graham was felt to be the right person to lead Mission England in 1984:

1 He would attract far more media attention than any British evangelist.
2 He was likely to command more respect across all the Christian traditions than any British evangelist.
3 He was much the most experienced evangelist in the world for a large campaign.

Usually, in Britain, great effort is made to find a speaker who will not offend, and thus too many British preachers are so over-awed by the prospect of speaking for the churches to the churches that they reduce their content so as not to arouse abuse or cause division. Thereby, they risk becoming bland and innocuous. Not many are experienced in addressing large gatherings with inspiring messages, for so much of their regular ministry is given up to outlining theological or even political opinions carefully. Only a handful of Anglican evangelists spring to mind. It is characteristic of the British churches that they have failed to make adequate use of the most able and eloquent of their ministers, John Stott, giving him no role of leadership, no commission to speak or teach, no place of honour or distinction. Whether or not he wanted such a role, the churches should have insisted. Like John Wesley before him, he seems to have said, 'The world is my parish' and made his mark overseas more indelibly than at home.

Gavin Reid also comments on the problems of what he calls 'two agenda evangelism' – evangelism and renewal; though with David Watson 'three agenda' – evangelism, renewal and reconciliation (see Chapter 19) – would be more accurate:

A factor that has inhibited the rise of British evangelists capable of leading large events is the average seating capacity of the average town or city centre auditorium. This means that our biggest meetings are still fairly small – but the side-effects of these limitations are more subtle and far-reaching. When an evangelist comes to lead a mission in a 1,000 or 2,000-seater hall the problem is not how to get 'bottoms on seats'. The problem is how to keep the wrong bottoms off the seats. The local Christian community can usually fill such a venue night after night without much serious attempt to draw in the unbeliever or seeker. In other words, British evangelists are far too often preaching to the converted.

This leads to some undesirable consequences. First, the evangelist finds himself compelled to carry *two* agendas. He has his natural agenda to want to speak to the unconverted, but he feels he cannot overlook the fact that most of his hearers have other needs. Inevitably, therefore, he finds himself engaging in a teaching or renewal ministry. Equally inevitably, the desires and preferences of the majority in front of him tend to dictate the terms with regard to the nature of the meeting. Very easily we end up with evangelists presiding over jamborees for Christians.[14]

David's concern to spread the message of renewal as well as to preach the gospel certainly did mean that there was a high percentage of Christians at those meetings which were advertised as 'Celebrations' or 'Festivals'. As often happened with the Guest Services in York, Christians from a wide area would flock in to hear David and share in the joyful worship which they knew they would experience. Many were undoubtedly blessed through these gatherings, and returned to their own churches with a renewed zeal to serve Christ and to share the 'good news'. But there were uncommitted people at these meetings too and a surprisingly large number of these found a faith in Christ for the first time.

There is no doubt in many people's minds that David Watson has been the outstanding British evangelist of recent years – some have even likened him to John Wesley. Michael Green has said that, 'throughout the English speaking world he has had an impact both as an evangelist and teacher second only to Billy Graham'. Andrew Cornes has said: 'He was an extremely good communicator. He is the evangelist I admire most and whose style I appreciate the most. One of the greatest strengths was the conciseness of phrase he used, particularly when time was short. There was also the note of God's judgement – a theme many contemporary evangelists shy away from.'

If submission to the Holy Spirit was the real secret of David's success, and his immense dedication to the hard work of prayerful, Scripture-based preparation was his method of practising this, his command of the gospel itself was essential to his evangelistic ministry. A prayerful reading of the Bible convinced David that it contained a clear and consistent message which was truly life changing. God, separated from man by his rebellious choice, was always seeking to win him back into fellowship. To this end, he had come himself, in the person of his Son Jesus, to reveal himself to man and to redeem man to himself by the bloody sacrifice of the cross.

He was now offering free and full forgiveness and reinstatement to sonship to those who would accept it and not try to earn it. Central to this, the means by which it was provided and the guarantee of its efficacy, is the cross, vindicated by the resurrection and applied by the power of the Holy Spirit.

The 'good news' of this unspeakable gift is surely worth preaching.

19

Reconciliation in Ireland

BY NOW, RECONCILIATION WITHIN the Body of Christ had become an important part of David's message. And yet it was a lesson which he himself had had to learn over a number of years, particularly as he ministered in the Province of Northern Ireland. In common with most evangelicals, he had been taught that the Roman Catholic Church was an 'apostate church', and as such he had had very little contact with it during his early missions. This was certainly the case when, in 1969, he had conducted university missions in both Londonderry and in Belfast, and in the following year when he was invited to lead a United Mission in Holywood, Belfast.

David's friend and confidant in Cambridge, Dr Basil Atkinson, had held strongly anti-Roman views and at the time David had no reason to disagree. He had been rather surprised when Basil once asked him, 'Do you think it is possible for Roman Catholic nuns to be saved?' 'Why do you ask?' enquired David. 'Because I have just met two nuns who seemed to be radiant for Jesus. It seemed impossible, and yet it was true!' Over the years, David himself encountered many Catholics who seemed to have a genuine personal relationship with Jesus, but he still did not find it easy to explain how members of an 'heretical' church had come to such a position.

David's opinions about Roman Catholics can easily be misunderstood. In Chapter 10 of *You Are My God*, entitled 'Widening Vision', he sets out what may be thought to be the general view of evangelicals on this subject, summing up: 'My "anti-Rome" attitude was almost akin to that of the most extreme Protestants in Northern Ireland, although I was less vocal about it.'[1] It is hard to believe that this is really accurate. It is certainly true that most of those who belonged as firmly within the evangelical tradition as David did were severely confined by the centuries of anti-Catholic theology and propaganda to largely negative convictions. The Ulster Protestants, the most hardened and convinced in their attitudes, were confirmed in their position by a long history of violent conflict and cruel injustices on both sides. Those who are critical of the Protestants do well to remember the degree to which the Catholics also contributed to the general level of hatred and horrible violence. Neither side is free from blood guilt, and both are surely wrong to try to justify either their attitudes or their actions as stemming from a supposed loyalty to Jesus of Nazareth.

Within Northern Ireland, on both sides of the divide, one can find the worst sort of Christian bigotry. The prejudices inherent in the differences between the two traditions undoubtedly present the individual Christian with great difficulties. As prejudice becomes entrenched with the passage of time and the incidence of bitterness, so the Christian can become infected by similar attitudes; and Christian faith is infused and distorted by the totally alien attitude of hatred. Theological differences, whether large or small, are amplified and emphasised by cultural demands to build the dividing wall ever higher. Unfortunately, similar attitudes (though not actions) were present in the differences between Catholics and Protestants outside Ireland. So the young David Watson, enthusiastically learning the evangelical doctrines, was encouraged to find the Catholic dogmas not only inconsistent with his opinions, but actually contrary and opposed to them.

The evangelical emphasis upon 'the inwardness of true religion' rejected the systematic sacramentalism of the Catholics. This was compounded within the Anglican Church by the gulf which was dug ever deeper between the two parties by the rampant dominance of the Tractarians (the Anglo-Catholics) in the first half of the twentieth century in England, and the backs-to-the-wall, minority defensiveness of the evangelicals. That the gulf became a chasm was due especially to the lack of much contact between the evangelicals and the Roman Catholics. Christians in England in the final thirty years of the twentieth century are liable to overlook the extraordinary change which took place when Pope John XXIII opened wide the doors to ecumenical activity by encouraging Roman Catholics to attend Protestant services and celebrations, to share in local fellowship with Protestant ministers, and to contribute positively to discussion at all levels. Not all differences were swept away, of course, but at least evangelical clergy could now meet their opposite numbers. Thus, opportunity was given for consideration of those beliefs which were shared by both, rather than the previous embargo which only encouraged mistrust and misunderstanding.

In *You Are My God* David is putting the worst interpretation upon his opinions about Roman Catholics in order, no doubt, to sharpen the contrast with what he was to learn. But there is no evidence that he ever preached against them, or paid any serious attention to them and their beliefs. Probably, like many Anglicans, he hardly ever met any Roman Catholic priests and certainly never entered into any meaningful discussion with them. He would simply have concluded that since they did not share his evangelical faith, they did not merit any in-depth consideration. He would have been much more directly concerned by the dominance of the Anglo-Catholics and the liberal theologians. But David was not a controversialist and these sort of issues played little part in his thinking, which was almost always positive. As an evangelist, his primary concern was 'good news'.

In 1971, David was invited to be one of the speakers at the International Fountain Trust Conference at Guildford. He was a little startled to find that not only would there be quite a number of Roman Catholics attending the conference, but also that one of the other main speakers, Kevin Ranaghan, was a leading Catholic charismatic. He wondered whether his appearance on the same platform as a Roman Catholic might undermine his credibility as an evangelist in evangelical circles in Britain but, after praying about it, he felt it right to accept the invitation.

During the conference he was surprised to discover what God was doing in parts of the Roman Catholic Church. He took the opportunity to discuss matters of doctrine with some of the leaders in the Catholic charismatic renewal, and found that they adopted a very biblical position. There was little difference between their understanding of the essential elements of the gospel and his own. Many of the major differences of opinion which he had expected to find quite simply were not there. The problems were sometimes a question of semantics and emphasis, and the areas of agreement far bigger than the areas of difference. In the St Cuthbert's Newsletter for August 1971, David recorded his impressions of that conference:

There was an overwhelming atmosphere of love and worship. The barriers of denomination were broken down, and there was a spontaneous desire to praise and worship the Lord. There was an astonishing agreement as to the truth of the Gospel. But of course, the Holy Spirit is the Spirit of Truth, and I found to my joy that these Catholic Pentecostals were Christ-centred and Cross-centred, with a great dependence on the authority of the Bible. We had, somewhat to my surprise, the closest fellowship in the Lord, based firmly on his Word as well as on a common experience of his love.

Although David welcomed the renewing work of the Holy Spirit in the Roman Catholic Church, he found it difficult to understand why these renewed Catholics stayed in what he saw as a basically corrupt church. As he thought and prayed about this paradox, David heard God speaking to him: 'David, I'm not first and foremost concerned about your convictions, but I am concerned about your attitudes. And your attitudes towards those with whom you do not agree are all wrong. First get your attitudes right, then we can talk about your convictions.' He realised that the Roman Catholics he had met showed him far more Christian love and acceptance than he had shown them. He repented of his negative and critical attitudes, his spiritual arrogance and his lack of love towards other professing Christians with whom he did not fully agree. As he prayed, God gave him a new love for Roman Catholics, as well as for other non-evangelicals. During the next year or two, he developed a close relationship with Monsignor Michael Buckley in Leeds, and later took part with him and Mairead Corrigan in one of the Peace Marches for Northern Ireland.

David saw very clearly that the renewal of the Church in Ireland, both Protestant and Catholic, bringing Christians together in a fellowship of unity and love, was the best if not the only way of ending the sectarian hatred. He was not alone in this belief. The Christian Renewal Centre at Rostrevor, founded by the Rev. Cecil Kerr, the Corymeela Ecumenical Community, and a number of local groups under the umbrella of the Protestant and Catholic Encounter, were already seeking to bring reconciliation between the communities in Ulster.

Bishop George Quin of the Diocese of Down and Dromore in the Church of Ireland, a diocese which includes part of the city of Belfast and the whole of County Down to the border with the Republic, had called his diocese to a Campaign of Renewal, searching for a revitalisation of the whole life of the local church. In the early 1970s Bishop Cuthbert Bardsley and some of his diocesan mission team from Coventry had paid several visits to the Diocese of Down and Dromore, and several groups of clergy from Ireland had visited Coventry for periods of 'in-service' training.

By 1974, Bishop Quin and his Diocesan Missioner, Canon William Neely, sensed the need for some fresh input into the diocese. They had heard that there was some interesting post-ordination training going on in the dioceses of Durham and York, and Canon Neely went to investigate. While in York he met Archdeacon Leslie Stanbridge, who suggested that he should meet David Watson. A meeting was arranged and Canon Neely was impressed by what he saw and heard, and by the theological basis for David's approach to ministry. He invited David to visit Down and Dromore and speak about his work in York and the lessons to be learned by others. David instead suggested that Canon Neely should bring some of his clergy and laity to York, so that they could see and experience the life of St Michael's for themselves. A group of thirty-nine people, mostly lay but including four clergy, came to York for a weekend just after Easter 1975. Canon Brian Mayne recalls the significance of the visit:

That weekend from Saturday lunchtime to after breakfast on Monday had a far reaching effect on the majority of the party and ultimately on the life of the diocese. For most, it was the first experience of the worship life of a parish in renewal. Members of the party found their faith coming alive in a new way as they encountered living worship in the witness of sensitive hosts.

Several other groups of clergy and lay people from the Diocese of Down and Dromore came to York during the next few months. The impact of these visits on the Church of Ireland gradually spread to other Protestant churches in Ulster, and early in 1976 a group of seven Presbyterian ministers stayed for a few days at St Michael-le-Belfrey. Eventually Bishop Quin invited David to bring a team to launch Mission '77, a diocesan mission of renewal, during the week leading up to the start of Lent.

David was already looking forward to his more direct involvement in Ireland during Mission '77 when he received an invitation for him and Anne to attend the Third National Conference on Charismatic Renewal in Dublin in September 1976. David was asked to give the opening keynote address. The conference was held at the Royal Dublin Society Showground, and was attended by about 6,000 people, of whom 5,000 were Roman Catholics. David's address was on the text 'Blessed are the Peacemakers'. He reminded his hearers that the cross of Christ, the symbol of the Christian faith, is at the heart of the gospel. Its vertical bar speaks of how God in Christ reconciles us to himself, while the horizontal bar shows us that, in that very act of reconciliation, we are also reconciled with one another.

On the Saturday evening of the conference, there was a moving Service of Reconciliation led by a group of Catholic and Protestant church leaders. From an exposition of Ephesians 2 they saw that the cause of divisions in church life, as in home life and society in general, is always human sin. They were reminded that the only place for reconciliation is at the foot of the cross, to which all come, not as Protestants or Roman Catholics, but as sinners. They were urged to accept one another as brothers and sisters in the Lord, and to ask for forgiveness for anything they might have said or done which had grieved the Holy Spirit. David found himself surrounded by a crowd of nuns and priests wanting to ask for his forgiveness, as a representative Protestant, for their past attitudes; and he, in turn, had to ask their forgiveness for his own critical spirit. As they embraced one another, David knew that the message of reconciliation had to be a central part of his own ministry.

In the first instance, David had been called to evangelism and had practised this as hard as he could. To this work he had learned to add renewal, which he found to be the key to unlocking the energies of the Church. Now in Ireland he found himself confronted by a third vocation. Whereas the word of God revealed that there is but one Church, the eye of man could clearly see many. The Spirit indwelt every Christian who had found life in Christ and yet some of them were so bitterly divided from each other that the life of the Spirit was being quenched within them. Cultural differences were not unacceptable and even theological differences could be tolerated, but how could complete rejection and even hatred be allowed to remain among the children of a loving God? If they could not agree, so be it, but they must surely accept each other with attitudes of love. This must be the natural development of renewal, that Christians should be reconciled by the Spirit of unity whom the Lord had sent into their hearts. There did not seem to David, then or later, to be any way for reconciliation between Christians to be achieved other than by the power of the Spirit. From this time forward, evangelism and renewal was bracketed with reconciliation as the threefold aim of his ministry.

It was at the Nottingham Evangelical Anglican Conference in 1977 that David produced his most forthright comment on the disunity within the Church, which he was coming to see as so unbiblical:

In many ways, the Reformation was one of the greatest tragedies that ever happened to the Church. Martin Luther . . . never wanted to split the Church, simply to reform it. We no doubt glory in the biblical truths that were rediscovered at the Reformation (as I certainly do) but from the Reformation onwards the Body of Christ in the world has been torn from limb to limb into hundreds of separate pieces.[2]

To a 'party rally', even in the sober context of a Bible Reading on the mission of the Church, this was a foolhardy thing to say. The lions snarled at Daniel hungrily, at the time and for years to come. Nevertheless, it was a courageous attempt to make a point which David knew would be unpopular, but which needed to be made because he saw it as part of the biblical revelation. He was not denying the great benefits of the Reformation, and he was not blind to the fact that upheavals within society usually produce fractures in the structure. Nevertheless, the New Testament only knows one Church. It was unity, not truth, to which he was addressing himself. Reformation truth was as precious to him as to anyone at the conference. But he could not see that a licence existed for Christians to separate themselves from their brethren simply on the grounds of disagreement. The incident gave expression to a major development in his thinking.

He looked upon the ecumenical movement for reconciliation between churches at denominational level with mixed emotions. On the one hand, he welcomed everything that was done to bring about unity between Christians and believed this to be of very great importance in the Church. But on the other hand, he could see no value in focusing upon the differences between Christians rather than upon their unity in Christ, which needed to be demonstrated continually. At the end of the day, disagreement did not matter as much as disunity. It could even be healthy to have a whole spectrum of ecclesiastical practices so that every temperament and culture could be accommodated. What mattered were the relationships between the groups and this could only be changed for the better if the actual people, rather than the denominations, loved one another. David preached what he believed, but he did not waste time arguing that others were wrong because they did not fit into his pattern. The obsession to be right found no place in his philosophy and its absence did not weaken the force and authority of his gospel. Reconciliation as he pleaded for it was of relationships and attitudes. It was these which could be radically altered by the Spirit's power as the Christian draws ever closer to Christ. It was only from these reconciled relationships that any hope could be held out for a 'sea change' in the denominations. What is more, to him the broken, bitter relationships of the Church presented a scandal of disunity to the world.

Canon Jim Mehaffey (subsequently Bishop of Derry and Raphoe) succeeded Canon William Neely as Diocesan Missioner in the Diocese of Down and Dromore, and was responsible for the final arrangements for Mission '77. He asked David to visit Belfast for a preparatory meeting with the diocesan clergy and some representative laity in the autumn of 1976. Some of the clergy were still suspicious, having heard rumours that David was not only a charismatic but also an evangelical with rather fundamentalist views. However, most of them were reassured by his theological method and personal qualities, and were impressed with his concern to familiarise himself as far as possible with the complex problems of Northern Ireland, so that he could minister more effectively in the situation.

The opening meetings of Mission '77 took place in the Shankill Church in Lurgan, the largest church in the diocese. It was a convenient centre for people based in the western and southern parts of the diocese who were reluctant to travel the forty or so miles into Belfast, especially at night. The Church of Ireland was not used to the drama and artistic innovations that David's team represented and the Rector of the Shankill Church admitted that 'this sort of thing is new to us'. Bishop George Quin's faith in the advice of William Neely and Jim Mehaffey was rewarded when the church, seating nearly 1,500 people, was full for the opening meeting. John Scott reported the event in the *Yorkshire Post*:

The congregation sang traditional hymns and eyed the row of microphones in the choir. The much heralded dancing reduced the singing to a whisper as heads craned to watch. There were no protests and no walkouts. The mime plays were watched in rapt silence. 'Receptive but subdued', was how one of the group summed it up afterwards. The next night more than 1,000 people again packed the church, despite pouring rain and the sight of an Army patrol edging its way through the shopping centre. This time, there was a younger element in the congregation. The word had spread. More people joined in the singing, and the atmosphere changed dramatically.[3]

The climax was reached during five nights at St Anne's Cathedral, Belfast. Supervised car parking was arranged, encouraging many people to bring their cars into the city in the evening for the first time in seven years. The cathedral, seating some 2,000 people including a number of Roman Catholics, was full each night. David told them, 'There are no Roman Catholics in heaven, there are no Anglicans in heaven. There are no Baptists or Presbyterians. Only sinners saved by Jesus Christ on the cross.'

In the congregation in St Anne's Cathedral on Ash Wednesday evening was the Assistant Minister of First Carrickfergus Presbyterian Church, the Rev. David Armstrong. Although he was unhappy over David Watson's reported attitude towards Roman Catholics, and his beliefs concerning the gifts of the Holy Spirit, he was pleased that the gospel was to be preached in Belfast and was curious to hear this evangelist for himself. He came expecting to hear some heretical views, but instead found himself mightily impressed.

David announced that his subject was the Holy Spirit and that he would be speaking primarily to those who were already Christians. He reminded them that there had been 120 people in the Upper Room on the Day of Pentecost. When the Holy Spirit had come upon them they had gone out and turned the world upside down. 'Are there not more than one hundred and twenty Christians in Belfast?' he asked. 'Then why are you not having more impact in Ulster? Where is the evidence for the power of the Holy Spirit? Why is the fruit of the Spirit not seen in your lives? Where is the love in Ulster Christianity? Where is the joy, the desire for peace, the gentleness?' David picked up a glove and a book to demonstrate how the Holy Spirit can transform a person's life. 'Supposing I pick up a book in one hand, and place this glove over the other wrist. Then I say to the glove, "Pick up the book!" It can't do it. So I give the glove an example of what I want it to do; I pick up the book with my other hand. But the glove still cannot do it. It needs a living power inside and so do we. But look what happens if the hand is only half inside the glove. The glove can do some things, but it cannot do all the things I want it to. Sometimes we let God's Spirit into our lives, but only so far. We need to let his Holy Spirit come and fill every part of our lives so that we can work as God wants us to. Then maybe we will be like the first century disciples and turn Ulster upside down!'

David Armstrong and his wife were among many in that congregation who were convicted by David's words, and who responded to his prayer of commitment at the close of his address. The lasting impact of Mission '77 can be seen in a dramatic increase in the numbers offering for ordination. In 1983, three-quarters of those in theological colleges in Ireland came from the Diocese of Down and Dromore.

David Armstrong, whose book *A Road Too Wide*[4] describes how his own ministry was transformed as a result of that service in St Anne's Cathedral, visited York a few months later. Soon afterwards, with the full support of the minister and elders, David and his team were invited to lead a 'Festival of Light and Love' in First Presbyterian Church, Carrickfergus in November 1977. Once again, David's ministry was primarily directed towards Christians with a message of renewal and reconciliation. It was not long before David Armstrong started holding regular meetings with a group of ministers from other denominations, including a Catholic priest, to pray for the renewing work of the Holy Spirit in Ireland.

During the mission in Carrickfergus, David Armstrong was able to get David Watson and his team into the Crumlin Road Prison to speak to some of the terrorists held there. Knowing that prisoners were not used to listening to sermons, David felt it important that his team be utilised to the full. They were warned: 'You will probably see more murderers in the next half-hour than in the whole of the rest of your life.' The team were not unnaturally a bit apprehensive. Nevertheless, many of the prisoners were moved by the message which they conveyed. When David led a short prayer of commitment at the end there was almost complete silence, and several professed conversion. One of the prisoners later told the prison Chaplain, 'For the first time in my life I feel free.' David received other letters from prisoners saying that it was the vitality of the whole team, rather than anything he had said on his own, which convinced them of the truth of the gospel.

After the Carrickfergus mission, David and his team conducted a one-night Festival of Praise in Belfast Cathedral, which was even fuller than it had been during the Mission '77 meetings. On this occasion, the cathedral was picketed by members of the Rev. Ian Paisley's Free Presbyterian Church. They handed out leaflets protesting against David Watson's attitude towards Roman Catholics, and then gathered on the steps of the cathedral to sing a hymn in protest.

Each of David's missions, in different parts of Ulster, seemed to have a spin-off on other churches in the region, both Church of Ireland and Presbyterian. There are now several churches actively involved in seeking reconciliation with Roman Catholics, often in the face of considerable opposition. David Armstrong eventually found himself in serious conflict with the elders at his new church in Limavady. It was too much for some of them when he visited the neighbouring Roman Catholic church on Christmas Day to bring greetings, and invited the Catholic priest to come into the Presbyterian church. There were warnings of pickets by the Free Presbyterians, and he received threats for the safety of his wife and family. Eventually, lacking support from his elders, he felt that he had no option but to resign and leave Ulster. He has subsequently been ordained into the Church of England and begun a new ministry. Despite opposition from some quarters, many others have been able to carry on building bridges of friendship across the Protestant–Catholic divide in Ulster, and a quiet work is still going on.

David's last visit to Ireland and, in fact, the last major engagement which he was able to carry out was in November 1983. Arrangements for the visit were made by the Rev. Cecil Kerr, leader of the Rostrevor Christian Renewal Centre, and included meetings in Belfast and in Dublin. The visit took place just a week after a group of IRA gunmen had attacked a little Pentecostal church on the border, killing three of the elders and seriously injuring many others. The need for healing and reconciliation was never greater. Some 2,000 people of all denominations filled Church House in Belfast and were challenged afresh to love and to forgive.

In Dublin, David and the team were scheduled to take part in a meeting in Sallynoggin Roman Catholic Church, which was due to start at 8.15 p.m. People started arriving from 7 p.m. to be sure of getting a seat and found another service, the usual Friday evening Mass, already in progress. The priest watched as his congregation steadily grew, a motley collection of Catholics and non-Catholics joining in whatever parts of the service seemed familiar to them. This rather accidental togetherness is perhaps symbolic of what reconciliation in Ireland is all about. It mattered not then who was from which denomination, nor whether the church building was Catholic or Protestant, nor even that much of the service was unfamiliar to many. They were there together and they had come to praise God.

20

Travels Worldwide

THROUGH HIS EVANGELISTIC MINISTRY in Britain, through his writings, through publicity in the Christian press, and increasingly through the Renewal Weeks in York, David Watson had become a respected name in the worldwide Christian Church. As a result, invitations to lead missions or festivals came in from far as well as near. He was even invited to many places where his convictions were not exactly shared simply because they recognised that here was someone who had 'made Christianity work' in his own church, and who spoke with love and grace.

In 1979 David started to accept regular invitations from outside the British Isles. By this time, Graham Cray had relieved him of the wider responsibility for the parish and he was free to devote even more of his time to travelling. His team was by now an integral part of his activities and a group of five or six always travelled with him. He asked the team members to commit themselves to him for at least twelve months, to adopt a simple lifestyle (generally living in one of the St Michael's households), and to be prepared for a demanding schedule of travelling. Above all else, he wanted them to demonstrate the love of God by practical love and support for each other. David set out his reasons for working with a team:

a The reality of Christ can often be seen best in our corporate life, rather than in our separate contributions.
b Renewal affects the body of Christ, not just the individual. A small team is a picture of that body, sharing gifts, ministries and lives together.
c Worship is our foremost priority, and I want to set evangelism firmly in the context of worship. In this way we may be better able to hear God's word.
d I have seen the great impact of drama – enacted parables – to reach people for Christ. The team must be able to do that in many different situations, from churches to streets, schools to prisons, and theatres to concert halls.

The originally established team, which remained with David for some time, included Paul Burbridge, Murray and Julie Watts, Liz Attwood, Sue Hope, Mike Dunn and Judith Stevenson. Phil and Joy Potter joined at a later stage and Gale McBride while the team was on tour in New Zealand, her home country. Andrew Maries was a regular member for a time. Latterly, the team changed fairly frequently as the old hands moved on to other work and newcomers came to join.

Once it was known that David was available invitations came in at an amazing rate. Douglas Greenfield, who administered the whole pro- gramme, says that at one stage they were having to turn down over 70 per cent of the invitations which they received. Nevertheless, during the six- year period from 1978 to 1983, David and the team conducted no less than fifty-eight missions on five continents. Each mission or festival was preceded by careful on-the-spot research by Douglas. Three criteria were applied to help decide whether to accept an invitation: Is there a 'holy discontent' with things spiritual in the area and a genuine desire for change? Is there any evidence, however small, that God has already begun to work so that there would be something upon which to build? Are there those who are willing to pay the price for spiritual renewal, for the continuing effect of any ministry would depend upon dedicated leader- ship?

One of the first overseas missions, in May 1979, was to South Africa. David took with him five of his team, including Paul Burbridge and Murray Watts. Before they arrived, David took considerable care to ensure that everyone understood the racial and socio-political situation, explaining that they would see signs saying 'Whites only', or 'Non-Whites', in both English and Afrikaans, on toilets, buses and many other public places. When the team arrived at Jan Smuts Airport, Murray Watts was so con- fused by all the signs that he went into the ladies' cloakroom. The original invitation to visit South Africa had come from the Christian groups in the Universities of Durban and Cape Town, at each of which David was asked to lead a four-day mission. But in view of the expense of six air fares, it was proposed to hold city-wide missions in both places, so that local churches could share in the costs.

The Durban University Mission had been well planned and prepared for by the Christian students and, although the main meetings had to be held at lunchtime, they were well attended and David felt that it had proved very worthwhile. Many students responded to the challenge of the gospel, with its implications for the situation in South Africa. However, the Durban City Mission was not a great success, and in *You Are My God* David went so far as to describe it as 'frankly a disaster'.[1] The numbers at the evening meetings were very disappointing, due to a lack of commit- ment to the event by the churches in the city. Peter Lee, now Bishop of the Diocese of Christ the King, South Africa, who had himself been greatly helped by David's ministry prior to and after his ordination, and who helped organise the event, writes:

In my simplicity, I came in with enthusiasm to try to draw churches together, but there was neither the time nor the close relationships in the City of Durban at that time to make a really major event possible. In retrospect, we would have been better to take one of the big Anglican churches and run something for them at minimal expense and probably substantial effect in the life of the Diocese of Natal. Instead, we took a tennis stadium and had relatively small meetings. The Diocese contributed handsomely financially and many good things did happen, perhaps especially in some of the local churches. Many overseas speakers do not take the trouble to go to churches in the more deprived communities – certainly they did not then. David [went] to Anglican churches in two black townships on the edge of Durban, to one so-called coloured community, and to an ecumenical event in the Indian community which was very poorly attended, but [which brought] great encouragement to a group of Christian leaders there. It also meant being entertained to one of the hottest curry suppers David and his team ever met on their worldwide travels!

Peter Lee was impressed, as many others have been, by David's preparation for each event:

It was extraordinary to see him go off to his room for hours at a time, day after day, to put together each particular sermon with meticulous care and prayer. He very rarely – as he could have done – scribbled a couple of words on the back of an envelope and survived by experience and the stock of stories at his command. He carried his entire system of quotations in his luggage on pieces of paper which could be clipped into his preaching book at the appropriate place. I asked him how he collected this enormous mass of material and he replied, 'I work pretty hard at it all the time.' What he actually did was to cull quotations from books he was reading and to make a note of anything he saw as he went around – an incident, an advertisement, or a detail – and his secretary at home would then put these on to the right pieces of paper and cross reference the whole lot. He was something of a perfectionist as a speaker and the world benefited from it.

At Durban, as on all his travels, there were seminars for ministers during the daytime. During these seminars, David used an overhead projector with diagrammatic material which was later incorporated into the Study Guide to *I Believe in the Church*. Peter Lee felt that these seminars 'left a permanent mark', and David himself, in a letter to Peter, commented that 'the ministers' seminars seemed first-rate. I sense that a lot of good has come, or will come, out of the mission.' David also spoke at a businessmen's lunch but he left Durban in a state of deep depression as a result of the poor attendance at the main meetings there. It had been arranged for the team to travel to Cape Town by road on the magnificent scenic route through the Drakensberg mountains, but David sat with his head in his hands for most of the journey, neither looking at the scenery nor talking to anyone. It had quite a demoralising effect on the rest of the team.

These bouts of depression on his overseas tours (and, indeed, when on tour in Britain) were not infrequent. Douglas Greenfield has commented:

> The depressions were sometimes fearful to behold, and at times no-one could really reach him. This would rub off on to the team, and the fact that they worked through such times, were not destroyed, and kept the ministry going, speaks highly of their spiritual quality both as individuals and as a team. The Lord always undertook for these occasions, but little did observers know the agony we were sometimes passing through on our tours.[2]

David was well aware of the effect on other people of his depression but there seemed little that he could do about it. He wrote:

> The depth of our relationships in Christ depends on the degree to which we are willing to share our lives openly with one another, and such openness brings pain as well as joy. For example, sometimes I battle with depression. I never know all the reasons for this 'dark pit', as it seems to me. Some of it may be hurt pride. Sometimes it is obviously exhaustion, physical, mental, emotional and spiritual. At times, when I am tired and strained, I can get angry over an incident that may be quite trivial in itself; and then I get angry with myself for getting angry. As I suppress both forms of anger, depression is the result. I am then even more difficult to live with than usual. I do not want people to get too near to me, but I hope very much that that they will not go too far away either.[3]

For the two missions in Cape Town, in the University and in the City, David worked with a black evangelist from Soweto called Caesar Molebatsi, who gave a very moving testimony of God's work in his life. There were good numbers at both these missions and David felt that the main thrust of his ministry should be along the lines of renewal and unity, rather than evangelism. He was aware of the need for a deep healing of relationships between Christians in South Africa, who were divided on theological and cultural grounds and therefore were not bringing a united witness to bear on the problems of their country. Writing to his prayer supporters after he had returned home, David described the visit to South Africa as 'a tremendously stimulating time for us, [with] some evidence that God had used us to bring his love and healing to others'.

In fact some of the participants at Cape Town were disappointed at the mission held in the city. This may have been because it came at the end of an exacting tour when both David and his team were exhausted. Possibly something a little different was expected of them from what they attempted. David's shift of emphasis from evangelism to renewal and unity may have affected what happened. Perhaps understandably, South Africans are sensitive about the many visitors who come with confident instructions on how the Christian message should be applied to their national problems. They are not so receptive as they might be if the mission were to centre more on Christ and less on them. It is hard to imagine David committing this error, but it is also hard to understand why his mission was less than successful. Reconciliation in South Africa is a very hot potato and, if attempted by an outsider, should be handled with extreme care.

Although David valued the tremendous support which he received from his team, and at their daily team meetings would always listen to their views and be open to their suggestions, he was not a good pastor to them. He spent a lot of time on his own, in prayer and preparation, and did not adequately get alongside the individual team members so as to be aware of their needs and feelings. Phil Potter, who was the worship leader in David's team for several years, often had to undertake a pastoral responsibility for others in the team. Sometimes too, David seemed to have favourites whom he would notice and commend, leaving others feeling that they had been overlooked or neglected.

Yet there were times on their travels when he was totally relaxed and the life and soul of the party. On one occasion, when they were all waiting for their flight home at Toronto Airport after a programme in Canada, David suddenly dug into one of the luggage bags, found a peroxide blonde wig (one of the team's drama props) and put it on. He then proceeded to imitate a pop star, strumming the rhythm on an imaginary guitar, giggling with laughter as he did so, to the delight of the rest of the party and the amazement of the onlookers. On a day off in California when the team visited Disneyland, David's whoops and shrieks of delight as he rode in a roller-coaster could be heard for miles around. On another occasion in Banff, the dare-devil schoolboy in him came to the surface, and he insisted on walking along the top of a narrow wall with a sheer drop on the far side. Sometimes, in the evening of a day off, David and the team would go out to dinner together in a restaurant, and often David would unwind and regale them all with stories of his army days. He was a good story-teller, especially of stories against himself. Once he asked the man who ran the St Michael's tape library what he thought of the sermon he had just preached. 'Not much,' he replied, 'but hang on a minute, I'll ask my wife.' He soon came back and announced, 'She didn't think much of it either!' He enjoyed telling them about the first talk he had ever given at Iwerne. Bash's immediate comment was, 'You said "er" eighty times!'

David taught much about the importance of relationships but he himself never found real life relationships easy, and he was very honest about his failings. Few of those who worked in his teams ever felt that they really knew or understood him. He set high standards for himself, and drove himself to the limit. He also expected high standards from those who worked with him, and would not accept anything less than their best. Those to whom he delegated responsibility for leading worship were hesitant about trying anything new in case he did not approve. He was very sparing in his words of encouragement and often they did not quite know what he felt. After working with him for several years, one team member was astonished when David told her, 'You are worth your weight in gold.'

He was always impatient to get on with the task ahead. When the team stopped at a motorway café for a break, it was a standing joke that before they had had time to stir their tea, David would be looking at his watch and warning them that it was time to move on. If he arranged to pick someone up at 7 a.m. to start off on the next stage of their travels, he would be sure to arrive at 6.50. Yet they loved him and worked with him on sacrificial terms for months on end, counting it a high privilege. He imparted to them great spiritual gifts and blessings and, in spite of the hardships, life was never dull.

The strain on David and Anne through these frequent and often long separations was considerable. It was never easy for Anne to see him going away on tour for several weeks knowing that, while she held the fort at home, she could not share his work and that others would provide the companionship which she had to forgo. David always tried to phone Anne at least once a week when he was overseas, and he made time to write to her two or three times a week, and to Fiona and Guy from time to time. Towards the end of each tour the girls in the team knew that they would be asked to help David choose suitable presents to take home to the family.

Nineteen-eighty was an exceptionally busy year for David and the team. In January, following a Festival of Praise in Rochdale, he set off on the 17th for three weeks in the USA and Canada. In mid-February he was in Wales for Festivals of Praise in Cardiff and Swansea, where there was also a Day for Local Church Renewal. Then there were two days in Liverpool, following up the earlier Merseyside Festival. At the end of the month he was leading a five-day mission in Bedford School, where over fifty boys came to Christ. In March he was back in Liverpool for a Festival of Praise, before giving a keynote address at an International Consultation on Simple Lifestyle. Then he re-joined the team at Rochdale for a six-day Festival, and a week later he was in Poole for two days to lead a Festival of Praise and some seminars in preparation for the City-wide Festival there later in the year.

After Easter, he attended part of a National Congress on Evangelism in Prestatyn, North Wales, and was back in York for the Renewal Week from 11 to 17 April. This was immediately followed by the Poole Festival (two weeks), and then two days in Cornwall to take part in the Centenary Celebrations at Truro Cathedral. Mid-May saw the Chelsea Festival, 'To London with Love', which included three evenings in the Royal Albert Hall. Then in early June, there was an eight-day Cambridge Festival, using a 3,000-seat marquee. Later in the month, after attending a Consultation on World Evangelization in Thailand, there were two days in Swansea for a Festival of Praise and a Day of Renewal. David and the team then took part in the week-long International Officers Christian Union Conference at Swanwick in Derbyshire.

In July there was a Festival of Praise at Sheffield, after which a month was set aside for a much-needed family holiday before setting out on a gruelling tour of New Zealand and Australia, which started on 27 August and did not finish until 3 November. Later in November, there was another Festival of Praise in Poole, the St Michael's Leaders' Weekend, and then the Sheffield City Mission for a week. It was a daunting itinerary for anyone, let alone a man who suffered from bronchial asthma and depression.

The visit to New Zealand was at the invitation of the New Zealand Church Missionary Society, who had asked David to speak at the CMS Spring School in Wellington, but the itinerary included many other events in Wellington, Auckland, Christchurch and Dunedin. The attendance at the 3½-day Spring School broke new records, with some 400 people attending the morning meetings and seminars, and up to 650 at the evening meetings. Always the team played their full part at each session. David's seminars were so well attended that they had to take the form of open lectures, and many of them had to be repeated. At the seminars, he made use of the overhead projector with clear diagrams to illustrate his message. These have since been used by one of the participants, Canon Ronald Taylor, for teaching a Pastors' Course in Tanzania.

Canon Taylor recalls the impact of that Spring School:

The fact that David brought a team with him and they supported one another in Christian love and prayer was evident to all. His use of skits and plays and modern dance was introduced sensitively so that even older, conservative people enjoyed the new approach. His explanation of how to use repetitive choruses for meditation was well received. The breadth of his ecumenical sympathies and his ability to relate well to Christians who did not share his evangelical or charismatic convictions meant that he had a more widely accepted ministry than many overseas visitors. He helped to bridge the gap between evangelicals and charismatics. His sensitivity and discernment in preferring not to use the phrase 'the Baptism of the Spirit' because it meant different things to different people helped many Christians from mainline churches to be more open to his teaching than they would otherwise have been.

One evening soon after joining the team Gale McBride, a former CMS missionary nurse from New Zealand, found herself in the room next door to David's in the Bible college where they were staying. At bedtime, she was intrigued to hear the sound of David worshipping the Lord and singing aloud in tongues. It helped her to realise how much worship meant to David, and that private worship had a place, as well as worship with others.

In Christchurch the big public square outside the cathedral was used to great effect. Dance and drama drew a crowd of about 1,000 people who listened attentively to David's address. The locals were made aware of the strategic significance of the site of their cathedral in the very centre of the city of Christchurch, and were introduced to a new concept of evangelism. The meetings in Auckland were particularly well attended, and even hastily arranged overflow halls themselves overflowed. People with little or no church connections came to the meetings, and many came to faith in Christ. The final Festival of Praise attracted over 6,000 people.

The visit to Australia took them to many different centres and involved long hours of travelling. They went to Brisbane, Launceston, Hobart, Melbourne, Sydney, Armidale, Tamworth and Canberra. They found tension between charismatics and evangelicals, and many Christians were suspicious of what they called 'American-style Pentecostalism', being fearful of fresh and unscriptural insights into the Holy Spirit's workings. Although some people travelled great distances to come to the meetings, attendances were generally smaller than in New Zealand. Nevertheless, the British style of David and his team, their informality and humour, and their emphasis on reconciliation were much respected. David was introduced at one meeting as 'the gentle mannered rector from England'. They found the situation especially tense in Sydney, a stronghold of Anglican evangelicalism. David led a crucial seminar for clergy, calling for repentance for any attitudes that destroy unity in Christ.

Mrs Mary Walters was one of a group of clergy and wives who attended the seminars in Sydney. She recalls 'the shock of sheer delight' when his team performed their 'Parable of the Good Punk Rocker' (based on the Good Samaritan), and she was delighted by David's 'educated British accent' as he answered questions from all round the chapel. 'He preceded every answer with "Thank you" and then gave his answer. It was so gracious – there was nothing of the "visiting overseas expert" about him. He was a marvellous teacher – refreshing and vigorous with a wealth of simple and dramatic illustrations.'

Exhaustion became a problem for all the team including David, and one night Joy Potter actually fell asleep on her feet while narrating a sketch. They discovered that the strain of the long tour and the constant fatigue made them rely more than ever on the Lord. It is through human weakness that divine strength is made perfect. However, that eleven-week tour convinced Douglas Greenfield and David himself that no future tour should exceed five weeks.

David spent a week in 1980 touring western Canada with Bob Roxburgh, then pastor of a church in Vancouver. They discussed with local church leaders their invitations for city-wide missions and clergy seminars in various centres the following year. Plans were drawn up, and a month was set aside from 23 April to 24 May 1981, with Bob Roxburgh doing most of the on-the-spot administration and making himself available to accompany David and the team on their Canadian itinerary. They were, in fact, back in Vancouver in January 1981, lecturing at Regent College and leading two big renewal rallies. From February until Easter, David and the team had their usual full programme of engagements in England and Wales, and at one of the team meetings, God gave them a picture of what he wanted to do through them in Canada. It would be like taking an orange to people who had never seen or tasted anything like it, peeling it and offering them its juice and sweetness. As they tasted it, people would take the seed of the orange and plant it to grow the fruit themselves.

They were joined for the tour not only by Bob Roxburgh but also by Ron Reed, a gifted Canadian actor, who quickly became part of the team and was a source of strength and encouragement to them. The first stop was Vancouver, from whence they went to Victoria on 26 April where, though numbers were small, the response was good. At Calgary from 29 April to 2 May there was healing of relationships among some Christians and a spirit of love and praise. They moved on to Edmonton from 3 to 6 May where they had some good workshops for leaders and a beautiful Communion Service. The visit to Saskatoon was the most difficult because of local apathy and because both David and Phil Potter had laryngitis. At Winnipeg from 14 to 23 May, the seminars were well attended and David's teaching on reconciliation in the Body of Christ was much appreciated. The tour had taught both the team and their Canadian hosts some valuable lessons. David also discovered that a dish-washer can fill a room with bubbles if ordinary washing-up liquid is used in it.

A number of Lutheran pastors from Scandinavia who had attended the Renewal Weeks in York invited David to bring his team to Sweden for the first time in 1982. Although this meant working with a translator, the message was effective and the visit began a steadily developing link between St Michael-le-Belfrey and churches in Scandinavia. On one occasion the Swedish interpreter, who had a reputation for being unable to tell stories correctly, totally missed the point when translating one of David's funny anecdotes. Many in the audience could, of course, understand English, and there had been quite a laugh when David told the story in English. When the translator put it in Swedish, there was a far greater laugh and David, not realising the translator had got it all wrong, said, 'It sounds better when he tells it.'

There was always a growing feeling of excitement as they started on the journey home. On one occasion the petrol gauge on their minibus was near the zero mark and they were still quite a few miles from York. David suggested that they should drive a bit faster to get home before the petrol ran out. But David was often too tired to share in the initial happiness of Anne, Fiona and Guy at having him home. It was not easy to switch from the 'family' of his team, with whom he had been living and sharing everything for several weeks, to renew normal responsibilities and relationships with his own natural family when he was still tense from the strain of his travels overseas.

There was something of an anti-climax too in returning to St Michael's. Though a warm welcome always awaited David and the team when they returned from their missions, everything seemed to be running so smoothly without him. With ever increasing demands for his ministry around the world, he slowly began to wonder whether he was really needed at York.

Fuller and Wimber

IN 1980 DAVID WATSON WAS INVITED for the first time to lecture at Fuller Theological Seminary, Pasadena, California. He led a two-week course on Church Renewal and Evangelism in the Doctor of Ministry post-graduate class for practising ministers. David lectured for six hours each day, covering subjects from the personal renewal of the pastor to the training of the laity for mission. He also undertook several preaching engagements beyond the college. The D.Min. course as a whole was designed to give those who had been in ministry for a number of years some further training and something to think about, thereby sending them back refreshed and invigorated into their ministry. It was therefore practical more than it was theological. As such, David enjoyed it all immensely and readily agreed to return the following year, bringing some of his team with him and extending his stay over a month to enable him also to lecture to the current students in the Master of Divinity class.

To say that David was well received would be something of an understatement. He would be on duty from six o'clock in the morning to midnight, mainly so as to be able to fit in the hundreds of students who wanted a private interview. Moreover, Dr Ray Anderson, Director of the D.Min. programme at Fuller, was greatly impressed with the way that David combined theological integrity with an emphasis upon the Spirit-filled life and Spirit-empowered ministry. In 1981, one of the visiting students was the Rev. Eddie Gibbs, an Englishman then on the staff of the Bible Society, but now himself Professor of Evangelism and Church Renewal at Fuller. He writes:

The American students loved David's accent and sense of humour. His humility created a great impression. I remember one frustrated student interjecting halfway through his course, 'We have sat here for over a week and you haven't yet mentioned your own church.' When they asked him about his salary there was a stunned silence when he replied that his clothes were second hand and he received three pounds sterling a week pocket money.

One of the students from his first course, Dr Gerald C. Freeman, comments on what it meant to him:

David did more for my life and ministry the time I spent at Fuller than any other professor I have sat under. He was so kind, sincere and compassionate and our whole class loved him. I was in a period of indecision in my life at that time, and I met with David, and his kind love and caring advice blessed my life. [He was] a brilliant theologian with a fantastic mind. Here in America there are hundreds of us who will forever be grateful for his life touching ours, if only for a brief moment.

Not surprisingly, David found the whole experience enormously challenging and stimulating and it fed his deep hunger for personal affirmation. More significantly though, he was greatly impressed with Fuller itself. It seemed to be a much better model for a theological training college than that found in England. It was more like a university, both in its size and its campus structure. The students, of which there were over a thousand, lived in off-campus accommodation, thus avoiding any sense of being incarcerated in a small college with a strict disciplinary code. It was non-denominational, although it was evangelical in nature, and it succeeded in combining a theological education with practical training. Visiting lecturers came frequently and from all over the world, especially Asia. Thereby it was open to new developments, such as David's own team which made a big impact and led to the formation of a home-grown group at Fuller.

Perhaps more than anything, David found that he greatly enjoyed the experience of training people for ministry, especially in such an appreciative atmosphere. Over the years he had dabbled a little in training, but it had usually been a 'side show' during a mission, or preparation of a group for a specific evangelistic occasion. Certainly he never lectured at an English theological college, which he found a little disappointing, but perhaps their style of training would not have suited David in any case. Fuller actually invited him to join the staff and he found this an attractive proposition, the more so as his roots in York were apparently being pulled up. However, he felt that his call was to be an evangelist, and especially in England, and he refused the offer. He knew also that such a move would have been difficult for Anne and the children. Nevertheless, he thought very seriously about the possibility of founding 'Fuller in London' and using it as a context in which to develop his training ministry. Had he lived, this would almost certainly have happened.

David's visit to Fuller became an annual event each January, and was the booking to which he looked forward with the greatest eagerness and which he enjoyed the most. Moreover, the experience at Fuller prepared him to conduct further courses on evangelism at Regent College, Vancouver, Canada. When David was taken seriously ill in early January 1983, within a very few days of his planned flight with his team to Fuller, David MacInnes and David Prior took his place at extremely short notice. Subsequently, the courses have continued under the leadership of David MacInnes and John Finney, still largely based on David's material.

On his visit to Fuller in 1981, David asked Eddie Gibbs to suggest where he might worship one Sunday. Eddie's advice was that, rather than go to one of the well-known churches in Southern California, David might visit a new church at Yorba Linda, in Orange County's Anaheim Hills. It was pastored by John Wimber, who until recently had been a member of the Church Growth faculty at Fuller. John's story is remarkable and, when he tells it, quite hilarious. From a poor family with absolutely no Christian background, in his youth he had been a member of a rock and roll group called The Righteous Brothers. They were not particularly righteous, and certainly not religious, but they were very successful. John's marriage to a girl called Carol suffered the usual problems of a rock and roll star, until they became Christians. In time John became an assistant pastor at a Quaker church, proving singularly effective in bringing in the people, and the church was soon crowded out with an exciting and excited cross-section of Californians. After a while Peter Wagner, Professor of Church Growth at Fuller, recruited John to be Associate Professor, and he began a rumbustious time touring the United States, developing a very remarkable teaching gift into a dramatically brilliant ministry.

Meanwhile Carol, now with four children, was living in Yorba Linda, Orange County, where she had become a member of a group of rather disillusioned Christians. Not knowing what else to do, they began to worship God in largely home made songs and the group began to grow. Carol, her sister Penny and Penny's husband, Bob Fulton, shared in the leadership. For a time they dabbled half-heartedly with Pentecostalism, but when the group grew to over 100 members they became desperate to find a future for it. Unitedly, the group asked John to come and be their pastor. Although at first reluctant, he eventually accepted the invitation, resigned from Fuller and hired a school gymnasium for the new church to use on Sundays. It was eventually named the Vineyard Christian Fellowship. Within four years, when David Watson came to them for the first time, it had more than 1,000 members. By 1983 it had over 4,000 and had sprouted a number of other congregations, mostly in the Los Angeles Basin. They moved to new rented facilities near Disneyland in Anaheim.

By any standards, it was a remarkable success story and David was very interested in seeing it for himself. Eddie offered to arrange for someone from the church to fetch David and to fix up accommodation for him. It was John Wimber himself who came. He describes their first meeting:

It was one of those encounters that God had fore-ordained. I remember standing at the door and waiting. I didn't know who David was or what he looked like. I just knew from the clerk at the desk that this was his room. I knocked at the door, he opened it, and the moment I saw him I knew I was going to love that man in the Lord. He had the kindest eyes of any man I had ever met. It took three sentences before I started kidding him, and four before I was brutally teasing him, and I think ten minutes before we were fast friends.

David came to the meeting 'dressed like Englishmen dress, full ensemble' in about 100 degrees Fahrenheit, 'sat through the entire service and loved every bit of it.'

Without question this meeting, and the relationship which sprang from it, were by divine appointment for the friendship became of immense value to David during the last three years of his life. Besides, no one would have regarded them as potential soul-mates, apart from divine intervention. The two were absurdly different in almost every cultural respect. David was from the English middle classes, neat and trim in appearance, careful not to offend and anxious to be approved. John was a year or two younger, comparatively rootless, a 'man of the world', bearded, burly and rather overweight. He was dressed in jeans and a cowboy shirt.

David undoubtedly had a tendency to be aloof from his companions, which had been apparent even at Ridley and had surfaced from time to time through his depressions. He always found it difficult to believe that he was really loved and trusted. Yet he discerned that here was a man of God whom he could trust with his innermost feelings. He wrote in *Fear No Evil*: 'Every now and then in my travels I meet someone whom I feel I can really trust – someone who loves me and accepts me as I am, who is not trying to use or manipulate me, and who is full of godly wisdom. There are not many like this, but John Wimber is one.'[1]

Anne had been praying for just such a friend for David, intellectually and spiritually his equal, gifted with equivalent gifts of teaching and leadership, and experienced in the same fields of church growth and strategic vision. Here was her answer.

John was also in need of David's help and friendship, for in some respects he was peerless and alone as the pastor of a large church outside a denomination, in spite of the warm fellowship within the Vineyard. Of course in many ways David had already trodden this same road, building a church where one scarcely existed before. He had much to say to encourage John, listened sympathetically and advised with humility and sensitivity. It was this graciousness which impressed John most. 'I didn't know who David Watson was, that he had written a lot of books, that he had a big church back in England and that he had an international ministry. I just knew him to be a loving man.' In John's immediate circle of family, colleagues and friends it was the same story. His sister-in-law, Penny Fulton, has said, 'David Watson made such an impact upon us. He was an ordinary Englishman and we loved him for himself. He was such a charming, lovely person. We didn't think of him as the great David Watson.'

David and John discussed the basis upon which they were doing the work of the kingdom and the values to which a church must hold firmly if it is to be true to God's word, sharing their frustrations as well as their plans and principles. They found that, to a very large extent, what David had been establishing at St Michael's, John was also building into the Vineyard. Worship and evangelism were the main emphases, firmly rooted in the relationships between the members of the fellowship, who were nurtured in Kinship Groups (which were very similar to the St Michael's Area Groups). In many ways, since it had not grown out of a particular Christian tradition, the Vineyard had started with a blank canvas and had been able to return to first principles. As such, David found the experience of finding these values central to the life of a new church very exciting. The Vineyard was not schismatic, for it had not divided from any other church, and it was not heretical, for it held firmly to the traditional Christianity which David himself embraced. Indeed, in some respects it seemed to David to be more orthodox and more loyal to Christian traditions than many of the established denominations. It certainly throbbed with the life of Christ.

In one particular respect, the Vineyard was way ahead of the churches in England and indeed in most places. David writes:

What first excited me about John Wimber's church ... was the indisputable evidence of God's power to heal, coupled with a lot of biblical wisdom and human sanity ... For a long time I had theoretically believed in the truth of all this, and I had seen *some* healings ... in my own ministry. But never before had I found such a wholesome and powerful healing ministry.[2]

John Wimber believed that the Gospel records of Jesus' healing compassion were intended as models for the whole Church, as it had been in Acts. He believed that Christians have only to trust God and to obey him implicitly to see 'signs and wonders' in modern days. He began to teach this to his church and they began to practise what he preached. They experienced failure, as the traditional churches said they would, but they had persisted and the healing work of the Spirit was now a central part of their church life.

David was thrilled and challenged by what he saw. He had long been aware of the inconsistency which seemed to govern the understanding of the spiritual gifts in the Charismatic Movement. As a whole, the gifts were accepted and many were enthusiastically used; but others, notably healing, hardly seemed to be practised at all. This was mainly because it was supposed that they had only been given to an exclusive few to operate. Tongues were for everyone to use, and indeed in some rather Pentecostal circles were seen as the mark of being spiritually qualified to use any gifts, but healing was treated as a gift for only some to exercise. Thus, the sick simply tended to go to these 'healers' when they were conducting a 'healing service' or some such thing. Prophecy and words of knowledge, on the other hand, were generally supposed to be employed by anyone in the context of worship or in the course of ministering to or praying for someone. Yet certain people, such as Anne, seemed to have a particular ministry of prophecy which effectively put them in much the same category as the healers. The other gifts had lesser prominence and therefore less frequent use or none at all. It was somewhat confusing.

Part of the difficulty lay in the interpretation of 1 Corinthians 12:7–11. At face value, this seems to suggest that the Spirit only gives a gift to one or another according to his choice. However, if these verses are interpreted in the light of the problem to which St Paul was addressing himself in this section of his letter – disorder in church services – the difficulty may be overcome. The phrase 'when you come together', used in chapter 11 in verses 18, 20, 33, and 34, becomes the key to an understanding of the Spirit's distribution of the gifts in chapter 12. In church, order is necessary, and only a limited use of the gifts is appropriate so that disorder is avoided. Otherwise the gifts are available to all believers at all times because they have all been baptised with one Spirit (1 Corinthians 12:13). This is what John Wimber believed and taught in the Vineyard; all the gifts were for everyone, because the Spirit was for everyone and the gifts were his. They were to be exercised anywhere, any time as need and opportunity arose, but always with humility, compassion and absolute faith. No one was to presume upon God, and often for his own sovereign purposes he would not work the wonders asked of him. That was his prerogative as God.

Healing in the life of Jesus was not achieved through intercession but more by a word of authority. 'Lazarus, come out!'[3] 'Ephphatha, that is, Be opened'[4] 'Jesus rebuked the demon, and it came out'.[5] The disciples operated by the same method: 'In the name of Jesus Christ of Nazareth, walk,' said Peter at the Beautiful Gate.[6] John Wimber taught that the gift of healing released by the Holy Spirit to the Church was to be operated by precisely the same method. He did not believe that God is limited to any one method, but if the Church is to work under scriptural warrant, it should pay strict attention to Jesus' own method and that of the early disciples. Thus, there was to be complete dependence upon the power of the Spirit to heal, and not upon one's own prayers. If a healing took place, it would result from the operation of the Holy Spirit's power, activated by the authority vested in the believer in Jesus' name, and not by the operation of the believer, by his praying, his experience, his skill or his holiness. While those who did this frequently might well develop a ministry of healing, even the most practised and expert healer had no power of his own and might just as easily fail to heal as the most inexpert. It is God who heals.

Typically, David's excitement was tempered by caution and it took him time, prayer and thought to begin to build this into his system. He was not one to leap rashly on to a bandwagon. He wrote: 'Over the years I have been confused and cautious about the whole subject. I have not doubted that God *can* heal, and I have sometimes experienced healing myself, but it has very much been the exception rather than the rule.'[7] Of course, the activity of the Holy Spirit and the availability of his power to today's Church had been a cornerstone of his ministry for many years. But it had always been seen primarily as a source of power to perform better the everyday activities of the Church: evangelising, ministering, serving, loving, etc. Thus in *I Believe in Evangelism*: 'The Spirit of God is essentially a witnessing Spirit.'[8] In *I Believe in the Church*: 'The Church was born of the Spirit';[9] '[Mission] was the primary purpose of the gift of the Spirit';[10] 'It is the foremost concern of the Holy Spirit to pour God's love into the hearts of his people.'[11] In other words, whatever it is that the Christian is doing, it is the Spirit who will ensure success.

This, of course, does not exclude the possibility of the miraculous activity of the Spirit (and David was careful not to say so), but at the time of writing *I Believe in Evangelism* (published in 1976), David was not really expecting miracles: '[Whilst] "many wonders and signs were done among the people by the hands of the apostles", it is not to be assumed that the same astonishing power is available to all Christians in every generation.'[12]

Nevertheless, one can detect a subtle change in his thinking with subsequent publications. In *I Believe in Evangelism*: 'it is not to be assumed [but] God *may* give quite remarkable signs';[13] in *Discipleship* (published in 1981): the power for signs and wonders 'is still available to us who believe, [and the Spirit] longs, probably much more than we realise, to release us from physical sickness.'[14] By *Fear No Evil* (published in 1983): 'Remarkable healings take place [at the Vineyard] . . . Not *all* who are sick are healed, but a good many are.'[15]

In many ways, healing is the most difficult of the gifts of the Spirit to accept, simply because it is the 'most supernatural'. After all, the secular world recognises the gifts of teaching, service and administration. Prophecy, words of knowledge and tongues seem a little weird, but can nevertheless be accounted for by the unbeliever as luck, coincidence, extra-sensory perception, or simply over-exuberance. However, the blind seeing, the deaf hearing and the lame walking can only be accepted or denied by the world. Since they actually contradict the natural order as defined by medical science, they represent a challenge that demands a response. For the Christian, of course, the problem is slightly different. If it is hard to identify a scriptural basis for the supernatural *never* occurring any more, it is even more difficult to single out healing as being the only gift to be obsolete. Moreover, if one accepts that healing does take place occasionally, it is not clear why it should not happen all the time. The argument is often simply (and rather weakly) that it does not seem to happen very much; and yet at the Vineyard, David Watson saw it happening as the norm.

In fact the argument, especially from Christians, that healing does *not* actually happen, that it has never been satisfactorily documented, is the weakest of all. By now there are enormous numbers of cases where the incurably and even terminally ill have recovered. Many more would attest to having been unexpectedly and miraculously healed of more mundane ailments. No doubt a good proportion of these were not 'authentic' miracles, but simple statistics suggest that at least a few are genuine divine healings. After all, if one believes in an omnipotent God, why should they not be? The sheer worldwide scale of deception, conspiracy and delusion implied by denying it would in itself be miraculous.

David was so impressed with what he saw of the Vineyard on that first visit that he invited John to come to York and visit St Michael-le-Belfrey later in the year, and this was gladly accepted. He hurried home to tell Anne about John and to begin to prepare his people for the visit. In actual fact, through the offices of Eddie Gibbs, John was already discussing a visit to England with one of David's friends, David Pytches, erstwhile Bishop in Chile and currently Vicar of St Andrew's, Chorleywood. It therefore made good sense to combine the two, especially since Chorleywood was near to Heathrow and a good stopping-off place on the way to

York. Thus, in May 1981 John Wimber made his first ministerial visit to England. Unhelpfully, he landed at Gatwick.

When he turned up at Chorleywood with a team of thirty, David Pytches was appalled. He had not made proper provision to contribute to John's fare and was relying on the proceeds of a retiring collection, but how could he hope to find enough for all this team? Hesitantly, he broached the subject. 'Who said anything about money?' said John. 'We are here because God has sent us and we pay for ourselves.' In that short weekend a wind of the Spirit swept through St Andrew's, transforming its people and their lives.

It was the same at York as all sorts of prejudices were swept away and relationships were restored. In particular, of course, the difficult subject of healing was introduced with fresh authority. One young man under the power of the Spirit fell on the church floor and seemed to have passed out. His doctor, a very respected member of the congregation, moved forward to help. Wimber told him to leave him alone. The doctor, with understandable anger, expostulated that this was his patient who was having an epileptic fit. John bent over the young man and called him by name. He opened his eyes. 'Hello,' he said. 'I'm having a wonderful time with God. Please can I go back?'

John Wimber has said:

In those two visits God did more in a short period of time than we had seen altogether up till that point. It was an incredible week in York. We saw healings, deliverances, salvations and empowerings by the Holy Spirit. Even the children in the Family Service were touched by the Spirit, so that one boy of about ten or eleven began to sing in tongues in a beautiful treble voice, the sound being wafted up into the roof of the ancient building. When David came to see us off at the station, one of his friends asked him quizzically, 'Well, David, how are you going to report this ministry to the Bishop?' David just said, 'I don't think I shall have any difficulty. I shall just say that the blind have been made to see, the lame to walk, and the poor have had the gospel preached to them.'

Of course, reporting to bishops is never quite that easy. Nevertheless, the comment reveals the extent to which David had come to approve of John's ministry. Indeed, David's initial endorsement of the Vineyard teaching and his friendship with John opened the door for his remarkable ministry to the British churches after David's death. The fact that there is very little about supernatural signs and wonders in David's books is not surprising, considering that only two were written after meeting John in 1981. Moreover, in *You Are My God* (published in 1983) he is largely looking back over the period before he met him. By his final year and in his final book, David is a wholehearted advocate of a Spirit-inspired healing ministry.

Undoubtedly, the issue was focused in his mind by the fact that he was by then himself in urgent need of divine healing. Nevertheless, it would be cynical and most unfair to David's methods and integrity to conclude that this was the main reason for his new position. It ran deeper than that.

From his first exposure to it in 1981 he had slowly and carefully absorbed the Vineyard teaching, and with great satisfaction. It is true that Mark Slomka, who was to work closely with David from 1982 until his death, was still able to write, 'I was always slightly puzzled how David could be so identified with charismatic renewal and yet seemed to exercise many of the gifts so infrequently.' Nevertheless, he scarcely had any more hours in his day in which to begin doing it; he already had a fully developed and over-stretched ministry.

What is more, it was far-reaching in its implications and he was away so much that the task of teaching it to St Michael's, which was really now Graham Cray's congregation, was quite beyond him. Anne, too, was very little help. She more or less refused to take any part in it, not because she could not believe it, but because she was scared of the complications which would arise if they embarked upon a Vineyard-type ministry at this stage. Had they not got enough on? The problems in the church were already multiplying quite fast enough without adding to them a whole area of ministry about which they knew nothing. It was all right for David. He would be off soon on another mission and leave them holding the baby.

22

Leaving York

IN MAY 1980 DAVID WATSON WAS IN LONDON at the invitation of some of the churches in Chelsea to hold an evangelistic festival which they called 'To London With Love'. It involved his team, of course, and a series of events in Chelsea Town Hall as well as in the churches, with three evenings in the Royal Albert Hall. For these he enrolled the help of the Riding Lights Theatre Company who, under the leadership of Paul Burbridge and Murray Watts, had by now taken on their own identity and were operating independently of David. There were also two ministers' meetings at lunchtime in St Columba's Church of Scotland, Pont Street.

This festival was one of his best. It was promoted by an executive committee from eleven Chelsea churches and was widely supported by denominational leaders. The attendance at the meetings was very good and the acceptance of the message was general. David spoke of his three purposes – renewal for 'a sleepy, apathetic church', unity for 'a tragically divided church', and evangelism in 'a steadily ageing and diminishing church'. He was very pleased to have such response in the West End of London, where he had not previously attempted anything so far-reaching. It opened his eyes to the possibility of using London as a base, since it seemed the churches welcomed his ministry warmly. Other exciting contacts also were made at this time, including invitations to speak in Parliament to some of its members.

On Sunday 25 May the *Sunday Telegraph* carried a remarkable article by Peregrine Worsthorne, who had attended one of the nights at the Albert Hall. He wrote:

Truth to tell, Mr Watson is something rather special – a spellbinder without histrionic tricks, simply a conventional clergyman with a gift for preaching. Before he got up to speak, few were able to identify him. Nor was there anything at all unusual about what he had to say. His message was strictly orthodox, straight Christianity without frills. What struck one as singular about Mr Watson was not so much his ability to turn on [an audience] as his ability not to turn them off.

David was asked by a friend who sat next to him at lunch one day whether he had ever thought of leaving York and basing himself in London for the continuation of his travelling ministry. His reply was that he had been considering this, partly because the facilities of the capital would be much more convenient for his wider ranging ministry, and partly because he felt that Anne's position in York was not an easy one.

The appointment of Graham Cray to run St Michael's had greatly eased the pressure on David, but had also left him in no man's land. He was the founding father of St Michael's, still lived there and ministered whenever he could, but was no longer in charge or in control. The people still loved him, but he was no longer their leader and they only consulted him spasmodically. It could not be otherwise, for no one can ride two horses at once and his church and his travels had been pulling him apart for several years. When he had decided to major on his missions, his parish had discovered that he had only a limited relevance. In the Church of England provision is not made for a clergyman so to develop his church that he can grow his own support staff and systems to enable him to carry on his ministry as he chooses. The parochial system and diocesan oversight restrict him. Perhaps it is just as well.

A further difficulty for David lay in the authority he himself had given to the elders at St Michael's. The original purpose behind the appointment of elders had been to discharge pastoral responsibilities among the growing number of members of the church. David not only believed that this was a practical necessity, but also that it was scripturally sound, for did not St Paul 'appoint elders in every town'?[1] Maybe those Pauline elders were actually the ministers (presbyters) in the churches and more equivalent to what he was himself, but the biblical metaphor of the body encouraged him to think that a measure of democratic government was thoroughly appropriate for every church in addition to the administrative function of the PCC.

Finding in his congregation a number of men of ability and spirituality capable of undertaking pastoral work among the groups, it had seemed a natural step to call them elders and to extend to them a share in the leadership of the whole church. They offered him fellowship and support which became of great value to him, and he gave them the benefit of his personal oversight, sharing his vision with them and consulting them on all matters concerned with the ministry in the church. They met with him regularly and their meetings became the occasion for the making of decisions about the church on all spiritual matters. David called this 'shared leadership' and thought of himself as being subject to the decisions of the elders in all matters.

Unfortunately, however, one of the unintended effects of the ACE report's assessment of shared leadership was to tip the precarious balance against David's influence and to weaken the authority to lead given him by the Archbishop. The Church of England was swinging increasingly towards democracy and David himself, as well as ACE, was deeply infected with this. In this case, ACE's complaint was really that shared leadership was not true democracy, for the people did not elect the elders, and the PCC, which they did elect, was relegated to a rather more limited role. But, however they got into office, David did, in fact, give authority to the elders to lead the church alongside him and accepted their corporate decisions as taking precedence over his own judgment.

There seems to have been a confusion as to whether the point of shared leadership was true democracy (whatever that is) or corporate responsibility. This was only marginally significant so long as David's own standing was high in the church for, as ACE pointed out, he dominated the elders' meetings with his own agendas anyway. However, as his absences became more frequent, the elders very naturally and properly assumed that the leadership was theirs to discharge as seemed best.

It took David several years to see his mistake. By 1982 he had concluded that there can only be one leader in an organisation and it is not really possible for leadership to be shared. What he believed in, and the Bible clearly teaches, is shared ministry – the full involvement of every member of the church in some part of its ministry. All leaders should be subject to the higher authority from whom they receive their licence. They may then, in turn, delegate authority to leaders over particular sections within their charge. They can consult with whom they wish and take or reject advice, and there may well be areas over which they do not have sole responsibility (i.e. church finance, etc.). However, they cannot share the office of overall leader with others who have not been commissioned to it. There has to be a leader of the leaders.

After the ACE report, David's position became gradually more difficult, not so much because of Graham Cray, to whom he had delegated part of his leadership and who operated under his authority and the Archbishop's, but because the elders group was increasingly in charge of the church. There were three major eruptions resulting from this change. The first was the closure of the Mustard Seed when the elders, heavily influenced by a few of their number who could not accept the leadership of women, and therefore unhappy with Wendy Wharton's headship role, acted pre-cipitously during David's absence on holiday. This has been recorded in Chapter 16. David's dismay was very clear.

An even more difficult and distressing clash took place in 1980 and

ABOVE
David preaching at a city
festival.

LEFT
David with John Wimber.

OPPOSITE PAGE
David's team performs street
theatre at Cape Town,
Christchurch and
Chichester.

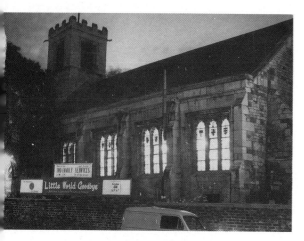

St Cuthbert's Church,
Peasholme Green, York.

RIGHT
David preaching in
St Cuthbert's.

St Michael-le-Belfrey, York.

LEFT
Inside the church.

centred on Anne's position in the church. Everyone knew that Anne had played a very creative and important role in the phenomenal growth of St Cuthbert's/St Michael's from the beginning, sharing with David the considerable hardships and sacrificial labours which had brought such remarkable results. If David's great gifts as a communicator, his warmth and humility, had been the most obvious force in building the work, Anne's dedication to it, her piercingly clear insights and unusual prophetic ministry were recognised by the membership to have made a major contribution. When new developments were attempted, Anne would be personally involved if at all possible, lending not only the weight of her authority but the strength of her back. But it was also well known that she and David sometimes had a difficult relationship brought about without doubt by his many absences, fuelled by her reluctance to accept the necessity for them, but also by her independent spirit. If he was happiest leading great missions and campaigns, she was at her best in the heat of building a local church. There was no secret about these tensions.

When the eldership was constituted, there was no place for women within it. Neither David nor anyone else supposed there should be, and it did not become apparent until afterwards that anything unsatisfactory had happened. Even then it was the omission of one particular woman that caused the problem, for Anne found herself excluded from the leadership which she had previously exercised. The issue of the role of women in the church was raised and given considerable exposure by the ACE report. Among the elders, a few traditionalists began to make their presence strongly felt. Since Anne was increasingly using her prophetic gift to influence the church, another prophetic ministry emerged, countering hers.

Prophecy is obviously a very subjective form of ministry, needing testing and strong control by the leader if a church is to benefit from it. In earlier days, David had always subjected Anne's prophetic insights to his prayerful study of the Scriptures. Given this careful and informed leadership, prophecy may be used rightly to lead the church forward. Nevertheless, even then it cannot ever be really safe because it involves the use of individual understandings and prejudices. A prophetic word may contain very personal impressions and preferences in addition to the message from God. It is certainly not infallible. Probably it has quite as good a chance of being sound as any synodical pronouncement. Actually, the inerrant Scriptures themselves are subject to human fallibility in translation and interpretation, however prayerfully they may be studied, and it is no surprise to discover that total safety in hearing and knowing God's word is not available to the Church. God has always been willing to reveal himself through a measure of distortion produced by the fallen nature of the human race, choosing to leave only the Scriptures as the basic deposit of divine truth and a yardstick for all other revelation.

So it is neither necessary nor possible to adjudicate in the power struggle then being joined, except to record that Anne seems to have left her flank rather exposed. On the one hand there were some problems with the leadership of the Heworth Area Fellowship, of which Anne was a member. On the other hand, it was also felt by some of the elders that David and Anne should make use of the space provided for them by the appointment of Graham Cray to seek to strengthen their own married relationship. Among the elders who took this view was David Smith, who had come from Gillingham to York at David's invitation in 1972 and became an elder and Reader in the church, though his real calling was as a conference speaker and missioner in parish churches throughout the country. These motives were entirely benevolent and encouraged by Anne's often repeated teaching that good relationships are the foundation upon which effective Christian ministry must be based. Such relationships needed to be seen in the Heworth Area Fellowship and in the rectory.

Eventually Anne was disciplined, relieved of all her responsibilities and instructed to spend more time with her husband. The irony of the situation was that her husband was just departing on his extended tour of New Zealand and Australia, and would therefore not be available to spend any time with his wife, who was not particularly minded to accompany him, even if she could. It was all a grave error which solved nothing, but which weakened still further David's allegiance to his York base. Surprisingly, it did not give Anne any desire to move but simply revealed to her, and to others, just where the battle lines were drawn and how necessary it was to match spirituality with reality. The elders continued to assume the authority David had given them with ever-increasing strength. His power to plot the right course and to lead along it had been surrendered.

But a further and more stunning blow was still to be dealt David. Graham Cray writes: 'The most powerful trauma which our church had experienced to date came in November 1980, when some members, including one elder and a number of experienced house group leaders left us, eventually to form a "house church". It was an experience of intense pain, a tearing.'[2] It was the nature of St Michael's as a church of 'committed relationships' which made the break so painful. Graham expresses the feelings of both sides when he says: 'The majority who remained felt betrayed and rejected. Those who left felt they had been pushed out and that there was no further place for them.'[3]

Since David's ministry contained so strong an emphasis on unity, reconciliation and relationships, it was for him a deeply felt wound. David described the causes for the split as growing from a theological disagreement and a difference over order:

The splinter group, as it was rapidly becoming, was preaching a dangerous idea, currently taught in some circles but with no theological basis, a distinction between the *logos* and the *rhēma* of God (both words being used interchangeably in the New Testament for the word of God). They held that the *logos* referred only to the general word of God in the Scriptures; but the *rhēma* was the prophetic word, God's word for now. Further, although there may be general agreement about the *logos* of God, our unity and fellowship depends in practice, they claimed, on our response to the *rhēma* of God.[4]

Since agreement on the *rhēma* could not be achieved, the group felt that 'they had no choice but to separate themselves from us'.[5]

David believed this was 'entirely fallacious' since Christian unity is 'quite simply in Christ'. It was a classic case of a division occurring because a difference of style demanded an independence which could only be achieved by theological disagreement. Because the structure of shared leadership could not be made to work, the new leaders could not find sufficient room to express their leadership beside him. Both rationalised the desire for this into a theological reason for separating. Church history is full of such events.

In *You Are My God* David records:

Perhaps the final straw came when Graham gave a masterly series of four sermons on leadership and, as vicar but with my total agreement, included three women in the next body of elders, one of these women being Anne. Many of us felt that the inclusion of women was long overdue, but that particular group found this altogether unacceptable.[6]

This, of course, was the difference over order which triggered off the split. It is interesting to speculate whether any split which may accompany the Church's decision over the ordination of women to the priesthood will cause as much suffering. Christians need to find ways of trusting each other and accepting division peacefully and without bitterness if they are going to continue to try to show God's love to an ungodly society.

Graham Cray puts it another way:

What we did not have the maturity to see at the time was that a minority spirituality had emerged within St Michael's that could not properly co-exist with that of the majority. The group who left had little sense of calling to the Church of England, whereas St Michael's is called to be part of the renewal of the Church of England from within the Church of England. Had we all had the wisdom and foresight,

our brothers and sisters could have been released with our blessing to fulfil their
own vision without the mutual sense of tearing and division.[7]

In other words, why argue and part company in pain, thinking that an
awful thing has happened when, with enough flexibility of attitude and
tolerance of others' opinions, a perfectly workable solution can be produced without breaking fellowship? The Acomb Christian Fellowship has
subsequently matured and developed as an independent fellowship in
York. But David's determination to keep people together under his leadership and within the ecclesiastic structures resulted in much misery and a
great sense of failure. It was a typically Anglican attitude.

All this helped to make David less committed to stay at St Michael's, and
more dedicated to his evangelistic ministry. The invitations kept coming at
a rate far beyond what could be accepted and he received so much approval
for it and so much joy from it that he had little difficulty believing this
was his true work. There were other factors. Anne had come successfully
through her 'disciplining' and was now an elder. Their marriage was going
along well, too. But whenever he was away, Anne found herself receiving
complaints from various people who were not as happy in the church as
they had been. Graham was now leading the church, not David, and those
who found that they did not like everything that Graham did decided that
Anne was just the person to tell about it. David knew that this situation
would be difficult to bring to an end.

David believed that Graham was now firmly in the saddle and doing
well. He had been throughout a loyal colleague and an effective leader
and David held him in high esteem. He knew his own position to be
anomalous. He was still the official leader of St Michael's but he was only
there sometimes and Graham exercised his office vicariously with success.
So long as David was around, Graham would never have the liberty he
deserved to develop his own work as he might wish. Indeed, David had
no real desire to stay around, however much he might love St Michael's
and his people.

In *You Are My God* David denies that the tensions in York were the
reason for his leaving. Without question they were not so much the cause
of his move as contributing to his frame of mind when considering a move.
There is no evidence in David's record that he was ever a quitter and it
is most unlikely that he would have left York in order to escape from the
pressures presented by the split or by the difficulties he was experiencing
over the powers he had given to the elders. He devotes considerable
space in the book to explaining and justifying shared leadership. If his
circumstances had been different and he had intended to stay in York

alongside Graham, it seems likely that he would have tried to modify the structure satisfactorily and would probably even have succeeded. He had certainly learned from his mistake by the time he came to London and knew what should be done about it. What is more, his relationship with the elders in York and with the church remained very fatherly and loving right up to the end.

The tensions told him that if he was to continue as a worldwide evangelist and grow into a national church leader as a result, he would not be able to become too involved in the parochial problems of St Michael's. He could have resigned as Rector and stayed on as a member, refusing to get involved. Whether that would have worked will never be known. But London beckoned and the advantages were obvious. He knew that he would be leaving behind an able vicar and magnificent group of leaders who were as capable as any, more capable than most other Christians of taking forward the work of a local church. They needed to do this and he needed to concentrate on the evangelistic work that he believed he was primarily called to do. In addition, he needed to do even more writing. He needed to respond to the invitations to be available to church and national leaders. He needed to be more professional over his missions and to make his team more so. He needed space to become a better husband and father within his family.

He began to consult his friends. John Collins had recently arrived in London as Vicar of Holy Trinity, Brompton (often referred to as 'HTB'), and was an early consultant, as was Teddy Saunders, Vicar of St Michael's, Chester Square. The value of being in London near the seat of government and so much else was discussed, and it was agreed that if he was to move away from York, it was probably strategic to make his base in London. What was quite as significant about London as its centrality to people and events was its excellent transport system. The long haul to York from Heathrow airport had presented David and his team with quite a challenge to endurance at the end of an exacting trip. There were also churches in London which he knew would welcome and support him, though in some the charismatic divide was still as strong as ever. When four evangelical vicars from churches in central London – John Collins, Teddy Saunders, Michael Baughen at All Souls and Dick Lucas at St Helen's, Bishopsgate in the City – invited him to come to London for a festival in May 1982, he felt confident enough to believe he was going to be well received.

In fact this 'Festival of Christ' was quite a disappointment. A student evening at the Barbican Theatre was well attended, as were two nights at the Royal Albert Hall and a Whit Sunday evening service in Westminster

Abbey, but the teaching evenings on St Luke's Gospel on Monday to Friday for three weeks were relatively poorly attended. By that time, David was already committed to London and this had been made public. Perhaps the expectation of his ministry in London for many years to come militated against a good attendance. Perhaps the hunger for his ministry was not deep seated enough to make the people turn out in any numbers over a long period.

Nevertheless, he believed that his acceptability among the churches as a whole was well proven and could be expected to grow rather than diminish. He approached the Archbishop of York, Stuart Blanch, who knew him as well as anyone and who fully understood the issues, and came away with the assurance that the Archbishop would support him if he decided to move and would do anything he could to help. Later Dr Blanch, perhaps with some hindsight, was to admit that he had some fears for the Watsons in making such a move, thinking that the loss of the York fellowship would be harder for them to bear than they recognised, but the Archbishop's support was a crucial factor for David in making his decision.

Archbishop Blanch made one particular decision which gave David and all his friends very great pleasure. He made David a Canon Provincial of the Northern Province, beginning his letter by saying, 'It seemed good to the Holy Spirit and to us' to make this appointment. He went on to say that David would hold it for the rest of his life, and his sole duty would be to pray for the Archbishop regularly. He made the appointment in recognition of David's services to the worldwide Church and within the Diocese of York in particular.

The practical matters seemed large. David and Anne had no house of their own, no capital with which to buy one, no income upon which to live, and two children still of school age. If he surrendered his incumbency of St Michael's, he would forfeit his rectory and his stipend, as well as the financial assistance given him by his church towards his expenses and the salary of his secretary. If he did not take on another church, none of this would be available to him in London, but the very purpose of the move was to be free to do his own work rather than parish work. His team, too, was by this time an accepted extra for St Michael's, but how would they be recruited and maintained in London and where would they be based?

The estimates for financial needs showed that about £40,000 a year would probably cover costs, assuming that the travelling expenses would normally be met by those who had invited them to travel. This had always been the way it had been done. The amount collected from each festival had never needed to cover the ordinary living costs of David and his team who had their salaries or household contributions to rely on for this. But now their entire subsistence would have to be found. It was quite a new situation.

A few years previously, an elderly Christian couple had given a capital sum and their home to David as a thank offering for the rich experience of being renewed in the Spirit. A Trust had been set up to provide for the wider ministry 'For the advancement of the Christian religion by the proclamation of the Gospel of Christ and the building up of his Body the Church.' David and the trustees felt it right to leave some of this in York for the support of David Smith's ministry, but it was decided to use the Trust itself and most of its capital as a vehicle for financing his new work in London. He had already begun to bestow the royalties from most of his books upon this Trust and to pay into it anything that was received as gifts or 'profits' from his ministry, so it was appropriate to use it in this way. Some trustees continued in office: Ian Anderson, Peter Collier and Crispin Joynson Hicks; and some new trustees were appointed: Teddy Saunders (to act as Chairman), Sylvia Mary Alison, John Collins, Douglas Greenfield and Michael Warren. Peter George was to be Treasurer. It was renamed 'The Belfrey Trust' to maintain links with York, and some publicity was given to the need for support. David wrote a News/Prayer-letter to an ever-increasing number of people who undertook to pray for him and much of the money received came from them.

The question of housing was quite difficult. It was decided to try to find somewhere within a reasonable distance of Holy Trinity, Brompton, and John Collins asked some of his people to investigate any possibilities. They worked very hard at it without success, mainly because of the very high prices involved in central London. Even property some way away was rather more expensive than could reasonably be afforded by the Trust. It was quite frustrating and David, still many miles away in York, got impatient. He wrote to Teddy Saunders to ask if there was anything he could do, and without much hope Teddy made an appointment to see the Duke of Westminster on David's behalf. The Duke was very sympathetic and agreed to see if something could be found from his London property, the Grosvenor Estate. Eventually, an ideal small house in Eaton Row, a quiet mews near Victoria, was offered at a greatly reduced rent. It had five bedrooms and two reception rooms, a garage and even a small garden. By putting David's study in a bedroom on the first floor and squeezing a secretary's desk, files and other equipment into the hall, it could be made very workable, but it was essentially a home and not a headquarters. David and Anne were delighted with it.

There was only one member of the existing York team who was available and willing to make the change to London, Diana Nairne, a graduate of Southampton University, who could sing, dance and act. Her links with the past were an enormous help in bringing understanding to a new team of what was expected of them and of the principles which were to govern the ethos of the future work. In addition, David had been approached by a young married couple who were students at Fuller on his first visit there in January 1980. Mark Slomka was preparing for the Presbyterian ministry in California and Carol was a gifted singer and oboist who would be very happy to dance and act as well. They reckoned that two years on David's team would be a wonderful preparation for any future pastorate. John Collins suggested some young people from HTB, and soon a small but well balanced team of actors and musicians were recruited including, for the first time, two professional dancers.

A young Christian couple who were going to work overseas came forward to offer their house in Battersea if David could use it. It became the team house, providing accommodation for the Slomkas, two other members of the team and David's secretary/PA, Hilary Saunders. It had been difficult to know how to choose an adequate secretary, for the Eaton Mews house was quite cramped and Anne was naturally concerned at having a total stranger so closely involved in the life of the family. Hilary was Teddy's daughter and had met David while working on the staff at St Helen's, Bishopsgate. A graduate of Durham University, she had limited secretarial experience but a high level of ability and dedication. She was accepted with enthusiasm, and her competence and cheerfulness soon made her invaluable.

So it was that in July 1982 the farewells were made in York and in August the new start was made in London.

23

London

As soon as they had settled into Eaton Row, the Watson family departed for a holiday in Portugal. Some friends in London lent them their villa in the Algarve where the sun shone in a blue sky, the sea, though cooler than expected, was very welcoming and the golf course was brand new, emerald green and almost deserted. Thoroughly restored, they returned to begin their new life.

David began by spending time with his new team. In addition to their learning new material, the main question which concerned him was the old one of relationships. They needed to know him and each other well; to trust and relate deeply to each other. They spent two hours together every morning as a group, sometimes with Anne joining them and sharing her insights with them. Sometimes they would have the Bible open and David would teach them, but always they would pray for each other; for their personal needs as well as their spiritual effectiveness, and for David in particular. They learnt worship songs and choreographed dance and mime routines for various parables and Bible stories. They also had to work very hard at drama rehearsals of the many sketches David used to illustrate his teaching. It was all quite intensive. Mark Slomka records how, when they fulfilled their first booking at Dartford in early September, 'David had invited Phil Potter to join us for his constructive criticism, encouragement, and to lead if we fell squarely flat on our faces.' Fortunately, David reported that he was very pleased with them and was confident that they would have a promising future together.

Douglas Greenfield continued his role as agent for David, covering many miles in investigation of the invitations which kept pouring in and arranging the first steps to be taken in those cases which seemed positive. His task was a difficult one, but he had rare discernment and became more and more skilled in sifting the invitations with David to decide which might be accepted. A programme of missions and festivals was booked through 1983 with the Fuller trip in January. The autumn of 1982 was taken up with settling into London and a long five-week tour in Canada, longer than David really wanted to stay away. In between excursions out of London, David was speaking regularly at evangelistic events or at small meetings for leaders both in the Speaker's House in Parliament and to military personnel at the Ministry of Defence. He also met a number of well-known actors, musicians and artists at evangelistic supper parties hosted by Cliff Richard at the Arts Centre Group. He was so acceptable and so incisive that many of his hearers were stimulated to want to hear more and came whenever he turned up to speak. For some years after his death, a group in Parliament met regularly to listen to his teaching tapes.

He was also able to attend consultations at the highest level in the Church such as a meeting between Evangelical and Anglo-Catholic leaders to which he was invited by John Stott. Soon after his arrival in London, he attended a gathering at which the Archbishop of Canterbury, Robert Runcie, was also present. Dr Runcie greeted him warmly, saying how glad he was he had come to London and was going to intensify his travelling ministry to the Church. 'Unless the Church of England can experience renewal,' he said, 'we are doomed.' It is most unlikely that either the condition or the conclusion in this remark was intended to carry any weight of theological precision, but David was delighted with the implied commissioning and assured the Archbishop of his firm intentions.

For Anne it was a strange and rather difficult time. She had lost her role as a leader and the fellowship of those who had been close to her for many years. Guy soon went off to boarding school (Pangbourne College) and Fiona was working hard for her 'A' Levels at St Paul's Girls' School in Hammersmith. On Saturdays, Anne and Fiona would drive to Wimbledon Common where Fiona would ride and Anne would walk her dog. Sometimes they all went to see Guy and often this was combined with a visit to Peggy Hawkes and Diana in Andover, which had been a filial relationship sadly neglected during the long years in York. But when David and the team went to Canada in October, Anne found herself more alone than ever and her weekly telephone conversations with David across the Atlantic revealed the danger of depression setting in. David rang their old friend Sylvia Mary Alison, now a Belfrey trustee, and asked her to call on Anne and investigate. He even considered coming home early if necessary. Sylvia Mary's report reassured him, but without question Anne found London life hard in spite of Hilary's cheerful companionship. The things which David enjoyed so much, Holy Trinity Brompton, the Arts Centre Group, Parliament, and the opportunity to mix and minister in London, attracted Anne not at all and she felt her isolation acutely.

After Canada, David began to write his autobiography. Since he was not yet fifty it seemed somewhat premature, but his literary agent, Edward England, who had previously published his books for Hodder & Stoughton, persuaded him to tell his story thus far before it became too dated and lost its topicality. Characteristically, he threw himself into the task and had almost completed the manuscript by the end of the year. He consulted carefully with friends over the balance and detail of the book, and was reluctant to leave any impression of criticism, even where it was justified. The book therefore may be said to lack punch in some places; his humility and the subjectivity which is necessary in an autobiography robbed him of the chance to spell out some of his views more precisely. Only the transparent integrity of the author, which shines out of the pages, may have saved it from sterner criticism. However, it was gratefully received by his many admirers the world over when published in October 1983. Unfortunately, his illness had made him even more widely known by this time and no doubt this added to the interest in his record.

When David informed his trustees in December 1982 about what he was writing, John Collins, with his usual perspicacity, questioned the wisdom of embarking on an autobiography at that stage, saying that it would make it much more difficult for him in the future to change his mind or to undertake anything inconsistent with what he had done before. What was more, not only David, but also many who had shared his earlier pilgrimage, might not benefit from the publicity given them in the book. By that time, however, David was committed to it and was well advanced in writing it. As it turned out, he had very little future to be concerned about. The book has inspired many by its revelation of what can be done by a gifted man prepared to seek God's face and to obey him without reservation. David's open admission of weakness and failure in some areas and times demonstrated his Christ-like character. David wrote: 'I have tried to write honestly about my life, my marriage and the Church, about the pains and joys we have experienced. No human frailty need be a hindrance to God's infinite grace.' *You Are My God* was reprinted ten times in its first year.

Preparations were well underway after Christmas for the visit to Fuller, which was to be the first with the new team. On 5 January, David went to see his doctor, Dr William Robarts, about his asthma medications, and as he was leaving asked conversationally if they could be having any side effects. 'I seem to be going to the loo rather a lot these days.' A short question-and-answer session was followed by a careful examination and then the truth came out: 'You have an ulcer in the colon. I would like you to see a specialist because you might need an operation. It could be serious.' David's protestations were swept aside and an appointment with

Mr Randolph Beard at Guy's Hospital was made for two days' time.

For weeks, David and his team had been looking forward to Fuller. Over sixty lectures were to be given in California within the next month and many pastors from different parts of the world were already gathering there, having spent hundreds of dollars on it. To David the shock of the diagnosis of his physical condition was compounded by the disappointment at being unable to fulfil his commitment to Fuller, and to enjoy the warmth of friendship with the people in the Vineyard who meant so much to him. But reality prevailed and within a week David was in hospital and undergoing surgery for a malignant ulcer. His team was at Fuller, with David Prior from St Aldate's, Oxford, for the first two weeks, and his old friend David MacInnes, then Diocesan Missioner in Birmingham, for the second two weeks. It was quite remarkable that these heavily committed men should have been able to make themselves available at such short notice.

Before going into hospital some of David's closest friends met to pray with him and for him, while Anne took Fiona and Guy out for the afternoon. Sylvia Mary Alison, John and Diana Collins, Jean Darnall, Margaret Knight and David and Mary Pytches came to Teddy and Margaret Saunders' home in Chester Square. During prayer, Jean had an increasingly strong impression, which she presented as a prophetic word, that David's 'ministry would increase and not diminish'. David was very comforted by this, but he quickly noted that it was his ministry and not necessarily his life which was to increase and his integrity prevented him from pretending otherwise.

The prayer gathering had been suggested by John Wimber. As soon as David had heard his specialist's diagnosis and had told Anne about it, he called John in California and told him what had occurred. They had prayed together over the phone and David promised to keep John informed of all developments. John called his church to prayer and fasting for the success of the operation, which, preceded by a biopsy, was carried out with great skill on Thursday 13 January. David and Anne were told by Mr Beard the next day that he had discovered secondaries in the liver, which was an inoperable condition. David had about a year of life left to him.

When John Wimber heard of this on the phone from Teddy Saunders, he said he would fly over to pray with David. Anne brought this good news to David and it lifted his spirits wonderfully. John flew in on Wednesday 19 January, bringing with him John McClure and Blaine Cook, two of his colleagues in the Vineyard. They went straight to Guy's Hospital to see David and prayed with him. While they were praying, David experienced 'heat as well as vibrations in my body, and I knew God was at work. This went on for half an hour or more.'[1] John Wimber remarked that he had seen other people healed who, at the time of the ministry of prayer, had described their experience in the same sort of terms which David had used. John writes: 'Through prayer and worship, our attitudes were transformed from fear and anxiety to trust and peace . . . We prayed fully aware of God's presence and peace. When we finished I said, "I sense that the work we came over to do is done."'[2]

Those who later were to seek for sticks with which to beat John have accused him of telling David he was healed when he was not. However, none of those who associated closely with David during the next thirteen months ever heard him claim to have been healed. He often said he believed he was being healed, but he might be wrong. He never said that he had been healed through John Wimber, and certainly not that John had told him he was healed. Indeed, John Wimber never tells anyone that they are healed, holding that the person concerned and their medical advisors are the only people to make such statements. He positively forbids his people from making such claims in any ministry to the sick which they may undertake. It is contrary to the principles on which the Vineyard ministers healing. John and his two colleagues returned to the hospital on the Thursday and the Friday, and left David feeling altogether better and even confident about the future.

During his hospital stay David was surprised and delighted by a visit from two friends from the House of Lords – Viscount Ingleby and Lady Sue Masham – both of whom are confined to wheelchairs. As such, the trip was not without logistical difficulties but as David writes:

They made it! They bundled themselves into a taxi outside the House of Lords, struggled out again at the hospital, and then wheeled themselves through seemingly miles of corridors until they sailed into my ward.

'How wonderful of you both to come,' I said. And I was so pleased to see them.

'You fight it! You fight it!' said Sue Masham . . . Here were two lovely people who knew all about suffering and facing uncertain futures, but who were undoubtedly winning the daily battle, and with enormous cheerfulness.[3]

There was a vast amount of mail from well-wishers from all over the world, which Anne and Hilary had to sort through. David was humbled to find the amazing love and concern shown to him by Christians of all denominations. There were letters from the Archbishops of Canterbury and York, and from many other bishops from all parts of the Anglican Communion. One letter told him that thousands of Christians were praying for him in Zimbabwe, a country he had never even visited. He learned too that in a prison in Northern Ireland, Catholic and Protestant terrorists who had come to faith in Christ were meeting together to pray for him. There were special services of prayer in many churches throughout the world, and at St Michael-le-Belfrey Bishop Morris Maddocks led a Healing Eucharist for him; similar services were held in at least thirteen other churches on the same day.

David was home again two weeks after the operation and settled into a new routine of life. Anne was in charge and her mother, also trained at Guy's, came to help. David had been advised by Randolph Beard that the best hope for the defeat of cancer in the liver lay in his faith and in leading an active, normal life. Together they agreed that chemotherapy would not be appropriate and that a resumption of David's ministry should take place after an initial six months' post-operative convalescence. Fiona came home from school every evening and was a joy and comfort to David. Guy came home from Pangbourne at half-term. About a fortnight after David's return home from hospital, Bishop Morris Maddocks and his wife Anne came and celebrated a Eucharist in the sitting-room of the house in Eaton Row. It was a time when they were very aware of God's presence and sensed his love and peace. Other special visitors in those days included Delia Smith and Cliff Richard. David was delighted by their concern and encouraged by their visits. Slowly strength returned, and normality, and David began to fret at his forced inactivity, but he was under orders from the doctors, reinforced by his trustees, to take a full six months off work.

The trustees had arranged for the team to try to fulfil as many engagements as possible under the leadership of Bob Roxburgh, Minister of Millmead Centre, a Baptist church in Guildford. Bob had recently come to this pastorate from Canada where he had helped David and the team on their tour, and his deacons most graciously agreed to allow him to fill in for David. Some invitations were cancelled when it was learned that David himself could not come, and David MacInnes managed to fit in the few which were deemed to be strictly Anglican in character. Occasionally the team operated on its own with Mark Slomka taking responsibility for leadership. Mark was a most valuable member, increasingly assuming a general oversight of the team throughout the eighteen months during which they remained together.

Later in the year, through the suggestion of Edward England, David wrote *Fear No Evil*, a vivid description of his own experience as a cancer patient, slipping gradually towards death but fighting for life every inch of the way. Published in May 1984, three months after his death, it has helped thousands to face the onset of death. The first draft which David sent to Edward England disappointed him because it was chiefly a treatise on the subject, warmly presented, but not exactly what had been asked for. Edward sent it back with the request that David wrote into it his own feelings and experience, the conversations held at home and the hospital, the reactions of his friends, and especially the effect on his faith.

The second draft, completed only during his last months, was a winsome and irresistible account of David's last year of life. He used his situation to teach with great clarity and power the wonderful truths of eternal life, salvation by grace and the heavenly inheritance. Hilary Saunders, who worked alongside him in writing and rewriting the book and who corrected it in proof while he was dying upstairs, remembers how, 'In the very process of writing it was as though David was facing up to his own fears and emotions and coming through it all with a deepened trust and faith. The end result was no less a testament to his willingness to allow others an insight into that process as it was to his certain hope for eternity.' What he was teaching others, he was applying himself to his 'personal struggle with cancer', the subtitle of his book. It is an extraordinarily courageous book involving considerable personal, even physical, effort to write and rewrite.

In April, the Watsons went off for a highly successful family holiday in North Devon at a hotel in Chittlehamholt, David playing tennis and golf with Guy. It was a great success and strengthened the new relationships they were building together as David realised how important his family was to him. He writes in *Fear No Evil*:

Although outwardly I seemed fairly peaceful about the present and the future, there was still a battle between faith and fear raging within. I noted with care, therefore, the advice of a Christian doctor who wrote:

'It is easier to prepare for healing than for parting. But to fail to prepare for parting is to leave a bitter legacy for those we love. David, if it should be that your disease progresses, make time for Anne, Fiona and Guy, to say thank you and to ask for forgiveness and to say goodbye.'[4]

In April also, David sought from his trustees permission to break his inactivity on one particular occasion. Chris Rees of the BBC asked if he would do an interview for radio with Nick Page. When it went on the air it produced such a remarkable response that it was repeated five weeks later. Sackfuls of letters arrived and Hilary was kept busy for weeks, sending out a general letter David wrote to meet the need and trying to answer particular questions where necessary. In the broadcast he said:

If God doesn't heal me, I think there's a mystery about it that one just doesn't understand. I think that God does have a purpose in our lives, and it is not measured by the length of our life ... Actually, there is nothing more glorious than to be with Christ for ever, free from pain, suffering and tears, and all the problems and injustices of this world. I genuinely am at a place now where I really want to be in heaven. The sooner the better! But I am willing to be on this earth with all its struggles, battles and problems, if he wants me here.

There will be times when we are actually angry with God; or utterly depressed or totally disillusioned because God appears to be doing nothing . . . But working through those moments of lostness ('the dark nights of the soul' as the mystics called them) so our relationship with God can deepen. If I only praise him when the sun is shining my faith is shallow.

The main thing that I worry about concerning death is my wife and children. It is very painful when I go away for a month and leave them behind. If I go away knowing that I am not going to return to see them this side of heaven, that for me is the most painful thing to come to terms with. Therefore, as an act of the will, I have had to put everything 'on an open palm' before God.

I've said, 'Lord, here's my wife, my children, my possessions, my ambitions, my all. You can take them.' The only place for peace and security for me in my heart is when I have all that on an open palm. Jesus said, 'If you lose your life you'll find it, but if you hold on to your life you're likely to lose it.'[5]

Michael Green, Rector of St Aldate's, Oxford, and a friend since Iwerne days, wrote to David after the broadcast and David mentions this in *Fear No Evil.*

[He] was kind enough to suggest that the radio interview might emerge as the most powerful and influential talk I had ever given! And yet all I did was to sit in my armchair, still very weak, trying to answer the questions that Nick Page put to me. If God had used that interview to touch the lives of many people in many parts of the world, it was (for me) another indication that Christ's power is most effective in our weakness.[6]

Then, in May, David and Anne were off to the Vineyard, with David buoyantly happy to see John Wimber again and to share the warmth of the fellowship at the church, and Anne nervous at meeting David's friends and genuinely perplexed to understand the significance of what she saw and experienced there. When David stood up in church to thank the people for their prayers, he was met by a spontaneous standing ovation which lasted over five minutes and moved him deeply. It was a very successful trip.

On his return, he preached at Holy Trinity, Brompton, and loved 'being back at work again'. He went to speak at the Hodder & Stoughton staff conference in the Lake District, just before the launch of *You Are My God,* and made a tremendous impression, even upon unbelievers who were present.

By July, when he began to work again, he was feeling remarkably well and stronger than ever, and he was beginning to believe that the power of

God really was working in his body as he had witnessed it in others. He was determined to keep his faith strong as his doctor had prescribed, to act on the basis that he would live, and that healing from the Lord had been given him. Back with his team again he visited Dartford, where he had led a Christian festival in the Orchard Theatre for a week the previous September. This time, they only stayed two days. During the summer and autumn he recorded some programmes for TV South in the form of conversations with Adrian Plass and his wife Bridget, and Bishop George Reindorp. Again he shared something of his faith and experience of God in the face of suffering and death. With the team and also the family, he led a week's Families' Christian Houseparty which was a great success in spite of some misgivings that it would not fit their style. It was quite intensive, for David spoke at least twice a day and gave many interviews.

They went off for a family holiday in Scotland, calling in at York on the way for David to preach at St Michael-le-Belfrey. He writes:

Emotionally, neither Anne nor I could have gone to York any earlier. Having lived and worked there for seventeen years, our roots had gone very deep and the tender transplant into London had been in constant danger of 'rejection' over the past year. Although we were not yet settled into London, we felt that we could at least meet those whom we had known and loved so much without being emotionally overwhelmed by it all.

It was wonderful being there, however. I knew how much they had suffered and prayed because of my illness, and just to be there to say 'thank you' was a marvellous experience for us. We loved the gentle and sensitive worship in the church services – a quality of worship that has melted many hearts in the past because it conveys the gentle, healing love of God. Conversations were inevitably brief, but even a minute or two with those who had been especially close to us, were full of silent eloquence. When you love someone deeply, you don't have to *say* very much. Even trivial comments convey a depth of feeling that is mutually understood.

On the Sunday night I preached. I must have preached many hundreds of sermons in that church, St Michael-le-Belfrey, next to York Minster. But this time it was a special, never-to-be-forgotten occasion. In spite of a cloudburst and torrential rain for over an hour before the service, the church was bulging at the seams with people ... It was tremendous looking round to see so many with whom I had shared my life deeply in the past ...

I preached, and Anne prophesied, giving clear directions for the church which confirmed the growing convictions of the leaders. And the service ended. Not quite. I stood at the door for about an hour and a half saying goodbye to each of the 1,000 or more present, shaking hands, hugging or kissing, whatever seemed appropriate. I thought of the farewell given to the apostle Paul by the Ephesian elders: 'They all wept and embraced Paul and kissed him.' To experience the godly love of God's family is one of the most treasured riches for those in Christ.

If heaven is like this, only much more so, why are we so reluctant to go there?

It was not yet heaven, however, since my back was almost killing me after all that standing![7]

He didn't realise it at the time, but this back pain was the beginning of a deterioration in his condition which gradually accelerated during the coming autumn. The pain persisted through the Scottish holiday, forcing Anne to do all the driving, and was still with him in September when he threw himself into a programme of activities as strenuous as any he had attempted before. It seems doubtful if Mr Beard's encouragement to him to fulfil his ministry as an alternative to letting his cancer take over would have been as unconditional if he had known the pace at which David worked. As before his illness, he was up early to pray and read his Bible, to prepare his addresses and to write *Fear No Evil*.

Virtually no concession was made to the fact that he was now an invalid. Team meetings continued every morning, and twelve speaking engagements in or near London were accepted in October as well as trips to Switzerland for a week at a Pastors' Conference, to Manchester for a three-day festival, and to Grimsby for two nights. In November, the pace never slackened and after five days in Ireland at the end of the month for a series of meetings arranged by Cecil Kerr from the Rostrevor Community, he returned to London exhausted. Thrush had broken out in his mouth so painfully that he could not give the last address and surrendered it to Cecil. His asthma was crippling and his back very bad.

Dr Robarts treated his asthma with massive doses of steroids, but expressed his opinion that the cancer was now growing fast in the liver. David cancelled his December programme and asked Teddy and Margaret Saunders to take him again to the Vineyard. Arrangements were made to fly out on 1 December. Four days before that, in the early hours of Advent Sunday morning, David had a deep and revolutionary experience of God's presence. Woken by an attack of asthma, he heard God speaking to him:

... so powerfully and painfully that I have never felt so broken before him (and still do).

He showed me that all my preaching, writing and other ministry was absolutely *nothing* compared to my love-relationship with him. In fact, my sheer busyness had squeezed out the close intimacy I had known with him during the first few months of the year after my operation.

God also showed me that any 'love' for him meant *nothing* unless I was truly able to love from my heart my brother or sister in Christ. As the Lord put various names into my mind, I began to write letters to about twelve people asking for forgiveness for hurting them, for still being inwardly angry against them – or whatever. It was the most painful pruning and purging I can remember in my entire Christian life. But fruitful! Already some replies to my letters have reduced me to tears.

Whatever else is happening to me physically, God is working deeply in my life. His challenge to me can be summed up in three words: 'Seek my face.' I am not now clinging to physical life (though I still believe that God can heal and wants to heal); but I am clinging to the Lord. I am ready to go and to be with Christ for ever. That would be literally heaven. But I'm equally ready to stay, if that is what God wants.

'Father, not my will but yours be done.' In that position of security I have experienced once again his perfect love, a love that casts out all fear.[8]

On the flight to Los Angeles, David's feet swelled up dramatically and, even more significant, his abdomen also increased. He stayed eight days in the Wimber home, being prayed for regularly and persistently, but the swelling in his abdomen continued, sometimes accompanied by acute pain. At one of the sessions, John McClure, Pastor of the Vineyard Fellowship in Whittier near Pasadena, was present, and had a vision, which he recounted and is here reproduced verbatim:

In the vision, we were all taken up into a long, narrow room; taken up into heaven. It had a ceiling, though you couldn't exactly see it, and it had walls, but the thing I remember clearly was the floor, because it was sheer crystal. At the end of the room there were these great doors that were closed. We were just standing there chatting, and I realised that we were waiting. We were outside the Throne Room.

All of a sudden, the doors at the other end opened up. A figure appeared in the doorway and motioned that we should follow. We walked together to where the door was and I realised as we got there that the door was opening into this room that was so massive that it was beyond description. It was like going into the most incredibly large coliseum you can possibly imagine. We could hardly see the other side of it, and it was filled with people and it was filled with song. Down in the centre of it, with everything facing towards it was this incredible throne. It was glorious, and over it there were angels all up above. It had a rainbow that ran over the top of it, except that it was a rainbow from wherever you sat. It was as if it were a sphere. One of the strange things was that every side of the throne was its front. The Lord was sitting there looking at us and yet it was as if he was looking at everyone. There was this vast crowd worshipping and praising, and the angels were worshipping and covering their faces. At that time I had never studied the Throne of God in Revelation. I just went in and there was all this. It was just incredible.

The angel said, 'Come with me,' and suddenly we just flew. We landed at the bottom, and by now we were carrying David in our arms. We walked up the stairs and Jesus got up and walked down. It was a terrifying thing in one sense, and yet I had no fear. I realised afterwards the reason why. It was because it had nothing to do with us. We were coming before the throne *with David*. It wasn't like we were coming for judgement. We were walking up and Jesus was walking down, and it was as if I saw him but I didn't see him; I didn't see his face. The Lord came down and we put David into his arms, and he then walked back up with David and we knelt down to worship. Then suddenly, we flew away; we were gone. I was expecting to be in the ante-room, but we weren't. It was over.

I was immediately perplexed because the strongest impression I had was that David didn't come back with us. And we had been praying for about two hours for him to be healed. I told the vision, but I didn't tell anyone that he didn't come back. As far as I told it, it ended at the throne. We were there and we handed David to the Lord, and then we just kept on praying. I was expecting him to be healed and then handed back, but we were just taken away. It was very sweet, there was nothing amiss, but I was left to figure it out. So I prayed for the rest of that time, and continued to pray that he would be healed.

I went home and a few days later, I woke up in the middle of the night, sat up and just thought, 'He didn't come back with us.' I remembered it just like that. I had thought it at the time but had put it out of my mind. I had thought, 'Well, that's just something I don't understand.' So at seven o'clock the next morning I called John Wimber and said, 'The vision I had, I think I'm supposed to tell you, David didn't come back with us.' And he said, 'What do you mean?' I recounted the whole vision to him and John said, 'What does it mean?' I said, 'I think he's going to go and be with the Lord.'

What impressed me so deeply was that he was in the Lord's hands and it really was the Lord's timing. Whatever the surrounding circumstances were in terms of spiritual warfare or our prayers or whatever else, the Lord was totally in control. There was no sense of anything being amiss; it was all completely right.

David and John Wimber agreed together that he was clearly dying. They parted cheerfully with their eyes on the eternal inheritance, but sadly aware that they would not meet again on earth.

David returned to London to die.

24

'The Best Is Yet To Be'

ON DAVID'S RETURN FROM CALIFORNIA, the Belfrey trustees decided to cancel all David's engagements outside London, but that his team would fulfil their existing programme until the end of April 1984, after which they would have to be disbanded. The team went ahead with their Fuller trip and were thus absent for most of January. In the event, David was unable to carry out any further engagements except for preaching twice at St Michael's, Chester Square. Not strong enough to climb into the pulpit, he sat on a stool to preach but his voice was as strong and clear as ever. On 8 January he preached from Jude 20–25 on our security in Christ, then on the following Sunday from Psalm 91: 'He is my refuge and my fortress, my God, in whom I trust.'[1]

David was very weak and exhausted after that sermon, and his strength steadily declined from then on. Anne and her mother provided all the skilled nursing that he needed, and Fiona gave them valuable support. Dr Robarts found a night nurse, which allowed Anne to catch up on sleep. David knew that he did not have much longer to live and was able to talk about this with both Fiona and Guy. He received a number of visits from close friends, including some of those to whom he had written following Advent Sunday. When David MacInnes came to report to him about the visit to Fuller with the team, David told him, 'I am completely at peace. There is nothing I want more than to go to heaven. I know how good it is.' When the team returned to England at the end of January, they were a little surprised to learn that David had survived so long, and were able to see him in twos for just a few minutes each. The Bishop of London paid a visit, as did the Archbishop of Canterbury, who said, 'I just want to thank him for all he has done for faith among God's people.' Bishop Morris Maddocks came and celebrated Holy Communion.

On Friday 17 February Teddy Saunders visited David and prayed with him. In the afternoon Guy came home for half-term and had a relaxed chat with his father about his school hockey team. In the evening David said to Anne, 'I'm very tired; let's go home.' Anne was in no doubt as to what he meant, but was able to go to bed as usual, while her mother sat with David. She prayed that God would wake her to be with David before he died. At midnight, she woke up and was able to be at David's bedside for fifteen minutes before the gates of heaven opened to receive him.

In the early morning Anne picked up her *Living Light* to read, asking God to give her some words of comfort.[2] Perhaps in the stress of the situation she was confused, for she turned to the reading for 19 February instead of the 18th – or perhaps it was in answer to her prayer. She read from Isaiah 26:19: 'Those who belong to the Lord shall live again. Their bodies shall rise again! Those who dwell in the dust shall awake and sing for joy! For God's light of life will fall like dew upon them.'

The previous day, Mark and Carol Slomka had given David a tape with all his favourite worship songs which the team had specially recorded for him. He writes:

He thanked us profusely, put on the earphones of his Walkman and began singing along. That was how we left him. Worship tape playing, eyes closed, face peaceful, and a smile on his lips. That evening as I slept I had a lovely dream. In it I saw David healthy and whole standing in a doorway – he had his usual look of confidence and joy about him. As I turned to him he waved and walked through the door. I woke up the next morning sure that David had died. To this day, while reason prods me to record Friday's visit with David as my last time to see him, my heart says no. It makes no difference in the long run . . . I have yet to see David for the last time.

Leaving Anne to get in touch with the family, Teddy and Hilary undertook the sad task of breaking the news to the trustees, David's team and closer friends and associates. By no means unexpected, his death was still something of a shock to all. However, with Anne's agreement, the death announcement in the newspapers ended with the phrase, 'The Lord Reigns!' – David's festal shout.

The funeral service took place in St Michael's, Chester Square. John Collins took the service, Douglas Greenfield read the lesson, Teddy Saunders gave an address and Bishop Morris Maddocks pronounced the blessing. It was attended by a limited number of friends, some of long standing, a few who met David only while he was living in London, and a group from York. Anne was there with their children and her parents. Peggy Hawkes came up from Andover with Diana. On the morning of the funeral Hilary wrote the Epilogue to *Fear No Evil* and then delivered the manuscript to Hodder & Stoughton.

Two great memorial services were held: the first in York Minster at which Stuart Blanch, recently retired from being Archbishop, gave the address and his successor, John Hapgood, pronounced the blessing. The great church was full to overflowing, people travelling from considerable distances to be present, whilst members of St Michael-le-Belfrey shared their memories and their thanksgivings with the wider Church, as they had had to do so often during David's lifetime. Graham Cray welcomed the congregation and led the prayers. Passages from some of David's books were read by Paul and Bernadette Burbridge. Testimonies were given by members of St Michael's and by John Curnow, Chairman of the Dartford Mission. Andrew Maries and Peter Seymour played the prelude from Bach's Easter Oratorio.

Two weeks later, the second service was held in St Paul's Cathedral in London. Again the crowds were enormous and many men and women of eminence within the nation and the Church attended. David MacInnes preached and led the congregation in David's festal shout, Robert Runcie, Archbishop of Canterbury, led the prayers and his predecessor, Donald Coggan, David's first Archbishop in York, read one of the lessons. Four ministerial representatives of the churches gave 'Words of Assurance' from different Scriptures and Sylvia Mary Alison prayed for the unity of the Church. David's team led three worship songs with style and vigour from a low platform under the dome.

There were other memorial services held in other places, notably in Ireland. Channel 4 commissioned a half-hour documentary-style television tribute to him which was screened that August. But in the Vineyard in California, John Wimber was too stricken with grief to tell his congregation for several months that David had died.

The Belfrey trustees gave the team notice to disband in the early summer and tried to treat them as generously as they could. Each has moved on to take on some form of leadership role in the Church. Mark and Carol Slomka returned to California and into the Presbyterian ministry. Hilary Saunders stayed on with Anne and the family through the summer, helping to clear up the affairs of the Trust in London, before developing a career in Christian journalism. There was never much doubt what Anne, Fiona and Guy would do. The trustees set up a fund in thanksgiving for David, of which the purpose was to buy the family a home in York, and gifts came in from all over the world. Archbishop Runcie offered his help in providing for them but expressed the opinion that there was 'so much goodwill out there' that he would not be needed. He was quite right. Over £60,000 was given for the purchase of a regency terraced house which suited Anne exactly for immediate needs and she moved in September 1984.

No doubt David's great contribution to the kingdom of God is largely to be found in the acceptability which he gained all over the world not only for himself but also for his message and his methods. It was not just the wisdom with which he spoke, or the particular things he said, but the sheer quality of the man which was so remarkable. He was heard and appreciated by people who were not on his side and who had no intention, before or after, of changing their views or their way of life, but who were quite unable to restrain their respect and admiration for him. Occasionally, an individual with a different theological perspective, usually a clergyman, would sound off an attack upon him, but these seem to have been lost in the murmurs of approval which greeted all he did in public. He was so open and so honest.

As such, his teaching was pursued and heeded. His books remain with the Church, many of them still in print. There are also many tapes of his addresses in St Michael-le-Belfrey and elsewhere. His book and teaching videos, *Jesus Then and Now*, are still widely used as Lent courses and for group instruction in churches who never knew David. All these are listed in Appendix II. Moreover, their ability to influence and affect people is undiminished by David's absence; their power was always from God, in any case. Businessman Graham Bridger, who never met or heard David speak, writes how in a Christian bookshop his

... eye was caught by a couple of books: *Is Anyone There?* and *Live a New Life*, both by David Watson. The titles were perfect. At 30,000 ft on a plane bound for America, I decided to read *Is Anyone There?* I was staggered by it and prayed the prayer of repentance at the end of the book. When I came home I told my wife Sue what I had done and she smiled in response. She pulled from beneath her pillow *Live a New Life*; she had committed her life to the Lord also. The only difference was that Sue was not a keen reader, and the prayer of repentance came very early on in that book. We found that we had made the commitment at the same time on the same day, 5,000 miles apart.

Still alive and active in Christian life and work are literally hundreds of those who came to faith in Christ through David or who learnt from him how to live with Christ and to minister in the power of Christ's Spirit.

As well as the direct influence that his ministry has had in the lives of individuals, the example he set has been followed by many of those engaged in God's work. Of course, anyone with a preaching ministry could do a lot worse than copy David's style and method. Moreover, his advocacy of lay ministry and the full use which he made of his team has encouraged many to develop the use of their gifts in the everyday activity of the Church.

He placed the creative arts at the centre of his ministry and thereby gave them a significant boost within the Christian world. As Mark Slomka has written:

David was theologically and 'spiritually' committed to the arts being integrated into Christian ministry. This did not simply represent an acquiescence on his part to culture and youth so that the Word could get around. The use of dance, drama and mime always provoked comment. Yet David was convinced that these were not mere novelties but could be central to the proclamation of the Gospel.

Many churches now have their own drama and dance groups, and groups for banner production. It is not unfair to say that over the last couple of decades, and partly due to David's ministry, Christian worship has taken on a new dimension.

Through his gentle but uncompromising advocacy of renewal David has had a great and lasting impact on the worldwide Church. There must be thousands of Christians who would never have gone near any overtly charismatic gathering, but who willingly went to hear David Watson. They found that renewal did not just mean the seeking of spiritual blessings and experiences for oneself, but was the Holy Spirit bringing new life and meaning into the whole Church. Thanks to David's ministry, many Christians have discovered that the Holy Spirit can renew them, transform them, equip them and give them a new love for each other.

Moreover, during his last year of life, David had extracted from John Wimber a promise that he would come to England as soon as possible to hold a big conference for the encouragement and inspiration of Christians. John arrived in October 1984 on the stage of the Central Hall in Westminster with a team of 200 from the Vineyard. He began the conference by telling the congregation that he had come because David Watson had made him promise to do so. 'David, if you can hear me, I promised I would come, and here I am.' This was the first of many subsequent conferences in different centres in the UK by which John Wimber introduced his model of ministry in the power of the Holy Spirit to the British churches. His movement has brought hope and liberty as David knew it would.

For years evangelism seemed to have been the province of the evangelicals. The strong emphasis they laid, very properly, upon evangelism, their insistence upon the precise form it should take and the impression they gave that they had almost a monopoly of it, had caused others to distance themselves from it. But David changed all that. He was himself so attractive and sensitive that almost overnight attitudes to what he stood for changed radically. Preaching the same exclusive gospel as the evangelicals, he was inclusive in all his relationships towards the other traditions within Christendom. Critics began to understand not only the force of his message, but also the need for it. Like David himself, evangelism became acceptable and appropriate. It must be conceded that the Decade of Evangelism owes most of all to the dawning realisation that the membership numbers were decreasing so rapidly that a real crisis of existence would soon be facing the traditional churches and a crisis of viability was already at the door. A missionary situation has been recognised in Britain for some years, although very little allowance has been made for it. It cannot be denied, however, that David Watson, more than anyone else, provided the demonstration which made evangelism possible. As the churches enter the Decade of Evangelism it may be that their capacity to do so owes more to David than any other single person.

Back in 1980, Peregrine Worsthorne had written: 'A single Mr Watson does not make a religious revival, and it would be foolish to exaggerate his significance. But it would be just as foolish to minimise it.' After his death, Robert Runcie, the then Archbishop of Canterbury, wrote: 'No sensitive observer of the Church of England over the past twenty years could fail to notice the impact of David Watson. So many people came to faith or were renewed in faith through his ministry that God's blessing upon his life and work seemed self-evident.' There may well have been greater, more impressive Christian men than David, but certainly none of his generation were as simply effective. When he was taken it seemed a terrible tragedy, but David's work was God's work, and God's work goes on. Jean Darnall's prophecy on that Sunday afternoon before the operation is surely being fulfilled daily: 'Your ministry will increase and not diminish.'

Nevertheless, behind the great David Watson and his spectacular ministry was a gentle, charming, slightly insecure and much-loved man. In an article in *Renewal* magazine, April/May 1984, Andrew Maries, with whom David had shared his home for a number of years wrote, 'Personally, I feel very sad at the loss of a friend and great influence in my life. I owe an enormous debt to both David and Anne for the sacrifices they made. Like many others, I have so much cause to be thankful to God for bringing them across my path.'

Six years after David's death God spoke yet again to Anne through a friend, comforting her and reminding her of Isaiah's prophecy:

> *The righteous perish,*
> > *and no-one ponders it in his heart;*
> *devout men are taken away,*
> > *and no-one understands*
> *that the righteous are taken away*
> > *to be spared from evil.*
> *Those who walk uprightly*
> > *enter into peace;*
> *they find rest as they lie in death.*[3]

APPENDIX I

It's Far From Being a Myth
Summary of ACE Report on St Michael-le-Belfrey

Is it true what is said about St Michael-le-Belfrey? Can its reported successes teach the rest of us anything useful? Or are the more important lessons the ones that come from weakness and failure? Is it all to do with David Watson personally? What happens when he goes?

This article tries to answer the first three of those questions. It will I hope establish that St Michael's is not all a myth. It is an extraordinary example of growth in a congregation within the charismatic renewal. And the points of learning are as much its weaknesses as its strengths.

There are four very positive statements which can be made from the study of St Michael-le-Belfrey, and we shall try to show the strengths and weaknesses of the congregation's experience under each heading.

1 People really pray believing God will answer. This goes right back to the tiny handful at St Cuthbert's when the Watsons arrived in 1965. It comes over as an attitude supporting every decision and activity of the congregation. Because people really do expect God to be answering their prayers, the Thursday prayer meetings in York have a sense of praise, thanksgiving and worship about them. There is a proper context to what can otherwise feel like a congregational 'shopping list' in the more normal prayer meetings of a church.

2 Living Worship discloses God as much as preaching. Morning or evening the clergy, lay elders and articulate lay people would say, what communicates is the whole event, not just the talk or the sermon. Over the last decade many have made the discovery, which is so obvious at St Michael's, that where God's Spirit is in worship, the proclaiming of Christ has already begun.

This does not make the preaching or teaching ministry less than essential. It serves only to redress a balance that needed redressing. Most of those who come to Christ do so through friends bringing them in to hear David Watson. Yet no-one merely 'hears David Watson'; they do so in the context of God's people enjoying worshipping him together. And what comes across is the sheer weight of testimony upholding the word preached by the word received, believed in and being lived by so many happy but ordinary people who are part of the proclaiming in themselves.

3 There are 'comfortable' numbers for doing different things. People like to be part of a big show, but at the same time are looking for fellowship which cannot be found in the larger group. The majority of the members of St Michael's said that this was what attracted them there. In October 1973 it was decided to encourage area house-groups for the pastoral care of the congregation. These concentrated on prayer, Bible study and general 'fellowship'. However they had attracted only about half of the congregation; had often gone as large as 50 in membership; and had not always been well led. The period of the ACE survey proved to be the time when overdue attention was given to increasing the number of groups so as to reduce membership to more comfortable dimensions. Increased attention was also to be given to leadership support.

St Michael-le-Belfrey stands at a cross-road of decision about its denomination-alism. It is virtually divorced from it, yet purports to be a parish church. A congregation of 700 or 800 in a 'parish' of 600 should be an extraordinary phenomenon. But a 1.3% penetration of the 600 living in its bounds is an incredibly *low* parish presence for an Anglican church. And a congregation of 700 in a city of 104,000 can only hold a peripheral place in its life.

In terms of numerical growth approximately two-thirds have come into St Michael's by transfer from other congregations. That leaves one-third as the 'conversion' ratio, but both transfer and conversion growth appear to be drawn from a highly mobile part of the population of York. This is not only class selective, but also tends not to reach the well-established, long-term York citizen.

The York congregation could now be poised for its third 'take off'. St Cuthbert's till it became uncomfortable; St Michael's till it became uncomfortable; now, growth groups of all sorts, with the developing of effective relations with other churches in the York area. The third stage, however, will not be as smooth and predictable a ride as the other two. In particular it involves an Anglican parish in some un-Anglican experimenting.

4 Man does not live by words alone. For a number of years there has been a full-time dance group at St Michael's. They take part on most Sundays in worship. Last September 'Breadrock', the acting group which had started out as street theatre and in young people's evangelistic work, took up residence as part of the full time team at St Michael's, and began work as 'Riding Lights'. Music plays a great role too: choirs, groups, orchestra, congregational training in full participation.

The ACE Study found that the dance and drama experiments which are so much part of the St Michael's scene, were mentioned often as the things most disliked in the activities of the church; but also as the things most liked. The team pleaded for the continued examination of the most effective blendings of dance, music, movement, drama, participation in liturgical prayer, and preaching and everyday witness as expressions of the Word within the Body of Christ.

Hopefully, as St Michael's goes on learning how to create worship services and evangelistic events in which all these things are made one in the Spirit, new levels of Christian communication will be discovered. Already there are signs of this in some of David Watson's university work where drama and preaching have become welded together, each reinforcing the other.

The report also asked four serious questions which had been raised by the team's survey of the work in York:

A Why have so few members a personal involvement in ordinary secular organisations in York? Some 65% of those questioned could not name any such involvement. There does not seem to be any regular encouragement to go out and help in the rest of life, or to see a need to express or bring God's kingdom there. This lack of personal involvement is reflected in what gets prayed about in church or at prayer meetings.

B Why does St Michael's not attract or hold more working-class people? The church is an eclectic congregation, drawing people in from a wide area. But of these very few indeed are from the council estates. Despite all the above-average attractiveness of worship patterns, of congregational drive, and of area support, St Michael's has no claim to any sort of break-through on the major frontier of our society.

C Can Pastoral oversight and decision-making be restricted to men in a congregation? St Michael's has a well-developed system of lay pastoral elders. They have always been men. There are signs that St Michael's is moving away from the situation where the lady parish-worker could not attend the elders' meeting; and where elders were automatically men. Nevertheless the full implications of 'neither male nor female, but all one in Jesus Christ' have still to be faced. Some area groups have assistant leadership by a woman. Some of the expanded number of groups now proposed may be under female leadership.

As things have been so far, the giving of 'prophecy' to the congregation has been one of the few possibilities for affecting decisions or suggesting new directions open to women. Inevitably and inexorably this issue will force St Michael's to face not only 'what the Scriptures say', but what we mean by such a statement. The debate cannot be narrowed to one of women in authority; that is not the point at issue. It is rather the question of women as people, God's children with gifts and ministries like anyone else.

D Is it unspiritual to teach about financial giving? On the face of it St Michael's does extremely well. It pays its way. It gives overseas liberally. It helps many mission agencies in this country too. It largely supports work among unattached youth in the city. Through its 'households' the congregation manages to keep many full-time staff in action. The graph goes on upwards, but discounting money given specifically for capital items like renovating church buildings, the graph turns gently towards a plateau. When corrected for inflation, the total giving is already seen to be in decline. This trend is emphasised by a graph showing giving-per-member corrected for inflation. This has been in steady decline since 1974. The 'worthship' of the congregation is seen to have decayed as the excitement of the move to St Michael-le-Belfrey wore off, and the area groups reached saturation point.

Should these facts be preached about, and 'put right'? Or is this something God looks after himself in times of specific need? One of the strange questions that kept recurring in the ACE Survey was 'Does St Michael's *always* need to be doing something new?' Maybe there is an unacknowledged *financial* pressure in an answer to that. Regular sacrificial giving if not part of life-style preaching needs the stimulus of new projects to be paid for.

Conclusion St Michael-le-Belfrey is not an ordinary Anglican parish. It represents the coming together of a particular person with his own gifts; a particular family with their own faith and vision; a particular moment in the life of the churches in a city and deanery; and in the processes of English society in the 70's.

Without attempting to answer the hypothetical question 'After David Watson, What?' a little must be said about him in order to explain all that has gone before. David Watson has tried very hard to create a fellowship in which a series of concentric circles of pastoral, loving contact and responsibility covers the whole congregation. To a degree he has succeeded, but his own management style and abilities play a determinative role in the whole set-up. He has developed a superb communications system, and has sensitively nursed the Christian fellowship, and this side of their pastor is at least as important to the people of St Michael's as his preaching. (Which means, of course, that the same style and gifts could hold a group together round a very different theology or churchmanship.) It is probably true to say, therefore, that if a parish wants renewal in the fashion of St Michael's, it must, in addition to prayer-and-fasting, be prepared to empty itself and to be led by a 'David Watson'.

We owe a great debt to the church for allowing the microscope to be used upon them, and for publishing the full report. To let yourself appear in public 'warts and all' is no easy thing. If this summary helps Christians elsewhere to derive hope from their experiences, it will have been worthwhile.

JOHN POULTON

Bibliography and List of Audio and Video Cassettes

Books, Booklets and Essays by David Watson

Learning to Lead Group Bible Study (booklet), London: Falcon Press, 1962

Towards Tomorrow's Church: A Practical Guide for the Church-based Youth Club, London: Falcon Press, 1965

My God is Real, Eastbourne: Kingsway, 1970

Hidden Warfare, Bromley: Send The Light, 1970 (originally published as *God's Freedom Fighters*, Croydon: Movement Books, 1972)

One in the Spirit, London: Hodder & Stoughton, 1973

In Search of God, Eastbourne: Kingsway, 1974

Live a New Life, Leicester: Inter-Varsity Press, 1975

I Believe in Evangelism, London: Hodder & Stoughton, 1976

I Believe in the Church, London: Hodder & Stoughton, 1978

Is Anyone There?, London: Hodder & Stoughton, 1979

Start a New Life (booklet), Eastbourne: Kingsway, 1979

My Path of Prayer, Henry E. Walter (ed.), 1981

Discipleship, London: Hodder & Stoughton, 1981

Be Filled with the Spirit (booklet), Eastbourne: Kingsway, 1982

Study Guide to I Believe in the Church, London: Hodder & Stoughton, 1982

Through the Year with David Watson, London: Hodder & Stoughton, 1982

Jesus Then and Now, Tring: Lion Publishing, 1983 (with Simon Jenkins)

You Are My God, London: Hodder & Stoughton, 1983

Fear No Evil, London: Hodder & Stoughton, 1984

OTHER RELATED BOOKS

Bash: A Study in Spiritual Power, John Eddison (ed.), Basingstoke: Marshall, Morgan & Scott, 1983

By My Spirit, Bill Burnett (ed.), London: Hodder & Stoughton, 1988

David Watson: A Portrait by His Friends, Edward England (ed.), Crowborough: Highland Books, 1985

Godparents, Anne Watson, Eastbourne: Kingsway, 1989

Joy Unspeakable, Martyn Lloyd-Jones, Eastbourne: Kingsway, 1984

Power Evangelism, John Wimber & Kevin Springer, London: Hodder & Stoughton, 1985

Power Healing, John Wimber & Kevin Springer, London: Hodder & Stoughton, 1986

Riding the Third Wave, Kevin Springer (ed.), Basingstoke: Marshall Pickering, 1987 (Introduction by John Wimber and contribution by Anne Watson)

Untitled contribution by Anne Watson in *Married to the Church*, Shelagh Brown (ed.), London: SPCK, 1982

Audio Cassettes by David Watson

There is an extensive range of tapes of David Watson's addresses, both from his pulpit in York and elsewhere, available from:

Anchor Recordings, 72 The Street, Kennington, Ashford, Kent
TN24 9HS
Tape Library, St Cuthbert's Centre, Peasholme Green, York
YO1 2PW

GROUP TEACHING COURSES

Christian Living, Parts 1 and 2

Christian Foundations, Parts 1 and 2

Spiritual Renewal

Available from Falcon AVA, Athena Drive, Tachbrook Park, Warwick
CV34 6HG

A Case for Healing?, David Watson in Conversation with Nick Page, BBC Radio 4, April 1983, available from:
Christian Broadcast Training Ltd, Severals House, 3 Bury Road, Newmarket
CB8 7BS

Video Cassettes by David Watson

In Company With David Watson (UK only)

Jesus Then and Now (UK video only, USA video and 16 mm film)

The Best Is Yet To Be – David Watson: A Tribute

Available from:

In UK – Anchor Recordings, 72 The Street, Kennington, Ashford, Kent TN24 9HS

In USA – Gateway Films Inc., 2030 Wentz Church Road, Box A, Lansdale, Pennsylvania 19446

Notes

Chapter 1

1 Wellington College Roll of Honour, kept in the Chapel at Wellington.
2 *You Are My God*, David Watson, London: Hodder & Stoughton, 1983, p. 14.

Chapter 2

1 *You Are My God*, David Watson, London: Hodder & Stoughton, 1983, p. 15.
2 *Ibid*, p. 16.
3 *Ibid*, pp. 15–16.

Chapter 3

1 *You Are My God*, David Watson, London: Hodder & Stoughton, 1983, p. 17.
2 *The Cambridge Movement*, J. C. Pollock, London: John Murray, 1953.
3 *Whatever Happened to the Jesus Lane Lot?*, Oliver R. Barclay, Leicester: Inter-Varsity Press, 1977.
4 *You Are My God*, p. 21.
5 *Becoming a Christian*, John Stott, Leicester: Inter-Varsity Press, 1968.
6 *You Are My God*, p. 24.
7 *Ibid*, p. 25.
8 *Ibid*, p. 25.

9 Ephesians 3:8, King James Version.
10 *You Are My God*, p. 36.

Chapter 4

1 *Bash: A Study in Spiritual Power*, John Eddison (ed.), Basingstoke: Marshall, Morgan & Scott, 1983, pp. viii–ix.
2 *Ibid*, p. 48.
3 *Ibid*, pp. 61–2.
4 *You Are My God*, David Watson, London: Hodder & Stoughton, 1983, p. 39.
5 *Book of Common Prayer*, Holy Communion Service.
6 *Ibid*, Articles of Religion, Article 6.
7 Psalm 27:8, Revised Standard Version.

Chapter 5

1 *You Are My God*, David Watson, London: Hodder & Stoughton, 1983, p. 35.
2 *Ibid*, p. 36.
3 *Ibid*, p. 36.
4 *Ibid*, pp. 36–7.
5 *Ibid*, p. 39.
6 *Ibid*, p. 40.
7 *Ibid*, p. 40.
8 *Towards the Conversion of England*, London: Church Assembly, 1945, p. 41.

Chapter 6

1 *David Watson: A Portrait by His Friends*, Edward England (ed.), Crowborough: Highland Books, 1985.
2 *Towards Tomorrow's Church: A Practical Guide for Church-based Youth Clubs*, Eastbourne: Falcon Books, 1965, p. 90.
3 Revised Standard Version.
4 Revised Standard Version.
5 Revised Standard Version.
6 Romans 15:13, Revised Standard Version.
7 *You Are My God*, David Watson, London: Hodder & Stoughton, 1983, p. 47.
8 *Fire in the Hills*, H. H. Osborn, Crowborough: Highland Books, 1991.
9 *The Hiding Place*, Corrie ten Boom, London: Hodder & Stoughton, 1971.
10 *You Are My God*, pp. 47–8.
11 *Ibid*, p. 48.

Chapter 7

1 *Honest to God*, John Robinson, London: SCM Press, 1963.
2 *Studies in the Sermon on the Mount*, Martyn Lloyd-Jones, Leicester: Inter-Varsity Press, 1959.
3 *You Are My God*, David Watson, London: Hodder & Stoughton, 1983, p. 52.
4 *Ibid*, pp. 52–3.
5 *Ibid*, p. 53.
6 *Ibid*, p. 53.
7 *Ibid*, p. 54.

Chapter 8

1 *Nine o'Clock in the Morning*, Dennis & Rita Bennett, Eastbourne: Coverdale House, 1974.

2 *The Cross and the Switchblade*, David Wilkerson, Basingstoke: Lakeland Books, 1964.
3 Ephesians 3:19, King James Version.
4 *You Are My God*, David Watson, London: Hodder & Stoughton, 1983, p. 59.
5 *Baptism and Fullness: The Work of the Holy Spirit Today*, John Stott, Leicester: Inter-Varsity Press, 1975. First published as a booklet entitled *The Baptism and Fullness of the Holy Spirit* in 1964.
6 *Joy Unspeakable*, Martyn Lloyd-Jones, Eastbourne: Kingsway, 1984.
7 2 Corinthians 5:17, King James Version.
8 *You Are My God*, p. 60.
9 *Ibid*, p. 61.

Chapter 9

1 *Commentary on Romans*, Anders Nygren, Minneapolis: Fortress Press, 1949.
2 Ephesians 5:18, literal translation.
3 1 Peter 1:16; Leviticus 11:44, New International Version.
4 Romans 6:6, New International Version.
5 Romans 6:11, New International Version.
6 Romans 6:12–13, New International Version.
7 *You Are My God*, David Watson, London: Hodder & Stoughton, 1983, p. 62.
8 *Ibid*, p. 64.
9 *Ibid*, p. 63.
10 *Discipleship*, David Watson, London: Hodder & Stoughton, 1981, p. 109.

11 John 14:27, New International
Version.

12 Galatians 5:22.

13 *You Are My God*, p. 70.

Chapter 10

1 1 Corinthians 7:32, Revised
Standard Version.

2 *You Are My God*, David Watson,
London: Hodder & Stoughton,
1983, p. 67.

3 *Married to the Church*, Shelagh
Brown (ed.), London: SPCK,
1982, pp. 79–80.

4 *You Are My God*, p. 68.

5 Luke 2:49, King James
Version.

6 *Married to the Church*, p. 82.

Chapter 11

1 Haggai 2:7, King James
Version.

2 *You Are My God*, David Watson,
London: Hodder & Stoughton,
1983, p. 74.

3 *Journey Into Life*, Norman
Warren, Eastbourne:
Kingsway/Falcon Books, 1964
(revised edition, 1980).

4 John 13:35, Revised Standard
Version.

5 *I Believe in Preaching*, John Stott,
London: Hodder & Stoughton,
1982, p. 229.

6 Hebrews 4:12, Revised Standard
Version.

7 1 Corinthians 2:2, King James
Version.

Chapter 12

1 *You Are My God*, David Watson,
London: Hodder & Stoughton,
1983, p. 84.

2 *Ibid*, p. 85.

3 John 15:4, Revised Standard
Version.

4 2 Corinthians 12:9, The Living
Bible.

5 Galatians 6:2, Revised Standard
Version.

6 *I Believe in the Church*, David
Watson, London: Hodder &
Stoughton, 1978, pp. 99–100.

7 Colossians 1:19–20, New
International Version.

8 John 13:35, New International
Version.

9 *I Believe in the Church*, p. 98.

Chapter 13

1 *My God is Real*, David Watson,
Eastbourne: Kingsway, 1970.

2 *In Search of God*, David Watson,
Eastbourne: Kingsway, 1974.

3 *Is Anyone There?*, David Watson,
London: Hodder & Stoughton,
1979.

4 *I Believe in Evangelism*, David
Watson, London: Hodder &
Stoughton, 1976, p. 85.

5 *Ibid*, p. 84.

6 *Runaway World*, Michael Green,
Leicester: Inter-Varsity Press,
1968.

7 *Hidden Warfare*, David Watson,
Bromley: STL, 1970.

Chapter 14

1 Luke 12:13–21.

Chapter 15

1 *I Believe in the Church: Study
Guide*, David Watson, London:
Hodder & Stoughton,
1982.

2 *I Believe in the Church*, David
Watson, London: Hodder &
Stoughton, 1978, p. 8.

3 The Mustard Seed, a coffee shop
run by members of St
Michael's, is described in detail
in Chapter 16.

4 *David Watson: A Portrait by His
Friends*, Edward England (ed.),
Crowborough: Highland Books,
1985, pp. 125–6.
5 Private report to ACE from Urban
Church Project.
6 *David Watson: A Portrait by His
Friends*, p. 136.

Chapter 16
1 *You Are My God*, David Watson,
London: Hodder & Stoughton,
1983, p. 121.
2 *Rich Christians in an Age of
Hunger*, Ronald Sider, London:
Hodder & Stoughton, 1978.
3 *Discipleship*, David Watson,
London: Hodder & Stoughton,
1981, p. 16.
4 *Ibid*, p. 18.
5 *Ibid*, p. 6 (Foreword to
Discipleship by Jim Packer first
published in the 1983 edition).
6 *Ibid*, pp. 62ff.
7 *Ibid*, p. 108.

Chapter 17
1 *I Believe in Evangelism*, David
Watson, London: Hodder &
Stoughton, 1976, p. 166.
2 *Ibid*, p. 156.
3 *Readings in St John's Gospel*,
William Temple, London:
Macmillan, 1961, p. 68.
4 *Community of the King*, Howard
Snyder.
5 *You Are My God*, David Watson,
London: Hodder & Stoughton,
1983, p. 131.
6 *Ibid*, p. 133.
7 *Tomorrow's Church*, 1981, No. 4,
p. 16 (a quarterly bulletin on
evangelism published from 1979
to 1981 by the former staff
members of ACE, after ACE itself
had been disbanded).

Chapter 18
1 See p. 44.
2 *Towards the Conversion of England*,
London: Church Assembly,
1945, p. 1.
3 *A New Canterbury Tale: The Report
of the Anglican Conference on
Spiritual Renewal*, held at
Canterbury, July 1978,
Nottingham: Grove Books, 1978,
p. 18.
4 Matthew 13:3–23.
5 *I Believe in Evangelism*, David
Watson, London: Hodder &
Stoughton, 1976, p. 9.
6 *Ibid*, p. 11.
7 *Ibid*, p. 10 (Preface to First
Edition).
8 1 Corinthians 2:2, King James
Version.
9 *I Believe in Evangelism*, pp. 77–9.
10 *Ibid*, p. 171.
11 Romans 15:4, Revised Standard
Version.
12 *I Believe in Evangelism*, p. 81.
13 *To Reach A Nation*, Gavin Reid,
London: Hodder & Stoughton,
1987, pp. 84–5.
14 *Ibid*, pp. 88–9.

Chapter 19
1 *You Are My God*, David Watson,
London: Hodder & Stoughton,
1983, p. 98.
2 *Ibid*, p. 102.
3 *Yorkshire Post*, 26 February 1977.
4 *A Road Too Wide*, David
Armstrong, Basingstoke:
Marshall Pickering, 1985.

Chapter 20
1 *You Are My God*, David Watson,
London: Hodder & Stoughton,
1983, p. 184.
2 *David Watson: A Portrait by His
Friends*, Edward England (ed.),

Crowborough: Highland Books, 1985, p. 78.
3 *You Are My God*, p. 190.

Chapter 21
1 *Fear No Evil*, David Watson, London: Hodder & Stoughton, 1984, p. 25.
2 *Ibid*, pp. 52–3.
3 John 11:43, Revised Standard Version.
4 Mark 7:34, Revised Standard Version.
5 Matthew 17:18, New International Version.
6 Acts 3:6, New International Version.
7 *Fear No Evil*, p. 52.
8 *I Believe in Evangelism*, David Watson, London: Hodder & Stoughton, 1976, p. 169.
9 *I Believe in the Church*, David Watson, London: Hodder & Stoughton, 1978, p. 165.
10 *Ibid*, p. 172.
11 *Ibid*, p. 175.
12 *I Believe in Evangelism*, p. 169.
13 *Ibid*, p. 169.
14 *Discipleship*, David Watson, London: Hodder & Stoughton, 1981, p. 105.
15 *Fear No Evil*, p. 51.

Chapter 22
1 Titus 1:5, New International Version.

2 *By My Spirit*, Bill Burnett (ed.), London: Hodder & Stoughton, 1988, p. 141.
3 *Ibid*, p. 142.
4 *You Are My God*, David Watson, London: Hodder & Stoughton, 1983, p. 167.
5 *Ibid*, p. 168.
6 *You Are My God*, p. 168.
7 *By My Spirit*, p. 142.

Chapter 23
1 *Fear No Evil*, David Watson, London: Hodder & Stoughton, 1984, p. 56.
2 *Power Healing*, John Wimber, London: Hodder & Stoughton, 1986, pp. 13–14.
3 *Fear No Evil*, p. 71.
4 *Ibid*, p. 69.
5 *A Case for Healing?*, David Watson in Conversation with Nick Page, BBC Radio 4, April 1983.
6 *Fear No Evil*, p. 94.
7 *Ibid*, pp. 145–6.
8 *Ibid*, p. 171.

Chapter 24
1 Psalm 91:2, New International Version.
2 *Living Light – Daily Light in Today's Language*, London: Coverdale House Publications, 1972.
3 Isaiah 57:1–2, New International Version.

Index

In this Index, the initials DW denote David Watson. No clerical titles appear in the Index.